Morningside

CHARLES J. SMITH

Illustrations by William R. Smith

JOHN DONALD PUBLISHERS LTD
EDINBURGH

To my family

© Charles J. Smith 1992
Reprinted 1994

John Donald Publishers Ltd,
138 St Stephen Street, Edinburgh EH3 5AA.

ISBN 0 85976 354 4

British Library Cataloguing in Publication Data

A catalogue record for this book is available
from the British Library.

Typeset by Pioneer Associates, Perthshire.
Printed & bound in Great Britain by
Scotprint Ltd, Musselburgh.

Contents

Preface and Acknowledgements   vii

1. The Village of Burghmuirhead — Churchill —
   East Morningside   1

2. Towards the Village   43

3. Morningside Village   62

4. The Land of Canaan   98

5. The Falcon Estate   135

6. The Jordan Burn   150

7. Beyond the Jordan — Morningside Station —
   Comiston   166

8. Plewlands — Craighouse — Greenbank   181

9. The Living Past   220

10. Morningside Today   239

11. Morningside's Changing Face   262

Further Reading   272

Index   276

Preface and Acknowledgements

Morningside as defined geographically by Edinburgh District Council for the purposes of its Community Council extends from Newbattle Terrace and Morningside Place on the north to the southmost end of the Braidburn Valley Park and along the boundary wall which divides the Braids from Mortonhall Golf Course; and on the east, Blackford Hill and part of the vicinity; westwards to Myreside, Craighouse Road and Greenbank. It is approximately within these boundaries that Morningside is presented in this book. Space precludes reference to certain districts and places such as Tipperlinn, the Royal Edinburgh Hospital and certain aspects of Canaan. Blackford and Braid also are given but passing mention. All of the above have been presented in considerable detail in the author's earlier books.

The district has been described by one writer as more than simply a geographical location but also 'a frame of mind' . . . 'a social attitude . . .' and 'a form of speech'. These characteristics are referred to in more detail in a later chapter. The suburb along with Newington and the Grange has been described by yet another writer as 'Edinburgh's other New Town'.

Within much the same boundaries as above, some of the history of Morningside was the subject of my earlier books written just over a decade ago. In more recent times my friend Malcolm Cant, one of Edinburgh's most popular local historians, has written about this southern suburb in his own characteristic manner, in his important work *The Villages of Edinburgh*, a prodigious study.

Our knowledge of the history of a district is never static or permanently defined, save perhaps as regards the Royal Mile and including the Castle and Holyrood Palace. Even there, excavation for new house building, continuing research of old records, could bring something new to light. The face of a district, as of a person, gradually or rapidly changes. In all of this Morningside is no exception.

In this new presentation much revision and updating has been carried out. Illustrations of places and people by now familiar, have been replaced by others, in many instances never previously seen or published. Noteworthy events of recent times are recorded. New organisations have been established and merit description. All of this signifies the district's ongoing development. Many strands of new insight into or revision of knowledge along with some consideration of 'Morningside Today' and 'The Changing Face' are brought together.

As always, the publication of local history, even if mainly an updating of previous material cannot be properly approached without reference to the resources of the Central Public Library, in particular its Edinburgh Room with its most valuable collection of relevant material as, for example old street directories, carefully documented press cuttings and of course reference books not readily available elsewhere. My first expression of gratitude, therefore, must be to Miss Sheena McDougall and her Edinburgh Room colleagues, for their well-known characteristic, professional and courteous service. Mrs Muriel Brown and Mr Phil Wark of Morningside Public Library were also most helpful. I am also much indebted to Mr Peter Milne of the Map Room at the National Library of Scotland, to Dr W. A. Turmeau, CBE, Principal of Napier Polytechnic and to Mr J. McDermott, Administrative Assistant to the Principal.

My appreciation is also expressed to Mr Ian Gow and his colleagues at the Royal Commission on the Ancient and Historical Monuments of Scotland, for important information on Falcon Hall; and likewise to Mr Godfrey Evans, Curator of European Metal Work and Sculpture at the Royal Museum of Scotland in Chambers Street for his expert information and assistance in my reference to the discovery and removal of the valuable piece of Roubilliac sculpture at one of Sam Bough's former residences in Jordan Lane. For a new appraisement of

Falcon Hall, Morningside village's one-time impressive 'big house', and the possible association of its owner Alexander Falconar with the Palazzo Falconieri in Rome, I am very greatly indebted to Mr Joe Rock, of Edinburgh University's Department of Fine Art, an authority on Falcon Hall and its architect Thomas Hamilton. In the same context I am most appreciative of the expert assistance of Mr Brian Phillips, formerly Senior Lecturer in Edinburgh University's Department of Italian, for obtaining the necessary books dealing with and illustrating the Palazzo Falconieri. The Visitors Centre, Royal Observatory, Blackford Hill was very helpful.

Within Morningside itself I have to thank so many people. If I do so, briefly, on account of space, I hope this will not seem merely a litany of formalities. Dr Margaret Oliver of East Morningside House kindly updated me on revived interest in Susan Ferrier; the Reverend George A. M. Munro 'fielded' many phone calls!; Councillor Kenneth Ferguson kept me right on many local developments *vis à vis* planning and other matters; again Mr Gilmour Main proved himself an oracle on Morningside's past; Mr Hunter Chisholm and Mr Cecil Moar, both former players in the Morningside Victoria Football Team kindly provided information and photographs; Mr James C. Allan of the Braid Recreation Club is a mine of information on this Club and much else about Morningside; Miss Peggy Hunter, originator of 'The Open Door' and Mrs Frances Cunningham, manager, and Mrs Doreen Tarbit, assistant, present-day successors; Mr John Chalmers FRCS, (E) an authority on John James Audubon; Mrs Sheila Durham for her invaluable documented knowledge of Morningside Cemetery and much other assistance; Mrs Elizabeth Notman for fascinating insights into the family dairy farm in Balcarres Street; Mr Dickie Laurie, himself a retired railwayman, for information regarding Blackford Hill Station and the Suburban Railway. Mrs J. McKean, daughter of Tom Moyes who succeeded his father as blacksmith at Balcarres Street, enlightened me on that era; Mrs Muriel Dickson filled in much that was missing in most people's knowledge of the Paterson 'dry dairy' in Jordan Lane; from the organisations I was kindly updated by Dr M. Keith, secretary of the Morningside Churches Council; Mrs Irene Burnie, Chairman of Morningside Association; Mrs Sheila Smith, Chairman, Morningside Heritage Association; and Mrs Neta Sinclair, Senior Committee Clerk, Community Councils, Edinburgh District Council. Mr Forbes Sinclair of Forbes Sinclair Associates, Cluny Gardens, architect of the Canaan Project, kindly provided most helpful information as did Mrs Marion Smith, Matron of Canaan Home and Mr J. R. S. Fraser, Appeals Organiser, The Royal Blind Asylum and School; Dr Andrew K. Zealley, Consultant Psychiatrist and Physician Superintendent, The Royal Edinburgh Hospital, was kind enough to provide a statement on the Hospital and the main changes in the 1980s; Mrs Deirdre Scott tried her skills with the brass rubbing technique on the early inscription on the wall at Tipperlinn but this would require further professional attention. For the preparation of illustrations I express my appreciation to Mr Neil Hanna of the University Photography Department in the main George Square Library; to Mr Bryan Ryalls for the use of his Location Map of Morningside; to Mr Malcolm Liddle for continuing assistance; and to my brother William R. Smith with whom this is very much a joint book. He drafted the chapter on the Jordan Burn. Mrs Maureen Smith provided helpful typing assistance.

I am also much indebted to Mr Neil Stewart. Mrs Barbara Simpson, Church Secretary, kindly provided much information and the photograph of Greenbank Parish Church.

I am grateful to a number of members of the Mortonhall Tennis Club for information kindly provided; and to Mr M. Shilland, Assistant Sub-Regional Engineer of the Lothian Regional Council's Department of Water and Drainage, Buckstone Terrace, for information regarding the old water pipes excavated at the site of the new premises of Canaan Lodge and Canaan Home at Canaan Lane.

Edinburgh, 1992   C.J.S.

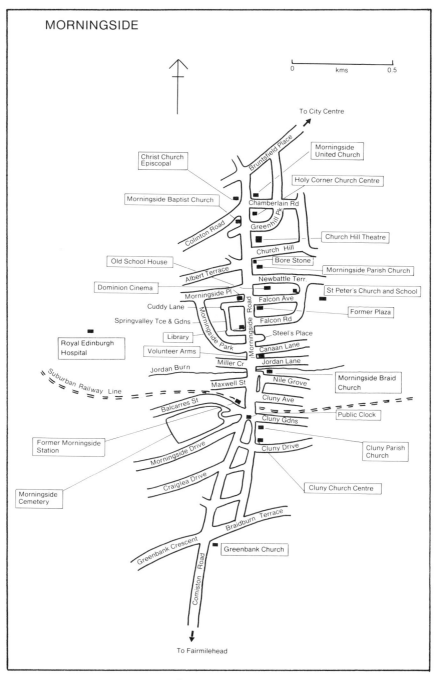

MORNINGSIDE

0   kms   0.5

To City Centre

Christ Church
Episcopal

Morningside
United Church

Holy Corner Church Centre

Bruntsfield Place

Morningside Baptist Church

Chamberlain Rd

Greenhill Pk

Collinton Road

Greenhill

Church Hill Theatre

Church Hill

Old School House

Bore Stone

Albert Terrace

Morningside Parish Church

Dominion Cinema

Newbattle Terr.

St Peter's Church and School

Morningside Pl

Falcon Ave

Cuddy Lane

Morningside Road

Former Plaza

Springvalley Tce & Gdns

Falcon Rd

Morningside Park

Steel's Place

Library

Royal Edinburgh
Hospital

Volunteer Arms

Canaan Lane

Miller Cr

Jordan Lane

Jordan Burn

Suburban Railway Line

Maxwell St

Nile Grove

Morningside Braid
Church

Balcarres St

Cluny Ave

Public Clock

Cluny Gdns

Former Morningside
Station

Morningside Drive

Cluny Drive

Cluny Parish
Church

Craiglea Drive

Cluny Church Centre

Morningside
Cemetery

Braidburn Terrace

Greenbank Crescent

Comiston Road

Greenbank Church

To Fairmilehead

Location map.

CHAPTER 1

The Village of Burghmuirhead Churchhill — East Morningside

While Morningside within the boundaries already described in the Introduction begins on the north at Newbattle Terrace and Morningside Place, Morningside Road commences, on its west side, in the vicinity of Christ Church, although on the opposite side, Bruntsfield Place for a short distance still continues. From 'Holy Corner', Morningside Road takes over, following the route of the ancient Wester Hiegait which skirted the Burgh Muir on this side. Dalkeith Road formed the Easter Hiegait. Here our account of Morningside begins.

The churches of Holy Corner have been referred to in recent times by Malcolm Cant in his well researched *The Villages of Edinburgh* and are therefore not described here. And while Merchiston has been covered in some detail in the present writer's earlier works, *Historic South Edinburgh*, nevertheless it is relevant to take a 'passing glance westwards into Colinton Road to note recent events there that have added lustre to the ancient annals of the beautifully restored fifteenth-century Tower.

When Napier College, built at a cost of £2 million in 1964, was officially opened by that distinguished scientist of world renown, Sir Edward Appleton, the then Principal and Vice-Chancellor of Edinburgh University, with the Tower as its centrepiece, this was an eminently appropriate means of honouring and commemorating John Napier, the Laird of Merchiston, who was born in the Tower in 1550 and died there in 1617, one of history's greatest mathematicians and of acknowledged genius and scholarship in other fields. Here Napier had worked out his system of logarithms, a process which was eventually to revolutionise mathematics and indeed,

1

'Holy Corner'. The beginning of Morningside Road. Below the steeple, centre, is the district of Burghmuirhead.

it has been said, to begin a course of developments leading in modern times to the invention of the computer.

Napier might well feel at home in the college bearing his name in the 'high tech' era and might well have watched with interest and no little pride as 'his college' gradually evolved to meet the demands of the years so as now to be on the verge of university status — surely an event of historic importance to add to the annals of Morningside.

Just over a quarter of a century since its establishment at Colinton Road, now the Merchiston Campus, Napier College has undergone many changes in name. From its original designation as a Technical College in 1967 it became a College of Science and Technology; seven years later, following amalgamation with the previous College of Commerce at Sighthill, it became a College of Commerce and Technology. In 1986 the College changed from the control of Lothian Regional Council Education Committee to that of the Scottish Education Department. Two years after that change it became Napier

NAPIER TECHNICAL COLLEGE

Napier College of Science & Technology

NAPIER COLLEGE
OF COMMERCE AND TECHNOLOGY

NAPIER POLYTECHNIC
OF EDINBURGH

The fifteenth-century tower, skilfully restored as the centrepiece of the Merchiston Campus; and the former Craiglockhart Hydropathic, War Hospital and most recently convent building becoming the Craiglockhart Campus. As it awaits being granted university status Napier Polytechnic can look at its succession of names. (*Napier Polytechnic; photograph designed by Neil Hanna*).

Polytechnic of Edinburgh. All will hope that before long the name above the College's entrance will be 'Napier University'.

During the steady development of the College over the years, with an increase in the number of courses and qualifications offered, and in student numbers, other premises have been acquired, viz., in the former James Gillespie's Boys' School in Marchmont Road, Sighthill, Redwood House in Colinton, part of North Merchiston School, and, most recently, the former Convent of the Sacred Heart and Roman Catholic Teachers' Training College at Craiglockhart.

While operating in these various premises, the Merchiston Campus will always in a special way commemorate the famous scientist whose name the College bears. At the same time considerable historic interest attaches to the College's most recent acquisition of the Craiglockhart Campus. These beautifully situated premises, described as 'a huge chateau' or 'giant Italian villa', built by Peddie and Kinnear during 1877–80, under the slopes of Wester Craiglockhart Hill, command an impressive panoramic view over the city, West Lothian, Fife and the nearer Highlands.

Opened originally as Craiglockhart Hydropathic, this became a war hospital from 1914 to 1918. It was to earn a place of importance not only as a hospital, but especially in the literary world, for here took place the first meeting of the two great war poets, Siegfried Sassoon and Wilfred Owen. As a result of their mutual inspirations, the war hospital magazine *The Hydra* first published some of their most important work.

The Craiglockhart Campus, which has undergone alterations costing millions of pounds, was opened by former Prime Minister, Mrs Margaret Thatcher, on 3 September 1987. Excellent facilities have been created, with pleasant outdoor recreational space, and a special asset is the former Training College's swimming pool. The convent and college chapel have been retained and are in regular use. In the Napier Polytechnic library there is a permanent exhibition of the life and works of Sassoon, Owen and other war poets. The number of students on the roll of the Polytechnic totals 5,500 full-time and 3,500 part-time. Of these, 93.4 per cent were domiciled in Scotland. Amongst them is an awareness of the history that surrounds them at Merchiston and Craiglockhart.

Burghmuirhead

Returning from Colinton Road and entering the locality of Burghmuirhead (alternatively Boroughmuirhead), we may recall that Robert Louis Stevenson knew this place well. He frequently passed it as he journeyed out this way on foot from the city to Swanston Cottage where he lived with his family for 13 summers, a period which influenced him profoundly and unforgettably. In his classic: *Edinburgh: Picturesque Notes* (1878), in the final chapter 'The Pentland Hills', he wrote: 'From Boroughmuirhead, where the Scottish army encamped before Flodden, the road descends a long hill . . .', and he describes his route through Morningside. We shall see that, in fact, the Scottish army did not encamp at this part of the Burgh Muir and we shall later follow Stevenson 'down the long hill'.

On our right, just beyond the Baptist Church as we proceed towards Churchhill, is a little lane leading to an open space now used as a car park. At the end of the lane a collection of small buildings tastefully restored and their adjacent walls remain from earlier days. In the car park stands a large, solid and sombre-looking villa, of a style common in Morningside and other parts of the city. Now the well-appointed premises of the Masonic Lodge Abbotsford, this impressive if gaunt house was for over a century known as Grangebank and, surrounded by pleasant gardens, it presided over the old village of Burgh-muirhead.

Located much further south than the district around the present-day post-office which still bears the name, Burghmuir-head was originally part of the lands of Greenhill, which constituted one of the several lots of the old Burgh Muir feued out by Edinburgh Town Council in 1586.

John Scoon, a 'meal-maker in Gorgie', obtained possession of Burghmuirhead in 1670 and built a number of houses there. In 1692 he feued out the southern portion of it to William Archibald, a writer in Edinburgh, who built additional houses. By the end of the seventeenth century Burghmuirhead had become a sizeable village, but still within the lands of Greenhill. John Scoon eventually sold his property to William Jamieson, a slater, and the transaction included 'that high house covered with slate in Burghmuirhead, with cellar, and little close built within the great close adjoining the said high house on the south, bounded by the King's Highway on the east . . .' This highway was, of course, the old 'wester hiegait' skirting the Burgh Muir, eventually to become Morningside Road. Scoon's sale also included another dwelling-house 'upon the north side of the said high house'. While this latter house has long since been demolished, the 'said high house' is that still to be seen and which had become known by 1852, and probably earlier, as Grangebank, although occasionally referred to as Burghmuir-head House. This house is thus nearly three centuries old.

In 1735 Adam Fairholm, owner of Greenhill estate (and the City Treasurer or Chamberlain already referred to), feued out two small cottages in Burghmuirhead village to John Mann, 'gardener at Foulbriggs', and a subsequent Greenhill owner conveyed another part of Burghmuirhead to John Mann's daughter. The latter married Thomas Steel, a surgeon of Burghmuirhead, and the Steel family, several of whom were doctors or chemists, resided in the village as owners of Grangebank House until 1819. Kirkwood's map of Edinburgh for 1817 shows the whole area of Burghmuirhead as 'Dr Steel's property' and Grangebank House is indicated.

The first Ordnance Survey Map of Edinburgh, that of 1852, shows the district of Burghmuirhead as triangular in shape, the base extending from the south-east corner of Colinton Road to the northern end of Abbotsford Crescent, with the apex at the meeting point of Morningside Road and Albert Terrace at the brow of Churchhill. Grangebank House is shown as surrounded by a wide area of well-planned gardens, which included a bowling green. Grangebank Cottage, apparently a substantial dwelling-house in 1852 and probably the house described as 'upon the north side of the said high house', stood a little to the north but was eventually demolished. A post office is marked in at the south-east corner of Colinton Road but it has now been replaced by that further north at the entrance to Montpelier Park.

In much earlier maps of Edinburgh and the Lothians, many of the then separate districts to the south of the city, which eventually expanded and amalgamated to form 'Greater Morningside', are clearly shown. Timothy Pont's map, *Lothian and Linlithgow* (1660) indicates Wrychtishousis, Grange, Merchiston, Tipperlinn, Craighouse, Blackford and Braid as distinct locations. J. Adair's *Map of Midlothian* (1735) — so wide-ranging as to include East and West Lothian, the Borders and Clydesdale — shows the districts indicated by Pont and also Greenhill, Whitehouse, Canaan, Plewlands, Comiston and

Greenbank. John Lawrie's map of Edinburgh and environs for 1763 adds Burghmuirhead. Among the most valuable and interesting sources from which one may trace the dates of Morningside's earliest houses and details of their successive owners are the old Edinburgh Directories. A complete series of these, the first dating back to 1773, is contained in the invaluable collection of historical material preserved in the Edinburgh Room of the city's Central Public Library. Perhaps, however, the first Edinburgh directory was *Constables' List of Inhabitants* (1682). Those listed resided mainly in the Old Town. They were grouped under each 'quarter' for which a constable was responsible. The people who earned a place in this earliest directory were titled or prominent in some sphere of public life, or were merchants or tradesmen of some standing. Morningside was then well outside the confines of Edinburgh, and in fact was no more than a short row of cottages. The great mansion-houses of Grange, Bruntsfield, Whitehouse, Greenhill, Merchiston, Craighouse, Braid and Comiston encircled the village, each with its own rural estate or farmlands.

The first attempt to produce a more comprehensive directory resulted in *Williamson's Directory for the City of Edinburgh, Canongate, Leith and Suburbs*, first published for 1773-4. It was not until 1832 that the city's residents (and, again, mainly those of standing) were grouped street by street as in directories of today. The streets were further grouped into districts. Bruntsfield Links, Burghmuirhead, Morningside and Canaan constituted District 43, while Leith and Newhaven formed the last District 55.

In the 1833-4 Directory, the pull-out map of Edinburgh for the first time extended to the Jordan Burn, the city's traditional southern boundary. Previous directory maps had reached no further south than Wrychtishousis. In the Directory for the previous year, the total number of residents listed under 'The Forty-Third District', divided into the sub-headings of Burgh-muirhead, Morningside and Canaan, was sixty-two! These were primarily the occupants of the district's principal houses, or important tradesmen and shopkeepers. From these old directories

and maps the successive owners of Grangebank in the village of
Burghmuirhead can be traced.

Grangebank passed from the Steel family in about 1850.
Among subsequent owners we may note a John Bartholomew
in 1859, founder of the now world-renowned firm of cartographers in Duncan Street, who died here in 1861.

In 1892 St Theresa's Orphanage for Girls was established in
Grangebank, latterly becoming a Catholic school of the same
name which at one time was well-remembered by a number of
Morningside residents who were pupils. This school closed just
after the outbreak of the First World War. After a period during
which it remained unoccupied, Grangebank was purchased by
the Lodge Abbotsford in 1920. This Lodge, originating at a
meeting held in Springvalley Hall, Springvalley Gardens in
1905, continued in that meeting place until 1914 when
alterations forced them to meet in other parts of the city until
the purchase of Grangebank. After considerable renovation,
their three-hundred-year-old premises were ready for occupation
in 1921, but further extensive repairs were required in 1955.
Deciding in 1963 to remain at Grangebank rather than move to
new premises, the members of Lodge Abbotsford have since
effected further tastefully executed improvements, especially to
their refectory. It is interesting to note the Lodge's Gaelic
inscriptions on the venerable interior walls of Grangebank.
'That high house', last remaining reminder of the old village of
Burghmuirhead, is happily still preserved.

Churchhill

At Churchhill we reach the summit of the ancient Burgh Muir.
From this vantage point, anyone venturing out here from
Edinburgh in early times would have enjoyed a magnificent
uninterrupted panorama on every side. To the north, gazing
back across Bruntsfield, the Castle would rise sharply against
the sky, dominating the old town, with the Forth and Fife like a
theatrical backdrop, while the crown steeple of St Giles would
tower like a milestone above the spine of the Royal Mile

descending steeply to Holyrood. To the west, Merchiston Tower would stand isolated amidst its surrounding orchards and farmlands, the open countryside beyond stretching as far as the eye could see. To the east, the turreted Grange of St Giles, the little chapel of St Roque and the Convent of St Catherine of Sienna would be the principal landmarks against the huge bulk of Arthur's Seat, and, on the horizon, Berwick Law, the Bass Rock and the Lammermuirs. To the south, down over the brow of Churchhill where today the villas, church steeples and tenements echo the roar of the ceaseless stream of traffic through the bustling suburb of Morningside, our traveller would have gazed on a very different scene: a farm cart and horse, perhaps, passing at leisurely pace between a row of cottages straddling a narrow country road descending steeply to the Jordan Burn; a hawthorn-lined lane leading to Braid, Comiston and Biggar, and, beyond, rising gently to the Pentland Hills. The mansion-house of Braid would lie hidden out of sight in the depths of the Hermitage; the ancient castle of Comiston might just be visible through its surrounding woodland; old Craighouse would be prominent on the eastern slope of Craiglockhart hill, while the whitewashed walls of the old inn at Hunters' Tryst would be the last outpost under the shadow of Caerketton and Allermuir.

The section of Morningside Road from the Baptist Church to Churchhill was originally known as Waverley Terrace, while the continuation to the corner of Abbotsford Park was named Marmion Terrace. Both names had their origins in the legends woven by Sir Walter Scott around this district with its famous Bore Stone, in which, it was for long believed, the Scottish Standard was raised prior to the muster of the Scots army about to depart for the ill-fated battle of Flodden in 1513. Colourful and romantically stirring as were such names as Waverley and Marmion, both names were lost, being incorporated in Morningside Road in 1886.

On the left, above the frontage of the shop at the north corner of Morningside Road and Abbotsford Park (originally the residence of the early medical superintendents of the Morningside Asylum), the name Marmion Terrace was once to be seen, but the passage of time and much paint has now almost obliterated it. This shop once belonged to a grocer named O'Hagan and was the subject of one of a classical series of old Edinburgh photographs by Balmain (now reproduced by Yerbury, the well-known Edinburgh photographers). Towards the end of the nineteenth century there was a small private school in Marmion Terrace known as 'Mr Baillie's School'. A copy still exists of a prize certificate awarded in July 1877 to Robert T. Patterson for map drawing; it is signed, 'James Baillie, Headmaster'. It is possible that the premises occupied by this school were those eventually acquired, and occupied until a few years ago, by Yerbury's. The 'life story' of one former pupil of Mr Baillie's school, David Yule, who became a very wealthy 'Merchant Prince' in Calcutta has been presented in one of the present writer's earlier books.

Through the commendable enterprise of Edinburgh Corporation, Churchhill came to be widely known not only to the citizens of Edinburgh but also to innumerable visitors from all parts of the world attending the city's annual International Festival. For here, on September 25th, 1965 was opened the Churchhill Theatre, soon afterwards to become an officially approved Festival centre.

The establishment of this excellently appointed theatre ended one chapter and began another in the history of amateur drama in Edinburgh. When the Little Theatre in the Pleasance, scene of so many successful amateur productions, was sold by the Pleasance Trust to Edinburgh University in 1960, the city's many amateur companies — and their large number of patrons — were far from happy. Alternative facilities were not readily available. Strong and repeated representation was made to Edinburgh Corporation for positive assistance. In 1960 Morningside High Church (which, until 1929 and the formation of the United Free Presbyterian Church, had been the last of a long succession of premises occupied by Morningside Free Church) became vacant as a result of its union with Morningside Parish Church at the corner of Newbattle Terrace. The spacious red sandstone building was purchased by Edinburgh Corporation for £6,000.

The cost of converting the former church into a first-class theatre was £67,000; the architect was George L. Walls. Apart from the excellent stage, seating and dressing-room facilities, there are two halls suitable for 'theatre in the round', the mounting of art or photographic exhibitions, public meetings and social functions. The Churchhill Theatre opening ceremony in 1965 was performed by the distinguished Scottish actor, Tom Fleming, and the theatre curtain rose for the first time on an inaugural production by the Scottish Community Drama Association of Oscar Wilde's *The Importance of Being Earnest*. First used for an Edinburgh International Festival production in 1966, the Churchhill Theatre now enjoys an established place in the official Festival programme of drama and ballet. For the rest of the year, the theatre is constantly booked by a wide variety of amateur companies and other associations which enjoy facilities unique in Britain.

As we turn into Churchhill Place, which, beyond its short row of substantial tenement flats, becomes Churchhill, it may be recalled that this street was formerly a narrow lane named Napier Terrace, probably after the distinguished mathematician laird of nearby Merchiston Tower. The street (and also the district of Morningside) was later to be known as Churchhill because there came to reside here the famous Dr Thomas Chalmers, who built the first house on the hill overlooking Morningside in 1842 and named it, originally, Kirkhill. Chalmers was instrumental in having Morningside Parish Church built just over the brow of Churchhill in 1838, 'the church on the hill' giving the names to the nearby street and district. This villa, now number 1 Churchhill, was re-named Westgate by a later owner, a name it still bears. A bronze tablet to the left of the front of the house briefly states: 'In this house Thomas Chalmers died, 31st May 1847.' Behind this simple statement lies one of the stormiest chapters in the history of the church, and indeed of Scotland herself, for Dr Chalmers, of course, was one of the

Dr Thomas Chalmers. *Courtesy of the National Galleries of Scotland.*

leaders of the Disruption which in 1843 tore the Church of Scotland apart.

Born in Anstruther, Fife, in 1780, of which busy fishing village his father was Provost, Thomas Chalmers studied at St Andrews University, where he later lectured in mathematics and chemistry before being appointed as Professor of Moral Philosophy. Divinity was, however, the subject in which he was most qualified. Entering the Church of Scotland ministry, he served in a number of country parishes before his appointment to Glasgow's important Tron Church in 1815. Here his sermons, frequently on the relationship between science and religion, gave an early indication of the eloquence and fire which were to lead to his recognition in later years as the most outstanding preacher of his day. This great talent was to play a decisive part in his leadership of the Disruption. He came to Edinburgh University as Professor of Theology in 1828 and his impact on the Capital was soon felt. His first residence in Edinburgh was in Forres Street, from which he moved to 7 Inverleith Row. In 1841 he went to live temporarily at 2 Morningside Place, where he was so impressed by the rural-retreat atmosphere of Morningside that he decided to build a house for himself in Churchhill. A man who led a deeply spiritual life, he perhaps had some feelings of guilt when he contemplated taking up residence in what was then a rather exclusive preserve of the wealthy who were able to spend the summer away from the city in the quiet rural environment of Edinburgh's southern suburb. He wrote in his diary: 'Mean to build at Morningside; but let me not forget the end of the World and the coming of Christ'.

Nothing, however, of the life of the idle rich entered the house which Dr Chalmers duly occupied at Churchhill. In the quietness of his study, the room to the right of the main door (looking in from the street), the remote peacefulness of Morningside was a stimulus to the man who, day after day, laboured relentlessly at his desk on a succession of sermons, speeches and articles which were to spur on events soon to burst upon Scotland like a revolution.

For some years a keen point of debate in the Church of Scotland had been Patronage, the right of the State or certain influential persons (aristocrats or landowners) to veto the appointment of a church minister chosen by a congregation. The age-old issue of Church versus State was involved. Most Church of Scotland leaders believed that, while recognising and professing loyalty to the Crown, the Church should be allowed independence in spiritual affairs and in the appointment of its ministers. This belief was outlined in a General Assembly resolution of 1834.

There were many test cases, notably at Auchterarder where Lord Kinnoull presented to a congregation a minister who was quite unacceptable to all but two members. The case was referred to a civil court and Lord Kinnoull's appointment was upheld. This decision was confirmed by the House of Lords. Other similar cases followed, and in each the local congregation's wishes were disregarded.

At a large meeting in London in 1838, attended by nine Church of England bishops, Dr Chalmers, in a speech of unprecedented eloquence, asserted the Church of Scotland's claim to freedom in the appointment of ministers, a matter in which he said, 'The King cannot . . . the King dare not' interfere. His rousing defiant words drew a great response.

The growing conflict between Church and State became a national issue. In Parliament, Robert Peel re-asserted the rights of the Crown. Many congregations in the Church of Scotland were, however, already flouting the law. The crisis was imminent. Some churchmen might have accepted a compromise, but not so Dr Chalmers: he and other prominent church leaders prepared to bring the issue to a head at the General Assembly of 1843.

The Assembly was to convene on May 17th in St Andrew's Church in George Street: forecasts and rumours of what might happen swept the country. The Assembly, it was generally agreed, would be stormy, yet on the evening of May 16th it was estimated that at most a mere twenty to thirty ministers, finding Parliament's ruling unacceptable, might secede from the established church.

Dr Chalmers and his colleagues had not been idle. They had already booked Tanfield Hall at Canonmills, having confidently predicted what was going to happen. Seating was available for three thousand. The day of the Assembly dawned. The seats in St Andrew's Church began to fill up. Outside in the city the atmosphere was hushed and electrified. Many stayed off work and there gathered outside St Andrew's Church a vast crowd

Church of Scotland General Assembly in St Andrew's Church George Street, 17 May 1843. The beginning of the procession of 474 ministers who 'came out' or seceded to form the Free Church of Scotland. The Moderator Dr Welsh and Dr Chalmers led the march. (From *The Annals of the Disruption* by Thomas Brown)

which included people from all over Scotland and many who had arrived specially from abroad. They had not long to wait.

The Assembly was hardly seated when the Moderator, Dr Welsh, rose, and, in the presence of the Lord High Commissioner, the Marquis of Bute, read the famous words: 'We protest that, in the circumstances in which we are placed, it is and shall be lawful for us . . . to withdraw to a separate place of meeting . . . with an assured conviction that we are not responsible for any consequences that may follow from this . . .'.

With this, the Moderator laid the protest on the table and, lifting his hat, bowed to the High Commissioner. He left his chair of office and proceeded to the door. Dr Chalmers, who had been close beside him throughout, immediately followed, accompanied by several other prominent ministers. Those in the gallery cheered the departure of the pioneers of the Disruption, then fell silent, waiting . . . How many others would follow? The stream of support began: first one minister left his seat, then another, and another; bench after bench became empty; a great mass crowded round the exit doors. Those who remained watched spellbound. Outside in George Street, as Dr Welsh, Dr Chalmers and their supporters appeared, the words were excitedly taken up by the crowd: 'They come . . . They come!' Those who counted their number, expecting a mere twenty to thirty, were amazed: the procession seemed unending. No fewer than four hundred and seventy-four ministers quit the Assembly. Before the eyes of the onlooker, the established Church of Scotland had been torn asunder.

At Tanfield Hall the first Free Assembly was constituted and Dr Chalmers was unanimously elected Moderator. The historic scene at Tanfield was recorded by David Octavius Hill, R.S.A., in a large oil painting, on which he was engaged for twenty-three years. It was purchased by the Free Church for £1,500 and now adorns the Presbytery Hall of their Offices on the Mound. Some years ago a modern building simulating Tanfield Hall has been built at Tanfield.

A few weeks after the Tanfield Assembly, Dr Chalmers resigned his professorship of Divinity at the University. When the Free Church College was built on the Mound, it was he who laid the foundation stone of this great landmark, designed by

W. H. Playfair. Dr Chalmers was also appointed first Principal, on June 4th, 1846, almost exactly one year before his death. After the reunion of the United Free Church and the Church of Scotland in 1929, the Free Church College on the Mound became New College, and it was incorporated in Edinburgh University's Faculty of Divinity.

Many writers have recorded sad scenes throughout Scotland as people watched long-serving and beloved pastors gather together their chattels and families and leave their manses to face the unknown. It was estimated that, in one day, those who quit their charges signed away more than £100,000 per annum in stipends. One third of the total membership of the Church of Scotland left to join the Free Church, and they were perhaps the most active and interested members. The Disruption had, indeed, seemed a mortal blow.

Such, then, was the impact on Scotland of the man whose sudden death at the first house in Churchhill is so briefly commemorated on an inconspicuous plaque.

Morningside experienced the effects of the Disruption no less than other parishes, as several churches in the district still bear witness. One of these is Morningside Parish Church, just over the brow of Churchhill (at the north-west corner of Newbattle Terrace). The establishment of this church had been pioneered by Dr Chalmers, who had also preached the inaugural sermon. At the Disruption, the Reverend Thomas Addis resigned his charge and, with many sympathetic parishioners, established the first Morningside Free Church.

These first Free Church members were, for a time, a congregation without a church: in the long pilgrimage which followed they were to occupy no fewer than five different places of worship before settling in the High Church opened at Churchhill in 1894.

For the first two Sundays after the Disruption, the Morningside Free Church adherents continued to meet in the Parish Church. On being threatened with expulsion, however, they sought permission to occupy the Old Schoolhouse opposite the western end of what is now Falcon Avenue. The committee of management of this little village school, then privately run, refused permission (not without a long and violent debate, it is recorded).

Dr Addis sought Dr Chalmers's advice and the latter immediately offered the use of his house in Churchhill. Thus, for three Sundays, a congregation of three hundred Free Church members in Morningside worshipped in Dr Chalmers's large villa, the considerable gathering occupying every room in the house. Dr Chalmers himself preached from the landing half-way up the staircase, while listeners sat on the upper and lower stairs and on forms in the lobbies and adjacent rooms.

In 1843 Morningside's Free Church gained their own premises — a large circular tent pitched at the south corner of Abbotsford Park. The four hundred who gathered there each Sunday, however, found the summer heat uncomfortable. The reaction was a mixture of annoyance and relief when the canvas church had one day suddenly to be vacated, 'a mischievous boy' having cut the guy ropes so that a gust of wind collapsed the tent on the occupants' heads.

By common impulse many of the congregation marched down Churchhill to the Old Schoolhouse, this time being granted admission. Here they continued to meet until the first Morningside Free Church building had been completed. This apparently stood a little back from the road near what is now 74 Morningside Road, and was opened in 1844. The little church is said to have been designed as a replica of Tanfield Hall at Canonmills where the first Free Church Assembly met. Strangely, there is no evidence of the exact site of this church either on old maps of the period or in contemporary street directories. Nevertheless, the church opposite the entrance to Churchhill served the Free Church congregation for thirty years, during which period a Free Church School was established near the present-day Public Library, and a manse in Morningside Place.

The second Free Church building, designed by McGibbon and Ross, was opened to the north of Churchhill in 1874 at a cost of £7,000. After twenty years, the accommodation of this church proved inadequate for the steadily growing Free Church congregation. Several sites proposed for a new church proved unsuitable and Sir John Stuart Forbes of Greenhill House refused to grant a site within his lands. A proposal to build a large church adjacent to Dr Chalmers's house was also rejected. Finally, the church which is now the Churchhill Theatre was built, two villas which occupied the site having been purchased and demolished. This spacious red sandstone building of Italianate style was opened in 1894. The vacated high-steepled church near the corner of Colinton Road was purchased by Morningside's small group of Baptist pioneers for £3,000, less than half the original cost of building.

The journeyings of Morningside Free Church were at last at an end. Morningside High Church remained its meeting place until the establishment of the United Presbyterian Church in 1929. Subsequently the Church of Scotland congregation re-united with Morningside Parish Church in 1960 and, after one hundred and twenty years, the wheel had turned full circle. Dr Alexander Martin, who succeeded Dr Addis as minister of Morningside Free Church, became Principal of New College on the Mound and played an important part in the move towards re-union with the Church of Scotland, achieved in 1929.

Dr Chalmers's funeral procession to Grange Cemetery on June 4th, 1847 is said to have been the largest of any in nineteenth-century Scotland. Innumerable memorials to the great Disruption leader are still to be seen in Edinburgh and other parts of Scotland, ranging from statues to churches bearing his name. One of the latter which he might well have treasured above all other reminders of his life's work was the Territorial Church (now demolished, but formerly sited on the West Port, almost opposite Portsburgh Square). Chalmers saw this church completed just before his death and he immersed himself in its outstandingly successful pioneering work amongst the illiterate and abandoned poor of the Grassmarket district. Drawing upon pastoral methods he had employed during his ministry in Glasgow, Dr Chalmers divided the West Port into a number of 'territories', each under the care of an elder or other

Morningside High (Free) Church built at Churchhill in 1892. This sketch of the proposed design is by the architect, Hippolyte Blanc. The tower was never built. The church eventually re-united with Morningside Parish Church in 1960, and became Churchill Theatre 1965. (*Royal Commission on the Ancient & Historical Monuments of Scotland*).

helper. These visited the families often experiencing severe poverty frequently caused by drunkenness leading to debt and despair. Temperance meetings were held and a school was started. Mothers were helped to manage their meagre budget and to look after their children. Chalmers described this work in which he took part in the last years of his life, in the district under the shadow of the notorious Burke and Hare, as the most important of his career. His involvement was short-lived. Perhaps the arduous work hastened his relatively early sudden death. The Chalmers Hospital, built in 1861 in Lauriston Place is named not after Dr Chalmers, but after an Edinburgh plumber, George Chalmers, who died in 1836 and bequeathed £30,000 for a hospital 'for the sick and the hurt'.

East Morningside

Leaving Dr Chalmers's house, which for a period in later years became a girls' school, and continuing eastwards along Church-hill, we may glimpse the white-walled East Morningside House beyond the green-domed private chapel at St Bennet's. This venerable mansion-house, the entrance drive of which leads from Clinton Road, was built by Gavin Bailie, an Edinburgh merchant, in about 1726. On his death in 1734, Bailie is described as 'of Morningside' and this is the earliest reference to the name of the district yet found in the City Records. The name may have been derived from the fact that the original entrance to the mansion-house faced east to 'the morning side of the sun'. The lands of East Morningside stretched from what are now Churchhill Place, Churchhill and Strathearn Place in the north to Newbattle Terrace in the south, and from the corner of Newbattle Terrace to Churchhill in the west to Whitehouse Loan in the east. The west wing of the house was added about 1850. It was because Sir John Stuart Forbes of the adjacent lands of Greenhill obtained part of East Morningside, and because of the subsequent marriage of one of his descendants, Harriet Forbes, to the 21st Baron Clinton, that the present-day Clinton Road was so called in 1858. Morningside Parish Church once paid a nominal feu duty to the Clinton descendants. The name of Pitsligo Road also recalls that Forbes of Greenhill and Pitsligo once owned part of East Morningside.

Whilst the story of Churchhill is associated with the ecclesiastical history of Scotland, that of East Morningside introduces us to one of the great literary figures who lived in Morningside. Many interesting and distinguished people have resided in the spacious and majestic mansion, East Morningside House, but none has received more widespread publicity than Miss Susan Edmonstone Ferrier, whose three novels *Marriage* (1818), *Inheritance* (1824) and *Destiny* (1831) had considerable impact and influence on the literary world of her day and on early nineteenth-century high society in Scotland, and indeed beyond.

Most of her first book was written at East Morningside House, in the oak-panelled study with its seventeenth-century pitch-pine fireplace. This room is still well preserved.

Susan Ferrier, whose novels drew the warm praise of Sir Walter Scott and once gained for her the title of 'Scotland's Jane Austen', was born in a flat in Lady Stair's Close, off the Lawnmarket, on September 7th, 1782. She was the youngest of the ten children of James Ferrier, Writer to the Signet and younger son of John Ferrier, Laird of Kirklands in Renfrewshire. Her mother was Helen Coutts, a famous beauty of her day, who, before her marriage, had lived in Holyrood Palace. Susan's early schooling was obtained at Mr Stalker's Academy for Boys and Girls in George Street. The Ferrier family subsequently moved from Lady Stair's Close to 25 George Street, and while there James Ferrier acquired East Morningside House as the family's summer residence.

Through the influence of John, 5th Duke of Argyll, whose estates he managed, James Ferrier was appointed a Principal Clerk of Session at the Edinburgh Law Courts. There he became a close friend of a legal colleague, Walter Scott. One of the many treasures preserved in the East Morningside House is a chair bearing the inscription: 'To my friend James Ferrier for happy days and hospitality at East Morningside House — *Walter Scott*'.

East Morningside House, Clinton Road. This was the first villa built in Morningside *c.* 1726. The house records bear the first reference to 'Morningside' in the area, the name perhaps deriving from main door facing east – the 'morning side of the sun'. Jacobite troops visited house while passing along to Holyrood in 1745. *Photograph by W. R. Smith.*

After her mother's death, Susan, then fifteen, made the first of many journeys with her father to Inveraray Castle, the Duke of Argyll's principal residence on Loch Fyne. These visits were to rouse in her the first stirrings of a lively imagination and were to be imprinted on a highly perceptive mind. While her father attended to his duties at the castle, Susan observed and experienced a whole new world of fashion and high life, encountering a fascinating variety of people who to her seemed larger than life and who, in time, found their way into her novels. There were 'red-haired Highland Chiefs, sniffing, sneezing and condemning everything that was not Scottish, and there were London ladies who brought their parrots, lap-dogs, macaws and doctors'. So one of Miss Ferrier's biographers described the scene. It was a potential novelist's paradise.

Nevertheless, young Susan might well have kept her impressions secretly and silently to herself (no doubt many of those who, to their embarrassment, later appeared in her books would have been much relieved had she done so) rather than present them satirically (though never wholly unkindly) to the Scotland of her day, had it not been for her friendship with the Duke of Argyll's young niece, Charlotte Clavering.

At first entitled *The Chiefs of Glenfern*, the novel was submitted in 1817 to the famous Edinburgh publisher, William Blackwood, the central, stimulating figure of a distinguished circle of Edinburgh writers including John Wilson (alias Christopher North), John Galt, Michael Scott, John Gibson Lockhart and James Hogg (the Ettrick Shepherd). Blackwood accepted the novel with little delay, writing to Miss Ferrier: 'The whole construction and execution appear so admirable that it would almost be presumption in any one to offer corrections to such a writer.' Not many writers receive such unqualified acceptance on the submission of a first novel!

'Anonymous Novelist'

Under the title *Marriage*, the book appeared in 1818. Miss Ferrier, in correspondence with Blackwood, negotiated and accepted a fee of £150. (This correspondence is preserved in the National Library of Scotland.) The novel, portraying with little disguise so many living people, laying bare their vulgarities, their selfishness and absurdities, was, not surprisingly, published anonymously. Susan's father, who had no time for female authors, was ill in bed at the time. On asking her to read to him, Susan obliged by taking up *Marriage*. She was eager to obtain his reaction before that of the general public. With the page carefully concealed behind a bedside curtain, she read on – to her father's apparent satisfaction. When he requested that she obtain another book by the same author, whose work he considered the best he had yet heard, Susan thought fit to point out that it had been written by a woman. Mr Ferrier refused to believe it: the book had been so good. His daughter then confessed her authorship.

In the literary world of Scotland and beyond, the appearance of Susan Ferrier's first novel was an event. Attempts were made to identify the author. London critics attributed the book to Scott, who, in later years, wrote: 'I retire from the field, conscious that there remains behind not only a large harvest, but labourers capable of gathering it in . . . If the present author, himself a phantom, may be permitted to distinguish a brother, or perhaps a sister, shadow, he would mention, in particular, the author of the very lively work entitled *Marriage*.' The mystery novelist was compared to Jane Austen and John Galt, and she was praised for diverting the Scottish novel into new channels.

Inheritance, Miss Ferrier's second anonymous novel, followed six years after *Marriage*, in 1824. While the first novel had been regarded as the work of an author of great promise, the second was generally considered to have fulfilled that promise, revealing a more skilful construction of plot and a much improved style. This novel Miss Ferrier sold to Blackwood for £1,000 (having rejected an earlier offer of £500). It seems that she had considered the sum of £150 received for *Marriage* as an underpayment. Scott also praised this second novel warmly. Another critic considered it 'the best of its class at the present day'. Others now saw a definite attempt at a style modelled on Jane Austen, though lacking that delicacy of treatment.

Destiny, or the Chieftain's Daughter, the third and last novel, was published in 1831. Critics saw in it signs of a decline — of which the authoress herself was perhaps only too well aware. *Destiny* was dedicated to Sir Walter Scott, now her close friend, who, it was said, had persuaded Blackwood to pay Miss Ferrier a record £1,700 for it. The book was widely read. Miss Ferrier had positive views on the role of the writer in society. 'The only good purpose of a book', she wrote, 'is to inculcate morality and convey some lesson of instruction as well as delight.' Whether or not her three novels put this into practice must be judged by her readers — and these she still has. The anonymity of her authorship was retained until 1851 when she allowed her name to appear on new editions.

Described as 'dark, tall, handsome, a brilliant conversationalist and herself no blue-stocking', Susan Ferrier never married. She was a most kind-hearted person, and especially helpful to Sir Walter Scott in his last years. When amidst his friends at Abbotsford, his speech increasingly impaired, she would tactfully help him over difficult moments in conversation. She herself suffered from near-blindness in her last days and was forced to spend much time in a completely darkened room. She died at her town house, 38 Albany Street, in 1854, at the age of seventy, and now rests in the family grave in St Cuthbert's Churchyard in Lothian Road.

Of East Morningside House, on one occasion she wrote: 'We are once more settled here, for seven months to come I suppose, and glad I am to find myself out of the smoke and dust of town which always disagrees with me at this season.'

In the winter of 1829 she wrote from East Morningside: 'The storm seems to be awesome and appears to be endless. Last night was almost as bad as any we have had — nine trees blown down at Morningside — the stack of chimneys of this house was discovered to be hanging on a thread. Except the Walkers and James on a Sunday we never see a soul.'

One map clearly indicates the fine avenue of beech trees leading from Newbattle Terrace (from the gateway near the present-day high voltage electric power plant) straight to East Morningside House. In Clinton Road it is still noticeable that one section of the southern boundary wall of East Morningside House was more recently constructed than the adjoining parts. This section was originally open and through it the main drive and avenue led up to the mansion-house.

The house, with its immensely thick walls, is set in spacious, well laid out gardens with stately trees. The grounds retain their rural atmosphere within the main gates, where little has changed in two hundred years, and they contain two interesting relics of earlier days. The ivy-covered square dovecote near the south wall at Clinton Road, which has two hundred and thirty-two nesting places — a reminder of times when pigeon-pie was a popular dish — merited description in Volume XXV of the *Book of the Old Edinburgh Club*. Its timber and slate roof inclines to the north, unlike those of most other dovecotes which are south-sloping so that the pigeons can bask in the sun. The entrances for the birds are also unusual: there are twelve openings in four rows, with landing ledges in a wooden frame set in a window cut into the angle of the south and west walls.

It is related that there was much rivalry between the dovecote at East Morningside and that at nearby Merchiston Tower. James Wilson, the famous naturalist who lived in Woodville at the top of Canaan Lane, a contemporary, close neighbour and friend of Susan Ferrier, once asked her in a letter whether she poisoned visiting pigeons to preserve her vegetables. One is reminded of how, two centuries earlier, the distinguished mathematician John Napier overcame the problem of invading pigeons by feeding them with grain soaked in alcohol. East Morningside House did not exist, of course, in Napier's time.

In many large Scottish estates, the dovecote has survived the manor house, perhaps on account of the special importance attached to it and the traditional belief that, if the dovecote were pulled down or allowed to deteriorate, the lady of the house would die within a year. James I decreed it a felony to destroy a dovecote and James VI introduced a law forbidding the building of a dovecote beside any house which did not possess a certain amount of surrounding land and adequate victuals cultivated in fields.

Close to the dovecote's south wall and hard against the Clinton Road boundary wall is a very old willow tree which was successfully grown from a cutting brought from Napoleon's garden at Longwood on St Helena. Carefully supported by splints, the tree still flourishes and a glimpse of it may be caught from Clinton Road. A white rose bush is said to have been in the garden when Bonnie Prince Charlie and his soldiers passed along Cant's Loan (now Newbattle Terrace) and on by Grange Loan in 1745 en route to Grange House, where they called, then on to Holyrood Palace. They plucked blooms to adorn their bonnets. Possibly linked to the same incident, the avenue of tall trees leading from Newbattle Terrace to what was an entrance to East Morningside House came to be known as 'Prince Charlie's Avenue'. The white rose still blooms.

Lord Fleming, Senator of the College of Justice, and a generous benefactor and active supporter of many causes, lived in East Morningside House for a long period. He and Lady Fleming are commemorated by a seat placed in Whitehouse Loan, which is inscribed 'Rest and be Thankful. This seat is placed here in memory of Lord and Lady Fleming who lived in East Morningside House from 1924 till 1944'.

For well over a century, East Morningside House enjoyed the rural remoteness of its secluded and spacious estate. In the nineteenth century, however, several other mansion-houses arose in quick succession in Clinton Road.

Directly opposite East Morningside House on the south side of Clinton Road, there stood until 1962 the stately Scottish Baronial-style mansion of Woodcroft. The original entrance gateway pillars bearing its name remain near the fine avenue of beech trees which once lined the main driveway from Grange Loan to East Morningside House.

Woodcroft was designed and built in 1858 by Colonel Sir David Davidson after his retirement from long and distinguished service in the East India Company. Standing in five acres of land purchased from the East Morningside Estate, the house was of fine pink sandstone quarried from its own grounds, and considered equal in quality to that then obtainable from Craigleith.

In his autobiography, *Memorials of a Long Life*, published in 1890, Colonel Davidson writes that he selected 'an amiable site on the ridge running east from Burghmuirhead, on which the Scottish army had camped before marching to Flodden, and commanding a view of the Blackford, the Braid and the Pentland hills stretching one behind the other like the scenery of a stage'. Standing three hundred feet above sea level, Woodcroft must then certainly have enjoyed a maginificent southern panorama. Dr John Brown, author of the Scottish classic *Rab and His*

Friends, was greatly impressed by Woodcroft. 'The best house in Edinburgh,' he once called it, 'and built of the rock on which it stands.'

Born in Haddington in 1811, young David Davidson had there been a close friend of the local doctor's daughter, Jane Welsh, later to become the famous Jane Welsh Carlyle, wife of 'the Sage of Chelsea'. While awaiting the completion of Woodcroft, Davidson had lived temporarily at St Margaret's Cottage in nearby Greenhill and there was visited by Jane Welsh Carlyle, on which occasion they exchanged reminiscences of their youthful days in Haddington. He also visited the Carlyle residence in Chelsea's Cheyne Row, where he met Alfred Tennyson. The meeting is said to have resulted in a most animated discussion. Colonel Davidson consulted the notable Edinburgh architect David Bryce regarding the design of 'Woodcroft'.

When Woodcroft was at last completed, the motto over its main doorway, *Meliora semper cogita*, was suggested by Jane Welsh Carlyle. It was the same motto that had been inscribed on her childhood home in Haddington. Frequent recollection of their early days at Haddington was at first a regular feature of Colonel Davidson's correspondence with Mrs Carlyle. This for some time she appears to have enjoyed, readily indulging in the nostalgia. Later, however, she began to find his constant references to the 'old days' increasingly upsetting and he was requested to write in such vein no more. The point, it seems, was taken.

Following Colonel Davidson's death in 1900 (he was in his eighty-ninth year), Woodcroft had a succession of owners. Towards the end of the Second World War, a part of the extensive grounds was requisitioned for the erection of a Post Office Telephones training centre. The old mansion-house was demolished in 1962 and three years later, on July 9th, 1965, there was opened by the Right Honourable Anthony Wedgwood Benn, then Postmaster-General, an important STD telephone trunk-call centre for south-east Scotland, operating in conjunction with sub-centres at Aberdeen and Dundee. Approximately half a million calls a week to all parts of the world passed through this most modern exchange, which retains the name Woodcroft. It is now an administrative centre.

Despite the impressiveness of Woodcroft, as a mansion-house, and also in its historical associations, and the beautiful and spacious gardens, illustrations of the house have 'disappeared without trace', despite extensive inquiries. The only known illustration which provides some indication of the house and its location is an aerial photograph taken by the Royal Air Force during their systematic coverage of the city. This photograph was not clear enough for publication.

Soon after the original Woodcroft was completed in 1858, two other houses of similar design were built to the east of it. Of pink sandstone from the East Morningside estate, they were again in the elaborate Scottish Baronial style.

That called Avalon, immediately adjacent to Woodcroft, bears the date 1860. Little is known of the original owner, Miss Fleming. The name of the house was probably chosen by a later owner. The architect was David Bryce.

A monogram carved in the stonework above the main door is now indecipherable, though the mottoes and philosophical injunctions inscribed on the walls may still be read. On the front is, 'He yt thollis overcummis', on the west wall, 'Feir God and honor ye King' and on the rear, 'Ponta labore quies'.

The wrought-iron coat of arms on the small gate to the left of the main entrance in Clinton Road is also of interest. The same heraldic design may be seen in many of the books published by W. Green & Son, the legal publishers of St Giles Street, in the stained-glass windows of Gracemount House off Lasswade Road (now an Edinburgh Corporation Youth Centre) and in the entrance hall of Avalon. These are the arms granted by the Lord Lyon in 1908 to Charles Edward Green of St Catherine's, Gracemount and Burnhead, who purchased Avalon in 1920. They show the scales of justice and an open book, and, surmounting these, a mailed fist holding aloft a sprig of holly. The accompanying German motto is, *Erst Wägenden wagen*.

Born in 1886, Charles Edward Green was the eldest of the

four sons of William Green, founder of the legal publishing house. On his father's death, he withdrew from his study of medicine at Edinburgh University to take over as sole partner of the firm. He continued to further the family's academic ambitions, however, by materially assisting his three brothers to graduate in medicine, law and architecture.

Charles himself never lost interest in medicine, the study of which he had obviously relinquished with regret, and the book he wrote on the possible causes of cancer attracted some attention in medical circles. Devoting himself assiduously to publishing, he produced four large encyclopaedias on medicine, accountancy, Scottish law and English law, the last of which was at the time the largest single work in the English language. From his own pen he published a standard work on East Lothian.

Charles Green's enjoyment of Avalon, with its magnificent garden and pleasant surroundings, was short-lived. He died at the age of fifty-four — within a year of purchasing the house. His widow (the younger daughter of John Dalrymple, an Edinburgh merchant) continued to live at Avalon until her death many years later. Possibly it was she who named the house Avalon, after the legendary paradise of King Arthur fame. Does the mailed fist and branch of holly in the coat-of-arms perhaps have some symbolic link with Excalibur, King Arthur's sword, rising above the water?

It is interesting to note that the garage door at Avalon is said to have come from St Giles' Cathedral. A sundial which once stood in the garden now graces a public park in Brechin.

Immediately to the east of Avalon, and entered from Whitehouse Loan, stands The Elms, the last of the trio of impressive mansion-houses on the south side of Clinton Road. It was built by Alexander Hamilton, W.S., formerly of Glasgow, in 1858. His monogram is carved above the main door with a motto reading *In arduis fortitudo: 1858.*

In 1884 The Elms became the residence of Andrew Hugh Turnbull, who was prominent in the world of Scottish insurance and was a director of the Royal Bank of Scotland. His wife Margaret was the youngest daughter of Adam Black, a former

Lord Provost of Edinburgh. Black was elected to Parliament in 1856 at the age of seventy, and served for ten years. He was for some time the publisher of the *Encyclopaedia Britannica* and the *Edinburgh Review*.

Passing from private ownership in 1957, this eminently suitable mansion-house became a Church of Scotland Eventide Home the following year. With additional purpose-built accommodation, The Elms now provides thoughtfully planned facilities for old people.

Facing Clinton Road, but entered (through a spacious and attractive garden) from the Whitehouse Loan, is Clinton House, built in 1877 by Mrs Kerr Ross, widow of Lieutenant-General James Kerr Ross, who served under Wellington.

Mrs Kerr Ross was a devoted member of Morningside Parish Church and a generous benefactress of the Dorcas Society and other charities for the poor. She presented the Communion Table to the church in 1877, when she first came to Clinton House, and the Kerr Ross Bequest of £1000 has brought relief and comfort to many beneficiaries over the years. A stained-glass window in the north transept of Morningside Parish Church was placed there by Mrs Kerr Ross in memory of her husband in the year of his death, 1872.

Of considerable musical talent, Mrs Kerr Ross at the age of ninety-one composed a march to celebrate the Diamond Jubilee of Queen Victoria, which the Queen graciously accepted. When she was two years past her century, this venerable and still alert owner of Clinton House bought a grand piano and continued to practise daily. She died in 1909 at the age of one hundred and three.

William Mair, in *Historic Morningside*, refers to The Elms as having been the residence of two distinguished brothers, George Wilson, M.D., F.R.S.E., founder and first director of the Scottish Industrial Museum (which became the Royal Scottish Museum) in Chambers Street in 1861, and Sir Daniel Wilson, author of one of the great classics on the history of Edinburgh, *Memorials of Edinburgh in the Olden Times*. In fact, George and Daniel Wilson lived not in The Elms but in Elm Cottage in Blackford

Road, opposite the gates of The Elms. Divided into east and west, it is now numbers 1 and 3. 'Elm Cottage West' is still indicated on the wall of number 1.

Professor George Wilson, son of a wine merchant, graduated in medicine, but his special interest was in chemistry. He published several books on this and related subjects, all the results of original research. His labours were directed particularly towards the foundation of a Scottish Industrial Museum, which was achieved in 1855. Soon after this he was appointed Professor of Technology at Edinburgh University. By the time of his death at Elm Cottage in 1859, he had collected over ten thousand specimens for his 'dear museum', as he once described it.

One of Professor Wilson's innumerable interests was the use of anaesthesia in surgery, prompted by a personal ordeal during an operation before Sir James Simpson's revolutionary discovery of chloroform as an anaesthetic.

The surgeon who operated on Wilson was Professor James Syme of the Chair of Clinical Surgery at Edinburgh University, reputedly 'The Napoleon of Surgery' of his day. Wilson wrote to Professor James Simpson strongly supporting him in his search for an effective anaesthetic, despite opposition in this by many surgeons. Wilson described to him the ordeal he had had at the hands of Syme, skilled as they were, but causing 'a black whirlwind of emotion, the horror of great darkness and the sense of desertion by God and man' that swept through him during the operation. Wilson also urged the use of oxygen in resuscitation. He was, in addition, the first in Britain to prepare colour-blindness tests for railwaymen and sailors.

His many years of crippling ill-health before his early death led him to seek the reputedly beneficial climate and peace of Morningside. After lodging in the district, he spent his last days at Elm Cottage. His elder brother Daniel joined him there for a short time before leaving to accept a professorship in Toronto, where he died in 1892.

Returning from Elm Cottage to Churchhill by way of Clinton Road, it may be recalled that this was the route taken by the

Professor George Wilson, the pioneer of the Scottish Industrial Museum, Chambers Street, the forerunner of today's Royal Museum of Scotland. He lived in Elm Cottage. (*The National Galleries of Scotland*).

early horse-drawn buses and trams which plied between Register House, at the east end of Princes Street, and, originally, Churchhill. Later they went as far as the Old Toll House beside the Jordan Burn at the foot of Morningside Road, and eventually to the Braid Hills terminus.

In 1879 a steam-operated bus was the pioneer in public transport but it proved unsuccessful. The Edinburgh Transport

Act of 1871 authorised tramways 'to be worked by animal power only'.

Horse-drawn buses were introduced in 1871. Some such 'buses' were old stage coaches; others known as 'brakes', consisted of rows of bench-style seats, with no sides, passengers clambering aboard by ladder. The horses had bells round their necks and the bus driver had a whistle to warn other traffic of his movements.

By 1872 the horse-drawn bus had been replaced by the more suitable horse-drawn tram. A journey cost three pence for passengers travelling inside and two pence for those perched, sometimes precariously, on the outside platform or on the roof.

An infrequent service was provided on the circular route from Register House via Salisbury Place to Churchhill (later to the Morningside Asylum gates) from the earliest days of the horse-drawn trams. The various city services were distinguished by buses or trams painted in different bright colours, and this Morningside service was red. The old circular route was not the same as the bus route of today, which goes via the Grange Road, Strathearn Road and Strathearn Place, since prior to 1897 Strathearn Place was a *cul-de-sac*. The horse-drawn bus and tram route to Churchhill and Morningside went from Salisbury Place to Grange Road, turning left at the top of Marchmont Road into Kilgraston Road and right into Hope Terrace, then across Whitehouse Loan into Clinton Road and, finally, half-right and half-left from Clinton Road into Churchhill.

By an Act of 1897, provision was made for the acquisition of the villa at the west end of Strathearn Place, then, as mentioned, a *cul-de-sac*. Duly purchased, it was demolished, opening Strathearn Place, and, by the same Act, horse-drawn trams were permitted to proceed directly from Grange Road, through Strathearn Place, to Churchhill. In this year, the Morningside service was extended to the Braid Hills terminus, and, that summer, to Fairmilehead, with occasional runs to Lothianburn. A carmen's shelter was situated near Morningside Station at Balcarres Street. The old tramwaymen's stone-built shelter and

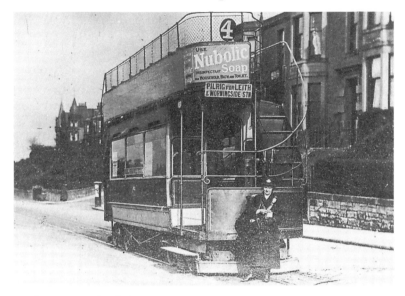

Cable car at Braid Hills Terminus.

rest place which was once at the end of the Strathearn Place *cul-de-sac* where the trams turned may still be seen within the forecourt of the Iona Hotel.

The year 1897 also brought other fundamental changes. Cable-cars were permitted by another Transport Act. Two power stations were built, at Shrubhill and Tollcross; the latter was demolished in 1971. The experience of cable-car haulage in San Francisco, a city with steep hills like Edinburgh, was drawn upon. Edinburgh's first cable-cars set forth in 1897 and during this same year a tram line, partly single and partly double, was authorised to run from the top of Marchmont Road, through Strathearn Road and Strathearn Place, to Churchhill and the Braid Hills terminus. By 1899 this line was laid and in operation. It was agreed that the old horse-drawn tracks from the Clinton Road route be removed, though this was not in fact completed until 1900. The new single cable-car line in Strathearn Place was specially designed to avoid the noise then associated with the changing of points, which offended residents.

Over the years, much concern had been expressed at the hardship suffered by horses on the city's steep hills. Icy roads in winter provided special hazards. One of the worst spots was the sharp turning from Whitehouse Loan into Clinton Road, apparently often the scene of horses slipping and falling.

Before leaving Clinton Road a recent historic event must be recalled. A few yards westwards from East Morningside House and situated in adjacent Greenhill Gardens is St Bennets, a large baronial villa built by John Henderson for a notable Edinburgh advocate and scholar, George Seton, in 1856. Henderson was also the architect of Morningside Parish Church just over the brow of Churchhill. This fine house was eventually acquired by the Roman Catholic Archdiocese of St Andrews and Edinburgh and has been the residence of successive archbishops. Here Pope John Paul II resided with Cardinal Gordon Joseph Gray during his visit to Scotland in 1982. The chapel was designed by R. Weir Schultz in 1907.

We return from East Morningside to Churchhill, from which prominent vantage point the extensive panorama of modern Morningside stretches out before us. In this district past and present are so closely interwoven that our descent over the brow of Churchhill into the heart of Morningside must again be delayed — but for the last time — as echoes from earlier days detain us.

Jane Welsh Carlyle, whose association with Woodcroft in East Morningside has already been described, records in her published letters some interesting impressions of the Morningside she knew in 1856, and her distinguished husband Thomas Carlyle related, in that year: 'My Jeannie has come across to Craigenvilla (fond reminiscences of Craigenputtock!) her aunts' new garden residence of their own in Edinburgh's Morningside quarter, some neat little place where the surviving two yet live.'

Craigenvilla, apparently a substantial villa, stood in its spacious garden at the south-west corner of Churchhill and what was then Banner Place (now Morningside Road) extending from this corner downhill to Newbattle Terrace. *The Edinburgh and Leith Post Office Directory* of that year lists 'The Misses

Welsh, Craigenvilla, No. 2 Banner Place'. The house, under previous ownership, had been known as Grafden Villa. The site is now occupied by tenements and a large house-furnishing business owned by a former City Councillor.

Thomas Carlyle's reference to Craigenputtock is to the house in Dumfriesshire which Jane Welsh's grandfather, and later her father, had owned; a house with deeply sentimental associations often referred to in the Welsh family chronicles. Whether Jane Welsh's aunts changed the name of the house at Churchhill from Grafden Villa to Craigenvilla in order to commemorate the old family house in Dumfriesshire is now difficult to discover.

During Jane Welsh Carlyle's short stays at Craigenvilla, from which several of her published letters were written, she made interesting comments on the Morningside of 1856, especially its Free Kirk atmosphere. This was just over ten years after the Disruption, when a substantial portion of the congregation of Morningside Parish Church, not many yards downhill from Craigenvilla, had 'come out' to found Morningside Free Kirk. The two Misses Welsh would appear to have been devout members of this new congregation.

Thomas Carlyle's reference to his wife's having gone to Craigenvilla continued: 'They had all gone deep into conscious devotion, religious philanthropy, prayer meetings, etc., etc., but were felt to be intrinsically honest-minded women, with a true affection for their niece, however pagan!'

'They were so unexpectedly tender and glad over me', wrote Jane, that she forebore to make her usual acid remarks on the morning prayers, grace before meals and general 'Free Church air' of the house. Just how great an effort of tolerance this demanded from her is made clear: 'One of your letters', she wrote to Carlyle, 'arriving as breakfast was served caused us all to fall quite unconsciously into *Sin*. Sin against 'T'olly Goast'. I was reading my letter, and had taken a sip or two of tea and bitten into my soda scone, and the others had done the same, when Grace suddenly shrieked out like "a mad", "Mercy! we have forgotten the Blessing". I started on my chair, and (to such a pitch of compliance with "Coostom in Part' have I already reached!) dropped *instinctively* the morsel *out of my mouth into my hand (!)* till I should see what steps were to be taken, for making our peace with Christ. But the case was judged past remedy – and the breakfast allowed to proceed unblessed.' Why, she complained elsewhere to an old family friend, did her aunts live 'in such a fuss of religion'? 'My dear,' explained the friend, 'they were idle, plenty to leeve on and nocht to do for't *they micht hae ta'en to waur!* So we maun *just thole them* and no compleen.'

Jane Welsh Carlyle refers again to Morningside's strict observance of the Sabbath in a letter to her husband on August 24th, 1857, in which she also comments on more earthly aspects of the village. 'Certainly is it a devil of a place for keeping the Sunday, this!' she writes. 'Such preaching and fasting, and "touting and praying" as I was never before concerned in.' The weather was apparently warm. '75 F in the shade yesterday. But there is plenty of east wind to keep one from suffocating, provided one can get it without the dust. I used to fancy Piccadilly dusty; but oh my, if you saw Morningside Road!' If Mrs Carlyle found Morningside Road dusty, she also appears to have found it noisy, reporting in another letter to her husband that she lay awake in the early morning 'amidst a tearing rumble of carts that seemed to drive over my brain.'

In her later years, when she described herself as 'a living miracle', she suffered much pain and frequent sleepless nights. While at Craigenvilla in 1862, four years before her death, she recorded in her diary her need for morphia to induce sleep, adding on one occasion: 'Am just going in an omnibus to Duncan Flockhart's for it.' Duncan Flockhart's, the chemists, were in 1862 established at 52 North Bridge.

Carlyle himself may well have resided in the villa at Church-hill – possibly in April 1866 when he was installed as Rector of Edinburgh University. Jane Carlyle, afraid of the climate in Edinburgh and the long journey north and also unable to contemplate the nervous strain she would undergo during her husband's installation and his Rectorial Address, remained in London. After the Address she received a telegram from her husband's close friend Thomas Tyndall, which read: 'A perfect triumph'. Jane, who lived for her husband's success, was overjoyed and waited eagerly for his return. An injury to his ankle, however, forced him to remain in Edinburgh. He was, at this time, the guest of Professor James Syme at Millbank in Canaan Lane. Carlyle, in his condition, could not have been in better company, Syme being the leading surgeon in Europe. The Sage of Chelsea's triumphant stay in Edinburgh, during which he was unable to cope with the number of invitations extended to him and receptions held in his honour, ended with tragedy. Two days before his eagerly awaited return to London, Jane, during a drive round Hyde Park, died in the back of her carriage. She was sixty-five. Jane Welsh Carlyle was laid to rest in the churchyard of her beloved Haddington. 'Her death', wrote Carlyle, 'has shattered my whole existence into im- measurable ruin.' He himself died fifteen years later.

Another echo from the past to claim our attention is from the 'city trained bands and proper bands of musick' which led to a great procession of city dignitaries and important citizens in Edinburgh's last official Riding of the Marches in 1717. Their lengthy route included Doo or Dove Loan (in more recent times renamed Albert Terrace in honour of the Prince Consort), one of the few streets in Morningside with a name not derived from local history. This narrow country lane was known as Doo Loan because of the many pigeons which resorted here from the nearby large doocot at Merchiston Tower. It led to the old village of Tipperlinn, and formed the northern boundary between the lands of West Morningside and Merchiston. The eastern boundary of West Morningside estate was Morningside Road, the old 'wester hiegait' through the Burgh Muir, extending from Churchhill to the southern boundary, the Jordan Burn. The western boundary, Tipperlinn Loan, ran uphill from the Jordan Burn, through the old village of Tipperlinn, to the Merchiston estate.

What is now Albert Terrace therefore formed an important

Albert Terrace, off Morningside Road at Churchhill and once the ancient 'Doo Loan', the name originating from the doocot of nearby Merchiston Tower. The street became Albert Terrace in 1863, with numbers 1 to 9 described as 'perfectly Georgian except for the pottery balustrade, with the figure of a heron at each end'. The reason for the herons could not be traced. *Photograph by W. R. Smith.*

'march line' or boundary between West Morningside and Merchiston, and hence was on the route of the great procession inspecting Edinburgh's internal boundaries for the last time in 1717.

The city records relate:

> About 9 of the clock in the morning the cavalcade 'sumptuously apparelled' and on horse-back rode out from the Bristo Port, by the Windmill and Siens, turning westwards to Brownsfield House and Merchiston Tower. From Merchiston then through the lane on the south side of the house, through Tipperling Lane to Boroughmuirhead Lane, thence to the village of Egypt and eastward by the cemetery wall of St Roque, next proceeding to the Grange House through Cant's Loan to Cameron, Priestfield, passing on the eastern side of

the gallows at Gibbet Toll Road, Bedford Hall, the Crackling House, the Pleasance, St Mary's Street, to Newhaven, and finally returning to the city.

This ceremony, 'the Beating of the Bounds', is of great antiquity, being recorded in Roman and Hebrew days. It is still observed each year, even if purely ceremonially, in the Borders. It was never carried out frequently in Edinburgh. The traditional biennial occasions were on the Feast Days of the Holy Trinity and All Hallows. The object of the Riding was to check that landowners had not, since the last tour of inspection, encroached on their neighbours' property. Records indicate that, in the vicinity of Tipperlinn Loan, successive Lairds of Merchiston regularly edged their way into the precincts of West Morningside.

CHAPTER 2

Towards the Village

The Bore Stone

As we take our last view from Churchhill before descending the steep hill into Morningside, we may recall those, prominent in the pageant of Scottish history, who, in varied circumstances, have traversed what became Morningside Road in successive centuries.

In early times Roman Legions marching up Watling Street from south of the Border reached the vantage point of Fairmilehead before descending by the old Braid road to what was to become Morningside and then climbing over Churchhill and Burghmuirhead on their way to the important settlement at Cramond. In 1298 Edward I of England, intent on suppressing the Scots, camped on the Braid Hills and from there, on July 15th of that year, marched with his well-equipped army along the route of what is today Morningside Road, then westwards to Falkirk, where he inflicted a serious defeat on William Wallace. A month later Edward returned by the same route to his base on the Braids.

In 1580 the Regent Morton, after his fall from power, was conveyed as a prisoner along Morningside Road on his way to Dumbarton. An unsuccessful rescue attempt was made by his friends, who leapt out from their hiding place amongst the rocky undercover of the Braid Hills. Just under a century later Oliver Cromwell, encamped with sixteen thousand men on Galachlaw, near Fairmilehead, sent foraging parties down into Morningside Road, where they met with stiff resistance from local residents.

Sixteen years after Cromwell's invasion, Morningside Road witnessed the spectacle of brave Covenanter prisoners, taken after the Battle of Rullion Green, being escorted to confinement

43

Morningside panorama from Churchhill. The one-time village 'High Street' stretches below to Morningside Station. The 'T' wood above Swanston and Caerketton are clearly seen. *Photograph by W. R. Smith.*

in the city. On September 17th, 1745, Bonnie Prince Charlie and his Jacobite army entered Edinburgh from the north via Slateford and by way of the Braid Burn. Seeking to avoid the

Shop formerly at No.102 Morningside Road, at the corner of Abbotsford Crescent. Note 'Marmion Terrace' on left, the name of this section of Morningside Road before 1885. Blanche was a well-known family business for many years.

range of the Castle's artillery, they proceeded up Morningside Road nearly to Churchhill before turning right along Cant's Loan (now Newbattle Terrace) into Grange Loan. Here the Prince paid a visit to his loyal supporters, the Dicks of Grange House, before continuing eastwards to Holyrood.

Grant, in his *Old and New Edinburgh*, described the Morningside which one would have looked down upon from Churchhill in the mid-nineteenth century:

> A secluded village consisting of little more than a row of thatched cottages, a line of trees and a blacksmith's forge still slumbered in rural solitude in 1850. There were a few large villas, some old, like East Morningside House and the Whitehouse, some comparatively new like Falcon Hall, but they and the nearby cottages were all in the country separated by fields of oats and barley from both Edinburgh and Newington until building began seriously in the 1850s.

The short stretch of Morningside Road between Churchhill Place and Newbattle Terrace was for long known as Banner Place, while the section on the other side of the road between Albert Terrace (the old Doo' Loan) and a point just opposite the Churchhill Theatre was known as Marmion Terrace. The old Waverley Terrace began just beyond this and extended as far as the Baptist Church. The villa at 65 Morningside Road which faces the entrance to Albert Terrace and Abbotsford Park still bears the name Flodden Lodge. All these names are derived from the tradition associated with the Bore Stone which stands high up on the northern boundary wall of Morningside Parish Church. The inscription on the metal plaque below the stone reads:

THE BORE STONE
In which the Royal Standard was last pitched for the muster of the
Scottish Army on the Borough Muir before the Battle of Flodden
1513
It long lay in the adjoining field, was then built into the wall near
this spot and finally placed here by Sir John Stuart Forbes of
Pitsligo, Bart.
1852
Highest and midmost was descried
The royal banner, floating wide;
The Staff, a pine tree strong and straight:
Pitched deeply in a massive stone
Which still in memory is shown,
Yet bent beneath the Standard's weight.

Marmion

Disenchanting as it may be to the many Morningside residents and visitors who stop to marvel at the stone, its authenticity and claim for an honoured place in Scottish history have been seriously challenged by Henry M. Paton in a lengthy and scholarly article in the *Book of the Old Edinburgh Club*, Vol. XXIV (1942). Paton's thesis is closely argued and well documented. The stone, he points out, exhibits no evidence of having been a bore stone: there is no bore, natural or man-made, in which the staff of a standard could have been implanted. It seems that the many writers who accepted the tradition established by Sir Walter Scott failed to seek for historical evidence to support it.

Prior to the publication of Sir Walter's romantic poem *Marmion* in 1808, there had been no suggestion of the stone's having held the Royal Standard. Several letters from Scott concerning *Marmion* and his other historical works make it clear that the great romantic novelist was not unduly concerned with historical accuracy. Nevertheless, it would appear from records that the Bore Stone did for long lie in 'the adjoining field' further up Churchhill, opposite the entrance to the old Doo' Loan. In earlier centuries it had probably been one of several march stones (also known as har, hare or hoary stones) which stood in the vicinity of Tipperlinn Loan. In later years it was moved further down Churchhill, near to its present site, when the ground now occupied by 67 and 69 Morningside Road was about to be feued. The Bore Stone was, as the inscription indicates, placed on its present pedestal by Sir John Stuart Forbes of Pitsligo in 1852.

It is Paton's second principal argument which is probably the most telling. The Royal Standard of James IV was, he points out, never hoisted on the Burgh Muir before Flodden. The accounts of the Lord High Treasurer of Scotland for the year 1513 make this clear. They contain several entries concerning expenditure on banners and standards prior to Flodden, including 'items for cloth to make the King's banner and the King's Standard, with fringes and cases', but, as Paton stresses, it is the following 'items' which are significant: '4s for the making of them [the banners] in haist' and '10s to ane man to byde on the standards and to bring them in haist that nycht that the King's grace departit furth of Edinburgh'. James IV in fact left Edinburgh on 18 August 1513 — before his Standard and other banners were ready. These were 'brocht in haist' after his departure and raised during the main muster of the Scottish army, which took place not on the Burgh Muir but at Ellem, a small village on the southern fold of the Lammermuirs, close to Flodden and the English border. This information destroys Sir

Walter Scott's tradition of the Royal Standard being hoisted in the Bore Stone and also discredits factually his colourful and eloquent description in *Marmion* of the vast assembly of the Scottish army on the Burgh Muir.

Mr Paton summarises his thesis thus: 'If there were no muster, then there was no Standard; if no Standard, then there is nothing of special note to be recorded about the Bore Stone. At best it is "just an old stone".' It is a coldly clinical dismissal of the romantic legends woven around Churchhill and its neighbourhood by the fertile imagination of Sir Walter Scott! The tradition of the Bore Stone will die hard, as will the association of this highest part of the Burgh Muir with the days preceding Flodden. Some writers have suggested that perhaps not a hundred thousand but possibly some thirty thousand men assembled there, on that part of the ancient Burgh Muir which today surrounds the Astley Ainslie Hospital in Canaan Lane.

Morningside Parish Church

The former Morningside Parish Church stands at the corner of Newbattle Terrace, its steepled clock a treasured landmark. Now the tall iron gates are closed and padlocked. Morningside village's earliest church has recently entered a union to form Morningside Braid. Something of this historic event is related in a later chapter. The establishment of this little church was also an historical landmark in the development of the district, important not only in ecclesiastical annals but for the part it played in changing Morningside from 'a secluded village consisting of little more than a row of thatched cottages' into a modern bustling suburb. The origin of the Parish Church was in a circular letter of 19 June 1837, distributed to people residing in the great mansion-houses of the district and also to those dwelling more humbly in the 'row of thatched cottages'. The circular announced:

Although a place of worship for the village of Morningside and its neighbourhood has for some time been felt to be highly desirable, in consequence of the gradually increasing population, no efforts have hitherto been made to supply the deficiency. It is now proposed to make an attempt to do so.

While submitting a proposal for this purpose it is impossible to omit referring to the unspeakable obligations under which the whole district has been long laid to both the Clergymen of this large Parish [St Cuthbert's at the West End of Princes Street], Dr Dickson and Dr Paul, for their indefatigable and unwearied labours among them, amidst all the conflicting claims of so overwhelming a charge devolved upon them as the West Church Parish, and to which no language can possibly do justice. Among other labours there may be mentioned that for considerably upwards of twenty years Divine Service has been regularly performed once a week at one time on Thursday evenings, and latterly on the Sabbath evenings, in the School Room of the village . . .

It is proposed that the district to be connected with the new Church should extend from Buccleuch Parish on the east to the Parish of Colinton on the west, and from the Parish of Liberton on the south to St David's Parish on the north.

It was estimated that this first parish church for Morningside would cost £1,600, excluding the site. There would be seating, including a front gallery, to accommodate 634 people. Side galleries, to provide for another 130 people, were to be built later. It was soon possible to delete the estimated cost of a site, Sir John Stuart Forbes of Pitsligo, owner of Greenhill House, donating a third an acre, valued at 200 guineas, from his estate.

Subscribers to the church building fund came forward readily. A list of these, dated 25 December 1837, was headed by Mr Alexander Falconar of Falcon Hall, followed by his five daughters. Other generous donors included Sir George Warrender of Bruntsfield House, the Rt. Hon. Lady Napier and the trustees of the late Lord Napier of Merchiston, the Governors of George Watson's Hospital, the Managers of the Royal Asylum (which had received its Charter in 1807 and which, with its recent acquisition of the village of Tipperlinn, occupied a large area of Wester Morningside estate), Charles Chalmers, Headmaster (brother of Dr Thomas Chalmers) 'and the young gentlemen of

Sir John Stuart Forbes of Pitsligo, of Greenhill House, granted land for the building of Morningside Parish Church. Local streets were named after him. (Courtesy of Mr and Mrs Espessias, Australia).

Merchiston Academy', General Robertson of Canaan Bank and numerous others.

Many notable people who resided outwith Morningside but who had some connection or special interest in the district, perhaps because they chose to spend part of the summer in its pleasant sunny seclusion, also contributed. These included Lady Colquhoun of Luss, Benjamin Bell (the famous Edinburgh surgeon) and Dr John Abercrombie (a celebrated Edinburgh physician).

It was therefore decided to proceed with the building of the new church. John Henderson was engaged as architect. As already mentioned, John Henderson built St Bennets in Greenhill Gardens and other houses in the Greenhill district. He built many other Edinburgh churches, including Newhaven, Holyrood Free Church, St Columba's by the Castle, Holy Trinity at Dean Bridge. The boundaries of the parish were defined more specifically as 'That part of the Parish of St Cuthbert's bounded on the north by the Canal, running south in a line to Braidhill to a point where Colinton and St Cuthbert's Parishes meet, and then eastwards to the point where the Parishes of Liberton and St Cuthbert's meet, then north by the east end of Blackford Hill.' This extensive area was to be disjoined from St Cuthbert's and created a new *quoad sacra* parish to be called 'the Parish of Morningside'.

Just nineteen months after the original subscription list had been issued, the opening service of the new Parish Church of Morningside took place, on Sunday, 29 July 1838. Dr Thomas Chalmers preached at the morning inaugural service and the Rev. James Begg of Liberton in the afternoon. A newspaper report of the event read: 'There was an overflow attendance and many went away unable to gain admission. Dr Chalmers preached with all his accustomed eloquence and power.' That Dr Chalmers should have delivered the inaugural sermon was most appropriate: not only did he live within a few yards of the new church, but none had advocated the policy of church extension more vigorously and eloquently than he.

Services were conducted temporarily at the new church by the Rev. David Davidson and the Rev. Dr John Paul of St Cuthbert's, until the Rev. George Smeaton, assistant at North Leith, was appointed the first minister on 14 March 1839. Three years later he was succeeded by the Rev. Dr Thomas

Addis, but this appointment was short-lived. Dr Addis resigned his charge in 1843 to join Dr Chalmers and his supporters at the Disruption, and was appointed minister of Morningside's first Free Church. Dr Addis's predecessor, the Rev. Smeaton, also 'came out' at the Disruption while serving at Falkland, becoming a Professor in the Free Church College. A permanent manse was not acquired until 1881 when Harlaw House, 52 Morningside Park, originally built by David Deuchar of Morningside House, was purchased for £3,230.

The annals of Morningside Parish Church have been recorded in great detail by the late William Mair and published at length in the church's centenary booklet, in one of the volumes of the *Book of the Old Edinburgh Club* and, in summary, in Mair's *Historic Morningside*. In these publications and in an earlier booklet by John Stuart Gowans (1912) are many interesting facts not only about the history of the church but also the development of Morningside during the latter half of the nineteenth century. The church's steeple clock, a familiar landmark in Churchhill, must have attracted the glances of countless Morningside residents over the years on their way to work in the city. No clock is provided for in the original architect's drawings but in 1840 the church records list: 'To school fund for clock including case, £19.12.5d' and 'To Mr Clark, Clockmaker, £14.2 shillings'. The 'movement' or mechanism of the Old Schoolhouse clock was transferred to the steeple of the Parish Church, but it must have been replaced by the school's managers, as photographs of the school in the latter half of the nineteenth century indicate that it was still functioning. When the school was eventually closed after the opening of South Morningside School in 1892, the clock stopped at twenty minutes to four and the hands have remained at this time ever since. When, some time ago, the clock face was repainted and the hands removed, many Morningside people waited anxiously to see what would happen. To their relief, the clock was restored to its original state, and the brightly painted gold hands replaced at their appointed hour. In 1929 a new clock was installed in the Parish Church steeple at a cost of £64, the original old school clock mechanism having become worn and erratic.

Within two years of its establishment in 1838, the congregation of the Parish Church were contributing to special funds for the poor of the village, especially for the provision of coal. Gas lighting was introduced in 1852. In 1862 a marked prosperity may be noted in the congregation, indicated by the generous collections. Morningside itself was by this time already beginning to develop rapidly.

In about 1880 the Parish Church entered upon a period of great activity and it was felt that the church building required to be enlarged. The alternative was to provide for the growing congregation by building a new church further south, slightly beyond the lower reaches of the village. After much debate this latter course was decided upon and an iron church costing £650 was built in 1884 at what is now 2 Cluny Avenue, a few yards from the future Parish Manse. This was in due course to become St Matthew's Parish Church in Cluny Gardens, now Cluny Parish Church.

Expansion of the congregation continued steadily and a plan for a proposed new steeple, put forward in 1887, was laid aside and, instead, the chancel was enlarged and the organ transferred to the east end of the church.

The fiftieth anniversary of the Church was celebrated on 10 May 1888 by an evening meeting held in the Morningside Athenaeum at the north-west end of Chamberlain Road. Even the extended chancel failed to provide adequate accommodation and a letter to the congregation dated 20 January 1914 made a revolutionary proposal: that the original church be demolished and replaced by a new and very much larger building. The First World War intervened, however, and this proposal was left indefinitely in abeyance.

An event of particular significance for Morningside was the reunion, in June 1960, of the Parish Church with Morningside High Church. The High Church (now the Churchhill Theatre) had been built in 1894 as the last home of Morningside Free Church, as already mentioned. The reunion with the original

'Mother Church' of the parish in 1960, nearly a century and a quarter after the Disruption, brought the wheel of history full circle.

A living link between past and present at Morningside Parish Church was the devoted service, through four generations, of the Gilbert family as Church Officers. The Rev. Robert William Macgoun, who succeeded Dr Thomas Addis as minister in 1843, had a gifted daughter, Hannah C. Preston Macgoun, R.S.W. who was a regular exhibitor in the Royal Scottish Academy. Miss Macgoun illustrated two of Dr John Brown's classics, *Rab and His Friends* and *Pet Marjorie*. The Rev. Macgoun lived with his family in Banner Villa, immediately north of the Parish Church and now 69 Morningside Road. In recent years there has been a revival of interest in and appreciation of Miss Macgoun's work. At least one of her original watercolours has been traced, as also a miniature and some artifacts that belonged to her. At present a lady is endeavouring to trace more details of her life, which has remained obscure. A Morningside resident kindly presented the present writer with a copy of a letter written by Miss Macgoun in 1912 when she was living in Craiglockhart Hydropathic. This was a year before she died.

The street now known as Newbattle Terrace, immediately beyond the Parish Church, has had a succession of names. Originally the southern boundary of the East Morningside estate, it used to be a country lane leading eastwards from Morningside Road, the old 'wester hiegait', round the Burgh Muir and past the Grange of St Giles to the old Dalkeith Road, the 'easter hiegait'. From the early sixteenth century and for a period of nearly 130 years, when the Grange of St Giles was owned by the Cant family, it was known as Cant's Loan or Loaning. Soon after the Parish Church was built it became known, at its western entrance, as Church Lane. The architect's sketch of the church shows Cant's Loan and gives the impression that this part of Morningside Road was then less steep than it is today. Eventually the name Newbattle Terrace was given to commemorate the marriage between one of the Forbes family of

Miss Hannah Preston Macgoun was a daughter of the Rev. Robert Macgoun, one-time minister of Morningside Parish Church. The family lived at No. 69 Morningside Road, next to the church. Miss Macgoun was a very talented artist, specialising in water-colours. She illustrated certain editions of Dr John Brown's classic, *Rab and his Friends*, and many other small books. She died on 20 August 1913. Self portrait, 1887. (*The National Galleries of Scotland*).

Greenhill and a member of the Marquis of Lothian's family of Newbattle Abbey near Dalkeith.

Several of the villas in Newbattle Terrace are of relatively early date, being indicated in the first Ordnance Survey Map of 1852. One of these was named Banner Lodge in perpetuation of the legend of the nearby Bore Stone. Morningside Parish Church Hall was built in 1899. The villa opposite, Kirkbank, which stands next to the church, was built a decade later, with a view to the extension of the church.

After the tragic sudden death of Jane Welsh Carlyle in London while her famous husband Thomas — 'The Sage of Chelsea' — was in Edinburgh delivering his University Rectorial Address, Carlyle was plunged into loneliness and despair. He was hopeless in domestic matters and was able to persuade his niece, as yet unmarried, to become his housekeeper and constant companion at his Chelsea home. Apart from other duties, she wrote down by hand much of his voluminous writing. He acknowledged her indispensability and left her a generous bequest. Having married her cousin, Alexander Carlyle, shortly before her uncle's death, they eventually settled at 30 Newbattle Terrace, to which they brought a great collection of Carlyle's possessions: books of his own, signed first editions from other famous authors, and much else of great value. Their two sons, Edward and Oliver, attended George Watson's College when this was situated beside the Royal Infirmary, overlooking the Meadows. Alexander Carlyle presented to the National Library of Scotland a valuable collection of manuscripts and gifted Thomas Carlyle's industrious fountain-pen to Edinburgh's Central Public Library. Alexander Carlyle, his sons and his second wife rest in Morningside Cemetery, but Jane Carlyle Aitken is buried in St Mary's Churchyard, Dumfries.

Pitsligo House, near the corner of Newbattle Terrace and Pitsligo Road, incorporates the former Newbattle House. In 1947 Newbattle House was purchased by the owner of a well-known Edinburgh bakery and it became the Martin Benefaction, a pleasant residence for elderly ladies, administered by Dr John Martin. Pitsligo House was built in 1970 by the Merchant Company of Edinburgh Trust as a similar residence and it incorporated Newbattle House. Here between thirty to forty women enjoy tastefully designed and comfortable accommodation. The Edinburgh Merchant Company's crest adorns the entrance to Pitsligo House.

After Jane Welsh Carlyle's sudden death Mary Carlyle Aitken became her famous uncle's housekeeper and companion at Cheyne Row, Chelsea. After her marriage to her Canadian cousin, Alexander Carlyle, in 1879, they both returned to London to look after Thomas until his death in 1881. They then settled at 30 Newbattle Terrace. Many of Carlyle's books, papers, etc. were temporarily kept at this house. This portrait of Thomas Carlyle and his niece bears his handwritten inscription. (*From* 'The Homes and Haunts of Thomas Carlyle', *Westminster Gazette*).

Returning to Morningside Road from Newbattle Terrace, one's attention is attracted by the quaint row of terraced shops on the opposite side of Morningside Road, extending from the southern boundary wall of Bank House to Morningside Place. Set in the wall beyond the last of these shops is an old milestone, now barely legible, indicating 'One mile from Tollcross'. This is one of three stones which marked the distance to Fairmilehead. The Fairmilehead stone still stands near the entrance to the water filtration works, three miles from Tollcross. The second milestone is opposite the Braid Hills Hotel, within the Braidburn Valley park railings.

Bank House, from its high prominence at the south corner of Albert Terrace and Morningside Road, commands a magnificent view over Morningside to the Braid and Pentland Hills rising steadily on the horizon. The conservatory at the top of the steep entrance steps in Morningside Road is something of a landmark, glimpsed over the twelve-foot-high wall (the height of which, incidentally, indicates the considerable earth-cutting which took place during the construction of the busy thoroughfare over Churchhill).

Originally named Morningside Bank, the house was built in 1790 on land feued by Lord Gardenstone, then owner of Morningside estate. This land was formerly part of the original West Morningside. Subdivision of the house into Middle Bank House and North Bank House was carried out about 1860.

Bank House is mentioned in the biography of Cosmo Gordon Lang, Archbishop of Canterbury from 1928 to 1942, by J. G. Lockhart. Archbishop Lang referred to the important childhood impressions absorbed in an 'old world' garden. His family, including his younger brother Marshall, came to live at Bank House when Cosmo was four, during his father's five years of distinguished service as minister of Morningside Parish Church, just opposite the house, on the slope of Churchhill. While Cosmo, converted to the Church of England when at Cambridge, was to become the head of that church, his brother was, remarkably, to achieve the parallel distinction of being appointed Moderator of the Church of Scotland in 1935.

Born at Fyvie in Aberdeenshire in 1864, where his father, the

Rev. John Marshall Lang, was parish minister, the future Archbishop of Canterbury was named Cosmo Gordon after the local Laird. In later years he vividly recalled his boyhood days in Morningside:

> At that time a quaint country village, with villas and quiet lanes and no houses built beyond it. Real scene of my childhood was the garden of Bank House, Morningside. I suppose it was quite a small garden but it was my world from the age of four to nine. It was my *own* world where my imagination for once had its unclouded day. It was a world of make-believe — a bundle of sticks on which I stood enduring the fancied flames of a Christian martyr — the great black roaring cat who to me was the Devil, walking about seeking whom he might devour.

An amusing interlude which occurred during the General Assembly of 1935, over which as Moderator, the Very Rev. Marshall B. Lang presided, is recorded in the Assembly Proceedings of that year:

> Professor Lamont drew the attention of the House to the fact that Dr Cosmo Gordon Lang, brother of the Moderator Dr Marshall B. Lang, was seated in the Gallery. It was with gratitude and joy, said Professor Lamont, that they had with them in the House the head of their great Sister Communion, the Archbishop of Canterbury. The Moderator, in welcoming him, said: 'Your Grace . . .' (the remainder of the sentence was drowned in applause and laughter). 'It is a very singular pleasure,' he continued, 'to welcome you to the floor of the Assembly, not only as one I have been familiar with in past years (renewed laughter) but as representing the great Sister Communion in England,' (Applause.)
>
> The venerable Archbishop said that he had not come prepared with an address worthy of the Assembly, or of its traditions. 'I must content myself,' he continued, 'in the fewest possible words, in saying with what satisfaction I find that the choice of Moderator this year has rested upon one of whom at least I can say that he belongs to a highly respectable family, and that he has retained its traditions of respectability, orthodoxy and fidelity to the Church of his fathers more successfully than his elder brother. (Laughter.) With all my heart I pray that God's blessing may continually rest upon the Church of my Fathers.' (Loud applause.)

Archbishop Cosmo Gordon Lang with Queen Mary.

The Moderator expressed the gratitude of the Assembly to the Archbishop for the words he had spoken and the blessing he had given to them as fathers and brethren of the Church of Scotland.

The life and achievements of Cosmo Gordon Lang after his steady elevation of office in the Church of England cannot be summarised here. He was of course at the centre of the national crisis during the abdication of Edward VIII, at a time when the attitude of his church to divorce and remarriage, regardless of a person's social standing, was much stricter than today.

The father of these two eminent churchmen, the Very Rev. John Marshall Lang, CVO, DD, LL D, had himself been Moderator of the Church of Scotland in 1893, and in 1909 he became Principal of Aberdeen University. His son, the Rev. Marshall B. Lang, who followed him as Moderator, was the author of *The Seven Ages of an East Lothian Parish*, and had at one time been Minister of Whittinghame in East Lothian. The brothers were cousins of the distinguished actor, Matheson Lang.

On the top of two of the railings beside the gate below the steps up to a private residence, No. 110 Morningside Road, attached to Bank House, are small ecclesiastical crosses. They may possibly have been placed here to recall that in Bank House itself there resided the Reverend John Marshall Lang, with his family, while he was minister of the Parish Church opposite. Bank House was the early manse. Here, too, of course Cosmo Gordon Lang resided with the family. He later became Archbishop of Canterbury. Perhaps the crosses on the railings are to mark where he once lived.

CHAPTER 3

Morningside Village

The much-weathered milestone built into the wall immediately beyond the last of the quaint terraced shops which stretch downhill on the right-hand side of Morningside Road, opposite Newbattle Terrace, provides an appropriate place at which to pause before entering the heart of what was the original village of Morningside. Wester Morningside Estate, the fourth of the lots into which the Burgh Muir was divided and feued in 1586, comprised twenty-six acres. Its northern boundary was Albert Terrace (originally Doo' Loan), and it was bounded by Myreside to the west and Morningside Road to the east. The southern boundary was the Jordan Burn, running from Myreside to the Briggs o' Braid at the foot of Morningside Road, just before Maxwell Street and Braid Church. On this estate, over several centuries, three villages arose: Morningside, Myreside and Tipperlinn, the last being of greatest antiquity.

While the keeps, castles and mansion-houses surrounding the area on which Morningside was to develop were all sixteenth century or earlier, the first map showing Morningside as a distinct location was Richard Cooper's Plan of the City of Edinburgh and Adjacent Grounds, 1759. The village of Morningside is indicated by three houses. In J. Adair's Map of Midlothian, 1735, various places surrounding Morningside are shown but the village itself is not. John Laurie's map of 1763 indicates two small groups of houses which may be assumed to be Morningside.

James Grant, in *Old and New Edinburgh*, described Morningside as 'a row of thatched cottages, a line of trees and a blacksmith's forge' (to which description other writers have added: 'and an alehouse'). The origins of this settlement may be traced to the steady growth of several farms in the district. The earliest of these, and the nearest to what was to become

Morningside village, were the farms of Canaan, Egypt and Plewlands. Of early origin, but more distant (yet no doubt providing work for the villagers of Morningside), were those of Greenbank, Braid, Comiston, Oxgangs and, more remotely, Swanston, to the south. The village soon became an increasingly important first stopping place on the principal drove road into Edinburgh from the prosperous farmlands to the south on the Biggar Road.

Morningside, therefore, had its origins in agriculture, the development of which was later boosted when the Edinburgh Suburban and South Side Junction Railway — as it was originally named — was inaugurated in 1885. This permitted crops and cattle from surrounding farms to be transported to and from the busy goods depot at the end of Maxwell Street, next to Morningside Road Station.

The second important factor in the development of Morning-side village was the movement of Edinburgh's wealthier citizens southwards to the sunny 'morning side' of town. They built their villas and mansion-houses on the new, generously proportioned plots which resulted from the sub-division of the lands of Canaan and, later, neighbouring estates. In meeting the needs of the newly-resident gentry, the hamlet of Morningside became an important and bustling village. The systematic development of Morningside probably began very soon after the beginning of the nineteenth century, though existing records date only from 1812. In that year, James Knox's *Map of Edinburghshire* provides some indication of the layout of the village, its principal dwelling houses and streets. More comprehensive and valuable detail is given in Robert Kirkwood's map of 1817. This provides us with a good picture of the Morningside which had then become an early suburb of Edinburgh. It can be clearly distinguished, along with the estates derived from the 1508 and 1586 feuing of the Burgh Muir and the mansion-houses built within them by 1817.

By the time of the first Edinburgh Ordnance Survey Map of 1852 Morningside and its environs were well delineated and readily recognisable in relation to present-day houses and streets.

As regards the demographic development of the district, *Gray's Annual Directory* for 1832-3, the first Edinburgh directory to group the city's residents into districts, lists under Morningside and Canaan a total of 37 people, these, however, being only the gentry, professional people, tradesmen and shopkeepers. This selective listing of the local population in Edinburgh street directories continued until the late nineteenth century. In 1884 Morningside Road for the first time appears divided into a series of short individual sections, each with a different name. Commencing at Churchhill, these little streets, proceeding downhill, through the village to the Jordan Burn, the city boundary, were: Waverley Terrace, Marmion Terrace, Banner Place, Morningside Bank, Esplin Place, Blackford Place, Falcon Place, Reid's Buildings, Morningside Terrace and Morningside Village. The total population in 1884 listed in these various streets, the forerunners of Morningside Road, was seventy. Again, this figure is confined principally to professional people, tradesmen and shopkeepers. A year later, in the *Edinburgh and Leith Directory* for 1885-6, Morningside Road is no longer shown as a series of individual streets but as one major road which had absorbed its constituent sections, whose names were gradually to fade into obscurity. In this directory properties in Morningside Road are, for the first time, shown in numerical sequence from the corner of Colinton Road to Morningside Station, numbering from 1 to 276. In this new Morningside Road 150 residents are listed. Such figures are, of course, no index of the growth of population, being exclusive of the increasing number of people by then residing in the various streets built on both sides of Morningside Road, and of the many people who did not qualify for inclusion in early street directories.

Morningside continued to develop. In addition to the earliest reasons for growth — farming and the building of large villas and mansion-houses which absorbed local labour and services — another more recent factor which contributed towards rapid development was transport. The year 1872 saw the provision of the first horse-drawn trams, and just over ten years later came the inauguration of the Edinburgh and South Side Suburban Railway and the opening of the passenger station, Morningside Road. With the advent of the horse-drawn and, later, cable tramcars, the growth of the village had still been gradual, but, with suburban railway services, the village atmosphere changed almost overnight as Morningside suddenly developed into a desirable and rapidly spreading residential suburb. Many old village cottages which had once straddled the ancient Wester Hiegait were swept away, despite the protests of their occupants. Those which survived had, by the beginning of the twentieth century, become museum pieces, dwarfed by the serried rows of tenements which towered above the busy new highway to the south.

In the Braid, Cluny and Morningside Drive districts 'villadom' was steadily established. Morningside Public Library was opened in 1904. A cinema and ballroom followed. It was not until the decade prior to the Second World War, however, that the Greenbank district to the south witnessed a vast building programme of bungalows. In the midst of all this development, the venerable mansion-houses of the old Morningside estates, dating back to the original feuing of the Burgh Muir, remained pleasantly surrounded by their ample gardens and orchards, still apparently as remote as when their first owners built them as summer residences in the country.

We must now proceed beyond the milestone at the corner of Morningside Place. From existing printed records and recollections, or memories passed down by generations of Morningside residents, a reconstruction may be attempted of the principal features of the village towards the close of the eighteenth century and their gradual alteration or disappearance amidst the final massive building programme completed by the beginning of the present century. This reconstruction is made in terms of present-day street numbers.

On the right, immediately beyond the milestone and almost opposite Newbattle Terrace, is Morningside Place, originally named Deuchar Street after the family who for so long owned Morningside House and its surrounding lands, which included this ground. The first villas were built here in the 1820s. At 2 Morningside Place Dr Thomas Chalmers resided for a year while awaiting the completion of his new villa at Churchhill. This little house has been demolished and replaced by the premises of a medical group practice. Opposite the substantial villa, 1 Morningside Place, was for a short period the Morningside Free Church manse. No. 4 was for long the home of the Cowieson family. In 1895 Peter Cowieson acquired the Old Schoolhouse of Morningside when the new South Morningside School was opened in 1892. At 6 Morningside Place resided the Misses Balfours, aunts of Robert Louis Stevenson, who, as a boy, was a frequent visitor to this house, where he carved his initials on a cupboard door. On one occasion, while seated on the garden wall with his air-pistol, he accidentally shot a pellet into the arm of young Miss Cowieson of No. 4. The incident was revealed only many years later when this lady, then in her nineties, was admitted to hospital, where she explained the small scar on her arm, for so long romantically concealed and, perhaps, secretly treasured. Trafalgar House, 3 Morningside Place, is believed to have been built by a close relative of Lord Nelson, who named it after the great naval victory. At No. 7 resided the sisters of Dr John Brown, author of *Rab and His Friends* and assistant to the distinguished Edinburgh surgeon, Professor Syme, of Millbank in Canaan.

While most of the original houses of Morningside village have long since disappeared, fortunately one of its oldest buildings remains largely unchanged. This is the Old Schoolhouse (a few yards downhill on the right, beyond Morningside Place), where the hands of the old clock remained permanently at twenty minutes to four after the little school was closed and South Morningside School opened in 1892. The tower of the Old Schoolhouse still clearly proclaims the date of its foundation, 1823. It thus pre-dated the Parish Church by fifteen years and, as already mentioned, some of the earliest meetings of the congregation were held in the Old Schoolhouse, where Dr Thomas Chalmers after his coming to reside at Churchhill on occasion preached.

The Old Schoolhouse, Morningside Road, opened in 1823. Children came from as far out as Swanston and Lothianburn. The school was closed when South Morningside Primary in Comiston Road opened in 1892.

The origins of the old school had been hitherto unknown. Some references to it are to be found in the archives of St Cuthbert's Parish Church in Lothian Road, now kept in Register House. Morningside was, in early times, within the extensive parish of St Cuthbert's. Other references are found in the minutes of the meetings of the School Board of St Cuthberts and Dean, filed in the Edinburgh Room in the Central Public Library. None of these sources, however, goes back as far as 1823. Fortunately, the original deeds of conveyance of the ground on which the school was built and the names of people involved in its establishment were eventually discovered among the papers in an Edinburgh solicitor's office. These refer to a Morningside resident, George Ross, who was to become so closely identified with the school that for many years it was to bear his name.

The origins of the school are identified with another notable Scottish personage of the early nineteenth century, Lady

Maxwell of Pollock, the large estate near Glasgow, a generous benefactress of Scottish education and other social needs of her day.

Some years before her death in 1810, Lady Maxwell established an Industrial School for Poor Children in Rose Street, which was later transferred to Horse Wynd, off the Canongate. John Wesley visited the Rose Street school on several occasions and was much impressed. One of the trustees of the Rose Street Industrial School in 1810 was George Ross, an advocate of distinction and later a Judge of the Commissary Court of Scotland, who resided in the stately and pleasantly situated mansion, Woodburn House, in Canaan Lane, Morningside. In the charter of 27 March 1823 by which James Robertson, factor of William Deuchar, owner of Morningside estate, conveys a small portion of land for the building of Morningside's village school, George Ross of Woodburn is the first-named of four men involved in the establishment of the school. The others were Alexander Falconar of Falcon Hall, James Evans of Canaan Park and Henry Hare of Newgrange. By 1849 James Hare had moved to London and the Rev. Dr John Paul and the Rev. James Veitch of St Cuthbert's Parish Church had been invited to assist in the management of the school. Later that year many other prominent local people became shareholders (at £10 each), thus helping to support the school. These included Sir George Warrender of Bruntsfield House, Sir John Stuart Forbes of Pitsligo (owner of Greenhill Estate) and Mrs Henry Craigie, formerly Miss Jessie Pigou Falconar of Falcon Hall. A portion of the substantial legacy left by Lady Maxwell for the continuation of her educational benefactions was apparently to be used in support of the school, which, by 1856, had been in operation for just over thirty years. In that year George Ross noted: 'I have settled the sum of £1,300, £1,200 of which is at present in City Bonds having 4% interest, on Morningside School of which from the interest, (say £48), £25 per annum is to be paid to the teacher of Morningside School and £12 per annum to the female teacher of the sewing school. I retain for the present the management of Morningside School.' In a postscript he added:

'The two ministers of the parish, namely the Rev. Dr Paul and Dr Veitch of St Cuthbert's, are trustees of both schools.' From the middle of the nineteenth century it would appear from records that George Ross managed the school largely unaided. It became known simply as the 'Ross School', and later as the 'Subscription School'.

Articles and letters which have appeared in Edinburgh newspapers over many years about the personal recollections of those elderly Morningside residents who once attended the school, give us some insight into its life in various periods. Information about early teachers is sparse, but a Mr Galgour appears to have been 'the maister' in 1837. In 1873 the *Edinburgh Post Office Directory* tells us that this position was held by a man whose name was well-remembered by all who attended the school during his long period in charge, Andrew Myrtle Cockburn. He was known to his pupils, and to Morningside villagers generally, as 'Cocky Cockburn'. A Moray House graduate, he came from the village of Redding near Polmont. After twenty years service as 'maister' of the village school, Cockburn was appointed First Assistant at South Morningside School in Comiston Road when this much-needed new primary school opened in 1892. His two colleagues at the old school, Miss Margaret Cameron and Miss Campbell, referred to in the records as 'from the Ross School', also served on the staff of South Morningside School for some time, as did Miss McAllister, former pupil-teacher at the Ross School, who, soon after being transferred to South Morningside, left to undertake further studies, presumably at Moray House Training College.

Andrew Cockburn's daughter, who continued to live in Morningside, had many memories of the Old Schoolhouse, which, she recalled, was for some time known as the 'Subscription School'. School fees were apparently levied on those parents considered able to contribute towards their children's education, and she remembered one parent, whose several children attended the school, who paid fees in kind. The man was an artist, and over several years he presented the 'maister' with a series of watercolours of various aspects of

Morningside and district. These paintings were sold some years ago and unfortunately cannot now be traced.

Pupils came to the old school from the village itself and also from places as far distant as Lothianburn and Swanston. Just how many children attended is not on record, but judging from the large enrolment at South Morningside School when it was opened in 1892, attendances at the village school just prior to that must have stretched the two small classrooms to full capacity. Pupils who lived some distance from the old school would have come on foot or horseback, or riding on farm carts. This use of horses may have accounted for the school's becoming known as 'the cuddy school'. The horses were tethered in the little lane beside the school (still there today with its two pillars to prevent entry by traffic) which leads to Springvalley Terrace. This lane became known as 'Cuddy Lane', though on old maps it is named Rosewood Place.

The great event in the old school's year was the annual prizegiving ceremony attended by most of the villagers attired in their 'Sunday best' clothes. For many years the prizes were donated and presented by the Misses Falconar of nearby Falcon Hall, and the closing vote of thanks to the 'maister' was proposed by John Johnstone, factor to the Deuchar family, the owners of Morningside estate. He was a man with fiery red hair and long beard, greatly revered by the people of the village. The schoolhouse, for long a popular social or community centre, was the meeting place of the Marmion Lodge of the Independent Order of Good Templars. This organisation enjoyed strong support and provided two annual social highlights, a winter soirée and a summer outing to Habbie's Howe at Nine Mile Burn.

Following the Disruption in 1843, many parents who 'came out' in support of Dr Chalmers and his colleagues and left the Parish Church, withdrew their children from the village school and sent them to the Free Church School, housed in a little building just beyond the village smiddy, where the Public Library now stands. As several contributors to the press recounted some years ago, many former pupils of the old village school achieved distinction in various walks of life, some in far-off parts of the world.

Sixteen years after Ross's memorandum of 1856, by the Education (Scotland) Act of 1872, education became compulsory. In Scotland it came under the Scotch Education Department, administration being in the hands of local School Boards until 1919. They were then succeeded in the city by the Edinburgh Education Authority and, in 1930, by the Edinburgh Corporation Education Committee. More recently, with the advent of new systems of local government, Lothian Regional Council took over. While no records survive describing how the Act of 1872 affected the old village school, fortunately there are papers relevant to the school which have been discovered so that it is possible to trace the various stages in its latter years when, as the result of the Act of 1872, it passed from private ownership. Ten years afterwards, the Educational Endowments (Scotland) Act of 1882 led to a body of Commissioners being appointed to supervise and administer the country's many small schools founded by charitable benefactors. By 1889 the Commissioners were administering the Ross School in Morningside, along with several other such schools in Edinburgh known as Dr Bell's schools. These included Lady Glenorchy's School, Wightman's School, the Canongate Burgh School and the Lochend Burgh School. The minutes of a meeting of the Commissioners in 1889 indicate their power, twelve months thereafter, to close the Ross School in Morningside, but it would appear that this step was not taken and that the little school continued to operate under the administration of the Edinburgh Educational Trust, established in 1882. This body, it seems, kept the old schoolhouse open until the early 1890s. The next reference to the school occurs in the Register of Sasines for 1895. In that year, three years after South Morningside School in Comiston Road had been opened, the old schoolhouse and its small surrounding area of land were sold to Peter Cowieson, owner of the villa at 4 Morningside Place, by the Edinburgh Educational Trust. He appears to have let the premises for various uses. In 1946 the little building was sold by the Cowieson family to the

Brethren, a religious group who still find the well-preserved simplicity of the old school particularly well suited to their weekly services. This little religious community has done much to restore and preserve the old schoolhouse and its clock, now brightly repainted and proclaiming distinctly the date of the village's earliest educational establishment. This was not the original schoolhouse clock. It was purchased by Morningside Parish Church in 1840 and transferred to the church tower. The present-day schoolhouse clock, which had been installed after the Parish Church acquisition, over the years, according to the strength of the wind, the hands had moved from 3.40 to 12.25 and other chance times, but in recent years, a member of the schoolhouse's owners, The Brethren, skilfully carried out a virtual complete reconstruction of the mechanism.

Morningside village was centred on the small area now occupied by the Public Library and the 'Merlin'. On this, the west side of Morningside Road, cottages stretched at irregular intervals from just beyond the schoolhouse, downhill to what is now Morningside Park. On the east side of the road cottages extended, again rather sparsely, from the present-day south-west corner of Falcon Avenue to the Briggs O'Braid over the Jordan Burn, the ancient city boundary running along the back of Maxwell Street and under Morningside Road, past the north side of the lawn surrounding Braid Church. The west side of the village, the more populous, in which were situated certain important institutions, formed part of the eastern boundary wall of Morningside Estate, while the cottages on the east side of Morningside Road lay on the western boundary of the extensive lands of Canaan. The Parish Church, further up the hill at the corner of Newbattle Terrace, was thus somewhat removed from the centre of the village, but, as already related, it was built on this site as a result of the free gift of land by Sir John Stuart Forbes of Greenhill. Before 1885 separately numbered 'streets' had, as already mentioned, formed the village High Street. After this date, they were combined and renumbered to form part of Morningside Road.

Stone sculpted plaque above the entrances to Nos.43 and 45 Springvalley Terrace, commemorating the one-time location there of Springvalley House. *Photograph by W. R. Smith.*

We have already noted the little lane (once known as Rosewood Place) immediately beyond the school, leading to Springvalley House, or Spring Villa as it is named in one old map of the area. This fine mansion-house, set amidst pleasant gardens and some acres of farmland, was demolished in 1907.

A stone plaque set in the tenement wall above 43 and 45 Springvalley Terrace commemorates the house which gave its name to this part of Morningside. Springvalley House was for some years the residence of James Grant, celebrated author of *Old and New Edinburgh*, that classic and monumental work on the history of the city which was first published in parts by Cassells in 1880. Grant, an Edinburgh-born historian and military expert, wrote 56 novels. His other works included *The Romance of War, Memoirs of an Aide-de-Camp* and *Memoirs of Kirkcaldy of Grange and Montrose*. Grant died in London in 1887, aged 64, much impoverished, having devoted the last years of his life to self-sacrificing charitable work amongst the poor. He is buried in London.

We return to Morningside Road by the former Rosewood Place, now Cuddy Lane. This little lane retains some of its original character, three old stone cottages of the village still being occupied. Viewhill Cottage is amongst the very few Morningside houses listed in Gray's *Annual Directory of Edinburgh, Leith and the Suburbs* for 1832-3. This cottage, No. 2 Cuddy Lane, of two storeys and recently restored, in the early 1900s housed Austin's Family Laundry, originally situated at No. 4 Jordan Lane. No. 4 Cuddy Lane, now named The Cottage, in its charming little garden has a deep well of spring water. This along with others nearby shown on old maps may explain the origin of the name Springvalley. No. 6 is Rosewood Cottage.

Immediately beyond what was Rosewood Place was an area of open ground on which the present small block of tenements was eventually built. The south gable-end of these was built against the end of the little row of two-storey shops and houses which appear on early maps. The ground-floor shops were among the earliest in the village and included a dairy. The shopkeepers lived in their back shops and on the floors above. At the rear of the row, reached through a little pend and now numbered 160 Morningside Road, is a group of original two-storey houses, still occupied and retaining something of the atmosphere of the old village. One of these houses indeed still has its outside stone staircase.

Beyond the last of those shops in Morningside Road was an open area, on the front edge of which there stood, until it was demolished to provide a forecourt for the Merlin a few years ago, a large rectangular two-storey building. The front of this was hard against the pavement, which was thus at this point made dangerously narrow. Originally occupying the ground floor of this inelegant building was one of the earliest and most important institutions of the village, Dick Wright's smiddy. In 1955 a writer to the press, recalling the main features of Morningside in about 1880, wrote of this:

> It was a recognised howff for gossip between the villagers and the ploughmen who brought in their horses from the farms to be shod, and there were always horses there and always a pile of 'singed sheip's heids', for in these days 'sheip's heids' were not skinned but were sent by the butchers to the smiddies to be singed, thus preserving the juiciest parts. But for the absence of the spreading chestnut tree, Dick's might have been the smithy of the song. Children on the way to and from school (almost next door) looked in at the open door. We loved to see the flaming forge, to hear the bellows roar, and to catch the burning sparks that flew like chaff from a threshing floor. All that belongs to a bygone day. Dick Wright was the beadle of Morningside Free Church.

After the closure of Dick Wright's smiddy in about 1900, the ground floor of this old building was occupied by a monumental sculptor whose yard extended some distance to the rear, this land now being occupied by the Merlin and its car park. The upper floor became the joiner's workshop of Mr Willie Cheyne. At one time part of the premises was occupied by a printer and the building was known for a period as the Blackford Press, the name probably being derived from the fact that this short stretch of Morningside Road — no longer than the Merlin's frontage — was once called Blackford Place.

While it may have been a popular howff, a centre of village gossip and a source of fascination to pupils of the old school-house — all of which tended to give it a somewhat romantic atmosphere — Dick Wright's was not Morningside's oldest smiddy. When Grant dsecribed the village as 'a row of thatched

DENHOLM'S SMIDDY.
MORNINGSIDE

Denholm's Smiddy, in the heart of old Morningside village. Here carters from
surrounding farms and the south stopped to have their horses attended to. The
Public Library was built on the site of this smiddy.

cottages, a line of trees and a blacksmith's forge', the reference
would appear from records to have been to Denholm's smiddy.
In Gray's *Annual Directory* of 1832-3, the first Edinburgh
directory to have a separate heading for Morningside, 'J. and W.
Denholm, smiths' are listed alongside a total of seven shops.
(There is no reference to Dick Wright's smiddy at this period.)
Denholm's smiddy occupied the site on which Morningside
Public Library was built in 1904.

   Just beyond the Merlin is a little lane with, at its end, three
small cottages. This group of cottages is the last and oldest
survivor of the heart of the original Morningside village. All
three of these quaint little houses, tastefully renovated, are still
occupied.

   Pictures published with such captions as 'Morningside
Smiddy' (as, for example, that in Mair's *Historic Morningside*)
would appear not to portray either Denholm's or Dick Wright's,

but a third smiddy which, according to the Edinburgh Ordnance Survey Map of 1894, stood somewhere amidst the little cottages just described. Three blacksmiths are shown on this map.

Denholm's smiddy and its adjoining cottage, described in the early Post Office Directories as being in Falcon Place, were, after 1885, allocated the numbers 186 and 188 Morningside Road. Both were demolished in 1903 to make way for the building of the library. The Edinburgh Public Library Report for 1905 states that, 'Three years ago, representation was made by the inhabitants of the district of Morningside in favour of a Branch Library in that part of the town.' The wishes of the inhabitants were granted, and Denholm's smiddy, one of the village's oldest institutions, second in antiquity only to the schoolhouse, having stood for over seventy years, made way for the establishment of the fast-growing suburb's newest institution.

Morningside Public Library was opened on 9 November 1904 by John Harrison, second son of Lord Provost George Harrison, who became Edinburgh's City Treasurer. The Harrison family had close connections with Morningside, having lived for many years in Rockville, the controversial Pagoda house in Napier Road.

When the library was opened, six thousand volumes were considered an adequate initial stock. Ten years later this number was closer to ten thousand. In 1929 the library building was extended. Today the stock of books held has, compared with the year of opening, increased tenfold. The annual issue is now nearly 500,000. On the site of the old village smiddy there now operates one of the busiest branch libraries in Scotland.

Adjacent to Denholm's smiddy, at the corner of what is now Springvalley Gardens, was the Free Church School. Its site is now covered by the shops and tenements at 190 to 196 Morningside Road. Immediately beyond the old Free Church School was Reid's Lane (leading to Reid's Cottages or Buildings) and then an extensive dairy farm, long owned by John Reid. The cottages, today well preserved and still occupied, once housed the workers of Reid's farm. Among those who at various times resided here was James Gavine, the builder responsible for the construction of the Midmar district of Morningside. Immediately beyond the cottages, a pend runs under what was once The Silver Slipper dance-hall and later the Springvalley Cinema, into an open area now occupied by car lock-ups. A small outside balcony with iron railings may still be seen above the entrance to the pend. Here there were doors which could open out to allow fresh air into the cinema projection box and on which the projectionist might also stand to breathe more comfortably. On the left, just before the lock-ups, is an old two-storey building, the upper floor of which has a very old door, possibly a relic of one of the byres of Reid's Dairy. Just beyond this building may be seen, built into a boundary wall, a number of interesting and apparently very old ecclesiastical stones of varied motifs. Local tradition has it that these stones were set here by the owner of the nearby sculptor's yard. This sculptor, it is said, was on occasion engaged in the alteration or demolition of old churches, from which the stones originated. They are much older than any that would have been obtained from local Morningside churches, but they may have been brought here from some much older church in the city.

From about the middle of the nineteenth century there were several dairy farms in the Morningside district, but Reid's byres and outbuildings extended over such a wide area in the vicinity of what became Springvalley Gardens and Terrace as to make this undoubtedly the principal farm of its kind in the old village of Morningside. Elderly residents remembered it as Springvalley Farm. The press article quoted below describes the dairy farm in its heyday.

> The cows were all numbered with big black figures painted on their flanks. Each morning they used to proceed in stately single file on their own to pasture in 'The Shooting Field' next to the Hermitage, and equally stately was their procession back home for the evening milking. I have counted up to 130. Milk for the villagers was delivered by the milkmaids picturesquely dressed. The milk pails and cream pitchers were hung on a large hoop which the milkmaid carried with both hands, she being in the middle.

This colourful era of rural Morningside came to an end when Reid's byres were demolished in 1899 to make way for Springvalley Gardens and Terrace, built soon after. Immediately beyond Reid's Lane, now Springvalley Gardens, and on what is now the site of the Morningside Branch of the Trustee Savings Bank and the short row of tenements extending to the great modern supermarket at the corner of Morningside Park, stood the principal manor-house of the old village, Morningside House. Of modest proportions and simple style, it stood a short distance back from Morningside Road, behind a pleasant front garden. There were extensive grounds and an orchard to the rear, now forming the back gardens of several houses on the north side of Morningside Park. A large pear tree still flourishes in the back garden of 8 Morningside Park, a last relic of the orchard of Morningside House. When Morningside Road was numbered in 1885, Morningside House became 200, now the number of the Savings Bank.

When Morningside House was built and by whom is difficult to determine. The lands of Morningside passed through a long succession of owners, the early 'lairds of the village'. This area, originally known as Wester Morningside and then simply as Morningside Estate, was one of the lots into which the Burgh Muir was divided for feuing by Edinburgh Town Council in 1586. Morningside remained the property of successive owners of East Morningside Estate for just over one hundred years — until 1764. Among later owners was John Orr, an army surgeon, and John Mosman, a merchant who had previously acquired the extensive adjacent lands of Canaan. Mosman, at his other estate at Auchtyfardle in Lanarkshire, had welcomed to his home, with much-appreciated kindness, Mrs Maclehose (Robert Burns's 'Clarinda'). She enjoyed there rural peace and hospitality 'such as makes one forget the past'.

Mosman's nephew, Hugh Mosman, sold Morningside Estate in 1789 to Francis Garden of Troup, the eccentric and benevolent Lord Gardenstone, Senator of the College of Justice. A considerable amount of information has come down to us about this owner of Morningside House, who was perhaps also its builder. Lord Gardenstone, who chose as his legal title the name of his birthplace in Banffshire, was raised to the Bench in 1764. He came to live in Morningside House just four years before his death there in 1793.

Kay's portrait of Lord Gardenstone highlights one of his many eccentricities: he is shown entering the city on horseback, 'on an animal somewhat mild and aged to compensate for his Lordship's apparent lack of horsemanship', while alongside runs a little boy in Highland dress. The boy accompanied Lord Gardenstone all the way from Morningside House to the courts in Parliament Square and there looked after the horse till the day's proceedings were over, when he commenced his return journey to Morningside, again trotting attentively behind his master.

A great lover of pigs, the noted judge developed a special friendship with one of them, which in winter served a useful purpose before the era of electric blankets: the small creature would be placed in his noble master's bed to heat it and would then complete his duties by sleeping all night on his master's clothes to ensure that these were comfortably warm in the morning!

While living at Morningside House, Lord Gardenstone regularly, and apparently to his benefit, partook of the mineral waters of St Bernard's Well beside the Water of Leith at Stockbridge. During the first year of his residence at Morningside, 1789, he erected over the well a little Doric temple and dome designed by Nasmyth and modelled on Sybil's Temple at Tivoli. A statue of Hygeia, the work of Sir John Steell, was later placed beneath the canopy, and the well with its surrounding enclosure was presented to the city by William Nelson, the publisher, in 1884.

Lord Gardenstone is the first person referred to in the records as having resided at Morningside House, and it is thus possible that it was he who built this simple mansion-house in the midst of Morningside village. Work may have been completed before he took up residence in Morningside Estate, purchased in 1789. Contemporary maps of Edinburgh either do not include the

outlying village of Morningside, or, if they do, do not indicate
Morningside House by name or show its exact location. The
earliest Edinburgh directories do not list Morningside House,
the first to do so being that of 1836-7. It seems very probable
that this house was built by Lord Gardenstone in about 1789,
shortly after his purchase of Morningside Estate.

Lord Gardenstone was known to be extremely generous to
his household staff and tenants in the various estates he owned
earlier, and it may be assumed that such benevolence was also
shown towards the people of Morningside Village during the
distinguished judge's few years as 'the laird'.

David Deuchar, who purchased Morningside Estate and its
mansion-house in 1795 from Lord Gardenstone's nephew, was
of note in his own right, and even more so on account of his
having 'discovered' a young man who was to become one of
Scotland's, and indeed the world's, greatest portrait painters —
Henry Raeburn. Deuchar was an etcher and engraver of some
distinction whose studio is listed in Williamson's *Edinburgh
Directory: 1790-92*. The entry reads, 'D. and A. Deuchar, seal
engravers to the Prince of Wales [afterwards George IV] opposite
the Cross, South Side'. The Cross was the Mercat Cross in the
High Street, Deuchar's premises being on the south side of the
High Street, near Parliament Square. Near Deuchar's studio
was the shop of his close friend 'James Gilliland, jeweller,
Parliament Close'. Almost daily the two met to exchange news
and discuss business of mutual interest involving both their
skills. During one such visit by Deuchar to Gilliland's shop, his
friend drew his attention to the remarkable talent of his new
apprentice, Henry Raeburn. Deuchar was shown some work by
young Raeburn, who at first had concealed it from view, and
was immediately and deeply impressed. He himself gave this
young protégé his first formal tuition in drawing, then introduced him to David Martin, one of Edinburgh's notable painters
and engravers, who had studied under Allan Ramsay. Raeburn
became Martin's dedicated pupil.

The young apprentice jeweller whose genius was first
recognised by Deuchar, and who was knighted by George IV at

David Deuchar of Morningside House, an artist and engraver, reputedly discovered Henry Raeburn, the future famous portrait painter, when he was apprenticed to Deuchar's friend, William Gilliland, a jeweller near Parliament Square. The latter showed Deuchar some of the boy's sketches. The Morningside artist recognised a genius and arranged expert tuition. He drew a miniature of Raeburn. The young artist reciprocated by presenting Deuchar with the above miniature of his patron. *The National Galleries of Scotland.*

The world-famous portrait painter, Henry Raeburn, drawn by David Deuchar of Morningside House in reciprocation of the miniature which Raeburn made of Deuchar who had 'discovered his talent. *The National Galleries of Scotland*.

Hopetoun House in 1822, was a former Heriot's foundationer, born in a small slated cottage at the side of a mill lade of the Water of Leith at Stockbridge. His father was a yarn boiler, but both Raeburn's parents were dead by the time he was six years old. After six years as a pupil at Heriot's Hospital, as the school in Lauriston Place was originally known, he began his apprenticeship with Gilliland, which was to lead to his discovery by Deuchar. To mark the happy accident of their first meeting in 1773, young Henry Raeburn soon afterwards produced a miniature portrait of Deuchar. The latter reciprocated with a pen-and-wash drawing of the young apprentice, then aged seventeen. Both relics of this friendship, so fortuitous for the world of art, were acquired in 1931 by the National Gallery of Scotland from the Deuchar family.

David Deuchar's own work has been overshadowed by his association with Raeburn, but it was in fact of fine quality and much in demand. Of special note were his seal engravings commissioned by George IV. In addition to engraving, the lapidary etching which he originally took up as a hobby earned him considerable distinction. In 1788 he published a series of 46 copper-plate etchings of the 'Dance of Death' paintings by Hans Holbein the younger, which portray all classes of men, from Pope to beggar, terrorised by death. In the Fine Art Room of the Edinburgh Central Public Library may be seen 'A Collection of Etchings after the most eminent masters of the Dutch and Flemish Schools, particularly Rembrandt, Ostade, Cornelius Bega and Van Vhet; accompanied with sundry miscellaneous pieces and a few original designs, by David Deuchar, Seal Engraver, Edinburgh'. Miss E. Ethel Evans, for long resident in Morningside before her death many years ago, possessed a rare collection of Deuchar's original works. The location of this collection is not now known.

Following Deuchar's death at Morningside House in 1808, his estate was inherited by his four sons, in unusual sequence: ownership passed first to the youngest, then progressively to the eldest. While the eldest son Alexander followed his father as a seal engraver, his youngest brother John entered the world of science, becoming a lecturer in chemistry at the University of Glasgow and, later, at Edinburgh University, where he was the first to lecture in his subject to female students. At this time the chemistry classroom and laboratory were in Lothian Street.

Finally, the property in Morningside, including Morningside House, passed to David Deuchar, FRSE, manager of the Caledonian Insurance Company. By 1871 he appears to have moved from Morningside House, for in that year the *Edinburgh Post Office Directory* lists John Reid, dairyman, as occupying the old village mansion-house. In fact, the last of the Deuchar family to reside in Morningside House had vacated it for the substantial villa, Harlaw Lodge, which he built at 24 Morningside Park, just a short distance west of Morningside House, in 1874. Here he resided until 1881, when he sold it for £3,230 to Morningside Parish Church as its first permanent manse. They in turn sold it some years ago and the manse was until recently at 5 Cluny Avenue. The large villa in Morningside Park today recalls its long Parish Church association by its name, Mansewood. Morningside Place, which passes the top of Morningside Park, was for long known as Deuchar Street.

The Reid family remained in Morningside House until it was demolished in about 1895. High up on the wall of the tenement block built on the site of the front garden is a carved stone plaque commemorating the Diamond Jubilee of Queen Victoria in 1897. The plaque is deeply embedded, almost flush with the surface stonework of the tenement, suggesting that it was inserted when the tenement was built, probably late in 1897. It is directly above the Savings Bank at 200 Morningside Road, once, as already noted, the number of Morningside House.

Immediately beyond the southern end of this row of tenements, the stables of the old house remained for many years after Morningside House itself had disappeared. They were owned by a well-known Morningside doctor who resided in the corner villa at 2 Morningside Park, later demolished to make way for the supermarket. At 3 Morningside Park are the premises of the enterprising Morningside Club, which has its origins in the Morningside Liberal Club established on 30

November 1889 in a two-storey house at what was then 247 Morningside Road (where the annual rent was, initially, £23). That house, the property of a Mr Johnston, was, along with a number of similar adjoining houses, demolished in about 1889 to make way for the tenement between Canaan Lane and Jordan Lane. The inagural meeting of the Morningside Liberal Club, the membership of which numbered 150, was attended by several Morningside Town Councillors and prominent residents. Subsequent meetings of the Club discussed many topical issues of concern to the people of Morningside: the need for a new and larger school to supersede the old schoolhouse; the state of footpaths; the possible removal from the district of the Edinburgh Asylum established in 1813 between what became Millar Crescent and Maxwell Street to the outskirts of the city; the need for improved suburban railway services, and the construction of a skating pond at Braid Hills. In November 1890 the Club considered purchasing the Morningside Halls at Morningside Drive (later the Dunedin Hall), but their offer was not accepted and the premises were acquired instead by the Morningside Unionist Club. In May 1899 the Morningside Liberal Club purchased 3 Morningside Park, where it continued to function until 1950, when it became a social club. In the 1960s the premises were altered to provide the excellent facilities now enjoyed. Morningside Club's deep sense of pride in the history and traditions of the district from which it takes its name was signified on an early membership badge, not now used, which portrayed an Egyptian falcon, symbolising the Land of Canaan and Falcon Hall, and the rays of the 'morning side' of the sun. In 1989, the Club celebrated the centenary of its earliest foundation with a dinner in the clubhouse of the Tipperlinn Bowling Club. During the evening, apart from other speeches, a short history of the Club was presented to a large gathering by the present writer.

At the beginning of the nineteenth century anyone proceeding down the west side of the old high street would, once he passed the whitewashed garden wall of Morningside House, have found himself in open country 'of pastures green, waving corn and sweet-smelling hawthorn hedges all the way to Fairmilehead'. There were no other houses on this west side of the road until the other side of the Jordan Burn, in the districts of Braid to the left and Plewlands to the right. Morningside Park was not built till nearly a century later. After 1813, in the area between what is now Morningside Park and Maxwell Street, 'the pastures green' would no longer have been quite so visible. In that year there was built, at long last, 'an asylum for the cure or relief of mental derangement'. This was originally the East House, forerunner of today's Royal Edinburgh Hospital. Its high enclosing wall extended from just beyond the garden of Morningside House to the Jordan Burn at the Briggs o' Braid near Braid Church. The large gates and little cottage-type lodge at the entrance to the new hospital stood almost opposite Jordan Lane. The southern boundary wall of the hospital extended westwards along what is now the back of Maxwell Street, on the north bank of the Jordan Burn. On reaching the Jordan Burn with its little bridge, known as the 'Briggs o' Braid', one had reached the boundary of old Morningside Village, which was also, for centuries until 1882, the southern boundary of Edinburgh itself.

Where the lawn surrounding Braid Church borders on Morningside Road there once stood the old toll-house. While not shown on Kirkwood's map of 1817 or on the Ordnance Survey Map of 1852, it does appear on the Johnston-Lancefield map of 1861, located on the south bank of the Jordan Burn, just beyond the city boundary.

On 20 January 1852 a meeting of the Commissioners of Supply and Road Trustees for Midlothian had before it a petition, signed by 120 Morningside families, about a lively and heated topic of village conversation — their objection to having to pay a toll at Wright's Houses (near the present-day Barclay Church) which they had to pass on visits to and from the city. 'We unfortunates of Morningside,' they protested, 'cannot even visit a friend in Gilmore Place without incurring this extraction.' There was no possibility of avoiding the toll by taking a route via Viewforth, since a check bar had been erected there too, while to make the even longer diversion along Cant's Loan (Newbattle Terrace), Grange Loan and Newington resulted in being caught at the Grange Loan toll.

One of Morningside's nearby 'lairds', Sir John Stuart Forbes of Pitsligo and Greenhill House, supported the Morningside villagers.

Another neighbouring 'laird', Sir James Forrest of Comiston, a former Lord Provost, commented, when it was pointed out that the Wright's Houses toll-bar had operated for fifty or sixty years, that, while this was true, there had been 'no Morningside at all at that time'. Sir James was opposed to all of the city's toll-bars being moved outside its boundaries on the grounds that this would lead to suburban housing development, to the detriment of rents for those flats in the city vacated by tenants moving to the outskirts, but he did nevertheless support the petition for the removal of the Wright's Houses toll-bar southwards.

The Morningside villagers won their case. Soon afterwards the new toll-house was built on the south bank of the Jordan Burn, just outside the city boundary, where it remained for nearly 30 years until the abolition of road tolls throughout Scotland in 1883.

In 1888 Sir John Skelton, owner of the Hermitage of Braid, obtained permission to have the then obsolete Morningside toll-house carefully dismantled and rebuilt as the gatehouse at the entrance to his drive. On a lintel at the rear of the house the number 259, the original number of the old toll-house in Morningside Road, may still be seen, very faintly now, above the built-up doorway at which the tolls were once collected. The toll-gate was operated from within the adjacent bay window.

In about 1880 the keeper of the old Morningside toll-house had been Mrs Mark, a reputedly forbidding lady of German or Dutch origin who struck terror into the hearts of Morningside children who enjoyed trying to slip beyond the toll-bar unnoticed.

Opposite the old toll-house, horses which had drawn the old

buses, and later tramcars, from the city, were tethered in the then open area beside the high enclosing wall of the asylum at the back of Maxwell Street. Suitably refreshed, they later resumed their arduous haul up the steep brae to Churchhill. While these horse-drawn buses and trams which plied from the city to Morningside were fairly well patronised, the old coaches or cabs were not so popular, colourful as they were, trotting down Morningside Road to the warning blasts of the driver's coaching horn. In summer, however, business improved.

In the summer of 1859 there was a great invasion of tourists and it was recorded that, 'One day one might see five hundred new faces in Edinburgh.' (The Edinburgh International Festival, with its immense increase in the number of 'new faces', was still a long way off!) During this mid-nineteenth-century tourist boom, one of the well-advertised mystery tours by 'coach and pair' was a visit to Morningside. When they reached the toll-house, the cabbies suggested to their passengers that they might wish to stretch their legs and enjoy a pleasant stroll along the lane which now leads to a social club and which in those days ran along the bank of the Jordan Burn. Some distance along the lane, the visitors were met by a group of well-dressed gentlemen who invited them to relax in a game of 'thimble and pea' or be entertained with card tricks. Many visitors returned to the city with much less in their purses than when they arrived at Morningside.

There is a reference to Morningside's old toll-house in Robert Louis Stevenson's *Edinburgh: Picturesque Notes* (1879). The author proclaims, in no uncertain terms, his views upon the development of Morningside:

> Just beyond the old toll-house at the foot of Morningside Road, the chisels are tinkling on a new row of houses. The builders at length have adventured beyond the toll, which had held them in respect so long, and proceed to career in these fresh pastures like a herd of colts turned loose. It seems as if it must come to an open fight at last to preserve a corner of free country unbedevilled.

Joseph Laing Waugh, the author of several novels which have become classics of their kind, resided in Comiston Drive. He

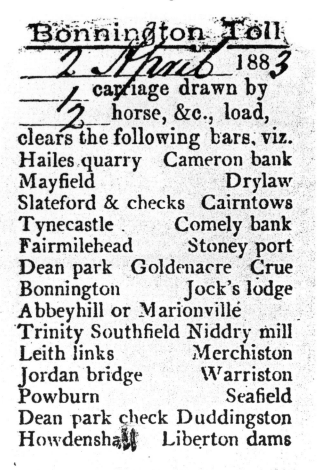

Bonnington Toll

2 *April* 1883

1 carriage drawn by
½ horse, &c., load,
clears the following bars, viz.

Hailes quarry   Cameron bank
Mayfield   Drylaw
Slateford & checks Cairntows
Tynecastle .   Comely bank
Fairmilehead   Stoney port
Dean park Goldenacre Crue
Bonnington   Jock's lodge
Abbeyhill or Marionville
Trinity Southfield Niddry mill
Leith links   Merchiston
Jordan bridge   Warriston
Powburn   Seafield
Dean park check Duddingston
Howdenshall Liberton dams

There were toll gates in various parts of the boundary of the city. This was a well-known one and the name remains. Morningside toll house would have its own tickets. Note 'Jordan Bridge' is shown. *City Libraries, Edinburgh.*

too refers to the old toll-house at Morningside, and the nearby low stone wall, overhung by a large and pleasant hawthorn tree, is also mentioned in his *Robbie Doo*. The broad wall was once a favourite haunt of schoolboys. Under its slabbed top were a series of little cellars, formerly pigsties, and subsequently used to house the delivery hand barrows of McIntosh's Dairy.

Proceeding uphill from the site of the old toll-house, we pass Jordan Lane on the east side of the old village high street. The short row of high tenements on the south side at the entrance to this street were the first to be built in Morningside, in about 1857. The stretch of Morningside Road extending from Jordan Lane to Canaan Lane was originally known as Jordan Place.

Grant's description of old Morningside might have included, 'and the village inn'. At the corner of Canaan Lane from at least 1800 onwards, and probably earlier, there stood one of Morningside's earliest institutions, an inn which came to be named The Volunteers' Rest, but which was known to many villagers as The Rifleman or, in later years, as The Volunteer Arms or The Canny Man's. Until relatively modern times this was Morningside's only hostelry. Some writers have claimed that there were at one time as many as seven public houses in Morningside, but this is difficult to substantiate, though there were a number of licensed grocers in the early days, on whose premises drink might on occasion have been available.

At the south corner of Canaan Lane and what became Morningside Road a cottage-type inn existed towards the end of the eighteenth century. This, the original village inn, was purchased by Mr James Kerr in 1871. He was the 'Canny Man', having earned this title because of his steadying influence on the carters who patronised his premises and tended to consume their drinks rather quickly. 'Ca' canny man', was the advice offered by Mr Kerr to such customers. His name stuck, and it also became the name by which the inn was commonly known during his ownership.

James Kerr was a native of Biggar, where his father was a blacksmith. He had first come to Edinburgh to take charge of Usher's the brewers' team of horses which pulled the old dray carts to various hostelries in the city. Successful in this job, he saved enough money to be able to purchase the little inn at the corner of Canaan Lane. The Volunteers' Rest, as he named it, became a popular rendezvous for the many carters coming to

Morningside with produce from many outlying farms. Here they would not only obtain refreshment and exchange the news of the day but also, if required, have an expert eye cast over their horses by Mr Kerr.

One of the great annual events in Morningside Village in the early nineteenth century was the Carters' Parade which took place on the first Friday in April. This was a lively affair: there were stalls selling sweets and spelderns in Morningside Road, which was decked with coloured flags. The day ended with a dinner, which may have been held in the Volunteers' Rest, presumably for farmers and leading participants.

While it was the patronage of the carters which was important to the village inn, it was from its popularity with a quite different class of clientele that its name originated. These were the men of the Edinburgh Volunteers. Not far from the village hostelry, a short distance up Braid Road, then the main road to Biggar and the south, a path led from a break in the hawthorn hedge on the east side to a large field (still unbuilt upon) on the south side of what became Hermitage Drive, facing the steep slopes of Blackford Hill. This was known as 'the shooting field' and was used by the Edinburgh Volunteers and, latterly, the Edinburgh and Midlothian Rifle Association. The targets were on the slope of the west side of Blackford Hill. In the interests of accurate marksmanship, it may be assumed that visits to the village inn were more fitting after than before practice at the butts. At any rate, the inn's signboard 'The Volunteers' Rest' was obviously appropriate.

Two water-colour artist's impressions of the old inn at Canaan Lane may still be seen in the public bar. A caption on each reads: 'The Golden Drop was first blended and sold here in the year 1871'. The initials F.D.O. on these paintings are interesting. The *Edinburgh and Leith Post Office Directory* for 1883 lists a 'Mr F. D. Ogilvie, artist, No. 1 Belhaven Terrace', who is presumably the painter of these pictures.

Frederick Ogilvie also painted a fine water-colour of the Braid iron church at the corner of what are now Braid Road and Cluny Gardens. Unfortunately no biographical details of this

The Volunteers' Rest, Morningside's earliest tavern at Canaan Lane and forerunner of the 'Canny Man', built nearby in 1871. The Edinburgh Volunteers who practised shooting at Blackford Hill frequented the hostelry. Johnny Kerr, the first 'Canny Man', so named for warning customers not to drink and drive – their horses! Ca'canny, man! (*Painting by Frederick Dove Ogilvie. By courtesy of Watson Kerr*).

Morningside artist could be traced. It is possible, though of course mere conjecture, that Mr Ogilvie was also the artist referred to earlier in connection with the old schoolhouse, who paid the fees of his several children in kind, with a series of paintings of Morningside and district.

In addition to the water-colours of the original Volunteers' Rest, the present-day premises, built in about 1890, house many interesting relics of bygone days. These include a complete range of copper whisky-blending jugs and measures, ranging from the minute to those holding several gallons, used in the production of the 'golden drop'. There is also an interesting collection of decorative bridles (perhaps preserved from the original owner's [Mr Kerr's] dray horses), a selection of coaching horns, and a quite fascinating old accounts book for 1892-3 in which regular customers were each allocated their own page, or several pages. The page headings reveal how the owner of the old inn knew each 'regular' personally, often simply by his Christian name or occupation. We find recorded such customers as, 'Old John, Shepherd with Falconhall', 'George the joiner', 'Hughy, mason at the asylum', 'Soldier Jock', 'Tom, labourer' and 'the gasman', and there are entries such as, 'Four quarts of beer during hay-making at Falconhall'. The prices of drinks in 1892 — for instance 'glass of whisky, 4d' — are such as to spark off the now frequent argument over the relationship between such prices and their modern equivalents.

In the old accounts book of 1892 most debts are shown as having eventually been 'squared'. Had a similar book been kept twenty years earlier it would, it seems, have revealed at least one customer whose debts were not so regularly paid — a fortunate occurrence, as it happens, because as a result the Volunteer Arms possesses its two most valuable treasures. The customer in question was the distinguished Scottish landscape painter, Sam Bough, RSA, who resided at the end of nearby Jordan Lane and who is given further attention in a later chapter. Whether to repay his debts, demonstrate his versatility, or simply as a commercial arrangement, the great and prodigious painter of landscapes presented to James Kerr in 1871, as the inn's signboard, a two-sided oil painting of a kneeling rifleman of the Edinburgh Volunteers, painted on a large oak panel and signed by the artist. Earlier Sam Bough had presented a picture of the same subject painted on canvas. These works would now bring a price large enough to settle a thousand-fold any debts incurred.

The eastern section of Morningside Road extending from Canaan Lane to Falcon Road West was once known as Morningside Terrace, now the name of the street branching off from the south side of Morningside Park. When Morningside was still a village what is now Steel's Place was called Steelies' Close or Steelies' Slip. Here there was once a cemetery for cats and dogs. Here too was set up by Dr Thomas Steel a small factory for the production of the magnesia for use in the famous 'powder' introduced by the celebrated Professor James Gregory

"THE CANNY MAN"

Soldier Jock
Glass Rum

Dr Old John with Douglas.

Post Office
12 Pint Aqua

Shepherd
Painter with D Howieson

Melville the Plumber   Old John the Plumber

Tom. Labourer.

Dr Gasman

Dr. M. Macfarlane Cyclist

Bob Lindsay Swap

Houghie at "Asylum

Names of 'the regulars' in an old ledger recording the running 'on account' purchases at the 'Canny Man'. (*Designed by Neil Hanna; Courtesy of Watson Kerr*).

of nearby Canaan Lodge, and which bore his name. Almost midway between Steel's Place and Falcon Road West were the main gates at the entrance of the drive leading to Falcon Hall.

From the Falcon Hall gates a row of low terraced cottages extended to a point almost opposite the old village schoolhouse, running the length of the short high street on the east side. Opposite were Esplin Place and Blackford Place. In the last cottage in this row, Falcon Cottage, which was larger than the others, lived the village doctor, Dr George T. Beilby, MD. This house stood on the site of what is now 161 Morningside Road. Here was born, in 1850, (Sir) George T. Beilby, LLD, FRS, a distinguished pioneer in physical and industrial chemistry. Another early village doctor was Dr John Airth.

Beyond these cottages, which stood on the west boundary of Canaan, lay open ground as far as the Parish Church at the corner of Newbattle Terrace. The tenements on the north side of Falcon Avenue were not completed until 1915, and the modern flats opposite much more recently. The last short section of Morningside Road, from the Parish Church to Churchhill, originally named Banner Place, has already been described. At this point the northern boundary of the village was reached.

The features and institutions of old Morningside Village which I have described appeared, flourished, and, in most cases, disappeared over a period of some two hundred years. In the chronological sequence of smiddy, inn, village school and Parish Church can be traced the development of the community. Until the mid-nineteenth century Morningside remained remote from the city. It was the transport explosion which transformed the accessible village into a suburb.

Among many recorded statistics concerning Morningside's development, two are important in showing the type of suburb it became. Despite the wide variety of houses built from the middle of the nineteenth century onwards, no instance has ever been recorded of housing, even in the most humble dwellings, becoming unfit for occupancy. Even today, in the heart of the old village, three of the earliest cottages remain comfortably occupied. Morningside's record is apparently unique in the history of Edinburgh's housing.

As a result of the vast growth of 'villadom' from about 1870 onwards, steadily effected by the chisels which tinkled beyond the old toll-house, much to Robert Louis Stevenson's regret, came Morningside's second distinction. In the pleasant residential districts of Cluny, Hermitage and Braid almost every villa originally had resident 'servants', usually spinster ladies with their own 'purpose-built' quarters. Thus the proportion of women in Morningside was considerably higher than in any other part of Edinburgh.

The village of Morningside, unlike its neighbour and one-time rival, the now non-existent village of Tipperlinn, did not merit a place on the earliest maps of Edinburgh and environs. Today, however, it covers a wider area and has a larger population than many small Scottish towns.

Tipperlinn

The 'High Street' of the ancient village of Tipperlinn, now Tipperlinn Road, Here was a famous community of weavers. The villa, left of centre, is Tipperlinn House, now the Royal Edinburgh Hospital's Young People's Unit. George Watson's College is seen on the left. On the wall, centre of the picture, under the last of the trees, is a now barely legible inscription, possibly initials on a marriage lintel from a weaver's cottage (1763). Tipperlinn gradually disappeared as the early Royal Edinburgh Hospital expanded. *Photograph by W. R. Smith*.

CHAPTER 4

The Land of Canaan

The high street of old Morningside village was bounded on its west side by Morningside Estate, stretching from Doo Loan (now Albert Terrace), at the brow of Churchhill, downhill to the Jordan Burn, the southern boundary of the village and of Edinburgh. On the opposite side of the street the boundary wall of the Canaan Estate extended from Cant's Loan (now Newbattle Terrace) to the Jordan Burn.

During the centuries following the feuing out of the western Burgh Muir in 1586, 'the land of Canaan', as it came to be picturesquely known, eventually enclosed an area of 65 acres. Its boundaries extended from Newbattle Terrace and Grange Loan in the north to the Jordan Burn in the south, and from Morningside Road in the west to Blackford Park and Blackford Brae in the east. It was thus by far the largest of the estates which had once formed part of the ancient 'Common Mure' and the most extensive of the various lands on which Morningside was gradually to develop. Amidst its rural spacious meadows, orchards and gardens arose many fine villas, and Canaan despite many changes has remained the most pleasant of the Morningside 'lands'.

Describing the varied features of Canaan involves reference to names such as Goshen, Eden, Hebron and Jordan, and the question of how such names originated in this district, described by the late Scottish writer, Wilfrid Taylor, as 'Edinburgh's Bible belt', immediately arises. Several explanations have been advanced. Henry Mackenzie, 'the Man of Feeling', who for some time resided in Canaan Lodge, wrote:

> At the distance of less than a mile from Edinburgh, there are places with Jewish names – Canaan, the river or brook called Jordan, Egypt – a place called Transylvania, a little to the east of Egypt. There are two traditions of the way in which they got their names:

98

one, that there was a considerable eruption of gypsies into the county of Edinburgh who got a grant of these lands, then chiefly a moor; the other, which I have heard from rather better authority, that some rich Jews happened to migrate into Scotland and got from one of the Kings (James I, I think it was said) a grant of these lands in consideration of a sum of money which they advanced him.

Another suggestion is that Morningside's Biblical names may be traced to Oliver Cromwell's occupation of Galachlaw Hill near Fairmilehead in 1650. Others claim to find an association with the farm of Egypt just south of the Jordan Burn. Such explanations have some element of probability but they must be looked at in relation to known historical events.

In the Edinburgh Burgh Records for 1585, an entry for 22 September states that Robert Fairlie, 'Laird of the Braids', had granted the city the use of his 'houssis callit Littil Egypt besyde the commoun mure for brewing thairin of the drink for the seik folkis in the mure and sic necessar usis as the toun hes found good to employ on the samyn'. This seems to be the earliest reference in the records to the existence in the district which was to become Morningside of a Biblical or eastern place name. The 'seik folkis in the mure' for whom Robert Fairlie was brewing beer were the unfortunate victims of the devastating plague of 1585 who were quarantined in wooden huts surrounding the little chapel of St Roque, which stood in the midst of what today are the pleasant tree-shaded grounds of the Astley Ainslie Hospital, a short distance from the original district of Littil Egypt.

The name Canaan first appears in the city records in 1661. The Edinburgh Town Council Minutes of that year record that on 28 August the Council agreed to set on lease to Mart (Margaret) Whilleis these 'aikers of the wester commoun mure commounlie called Canaan' for a period of eleven years. On the death of Margaret Whilleis in 1667 the land passed to James Russell, described as an 'indweller in Canaan'. Canaan is described as 'lyand betwixt the land of Braid on the south with a little stream [the Jordan Burn] the lands of Mr William Livingston some time'.

Egypt, then, is first mentioned in 1585, but Canaan only much later, in 1661. Neither reference, however, provides any indication of the origin of these names. In tracing this, probability must take the place of documented fact. The search must begin not in the district of Canaan but a short distance to the south, in the neighbouring estate of Braid.

In the mid-sixteenth century, Edinburgh's magistrates were hard put to it to deal effectively with the increasing crimes of theft, assault and vagrancy within the city. In 1566 a gibbet or gallows was erected at the eastern end of the Burgh Muir, on the site of what is now Preston Street Primary School. One particular group of people caused the authorities considerable trouble. These were the gypsies or 'vagabondis'. In earlier days, the gypsies claimed, their forefathers were Christian pilgrims expelled from Egypt and forced to wander through India and, later, Europe. They had come to be regarded as exiled Egyptians, and this name was eventually abbreviated to 'gypsies'.

The gypsies first appeared in large numbers in Scotland in the early sixteenth century. At first they seem to have been accepted wherever they established their communities. Indeed, their colourful dress and way of life and their gifts of music and dancing attracted the attention, perhaps not surprisingly, of James IV, who in 1505 received some of their community at Holyrood, presenting them with ten French Crowns. Likewise, the Lord High Treasurer's accounts reveal that on 25 May 1529 James IV's somewhat Bohemian son (later James V) also made a gift to the 'Egiptianis that dansit before the King in Holyrudhous'. In 1540 James V granted to 'Johnne Faw, Lord and Erle of Egypt and to his sons and successors power to hang and punish all Egyptians within the Kingdom of Scotland'.

Their fortunes were, however, soon to change. Perhaps Johnne Faw and his successors failed to maintain law and order within their communities, for in 1541 the Lords of Council issued an order for their expulsion from Scotland on account of 'the gret thiftis and scaithis done be the saidis Egyptians upon our soverance lordis liegis and quhair thai cum or resortis'. In accordance with the decree Edinburgh's magistrates forbade all gypsies residence within the city's limits. It was probably as a consequence of this that the first of Morningside's Biblical names arose. The principal Edinburgh gypsy community may very well have been established on the southern slopes of the Burgh Muir, in the future Morningside district, still within the city boundaries. To obey the magistrates' decree it would have been a simple step literally for the gypsies to have moved their encampment from the northern bank of 'the little strand' (the Jordan Burn) to the southern bank. They would then have been within the Braid Estate. If this is what did in fact happen, they must have been squatters, as in the records of the period there is no reference to the Laird of Braid granting them asylum within his lands.

The above-mentioned entry in the Burgh Records relates that in 1585 Robert Fairlie, 'Laird of the Braids', granted the City use of his 'houssis callit Littil Egypt *besyde* the commoun mure' — *beside* and not *on* it. The word 'Littil' preceding Egypt may be of significance in supporting the above suggestion as in gypsy communities establish in Britain their leaders were given the titles of Kings or Erles of 'Littil Egypt'. This was a peculiarly gypsy term and it therefore seems probable that the 'Littil Egypt' in which Fairlie's 'houssis' were located was or had been the site of a gypsy community. It is also interesting to note that the 'Lord and Erle of Egypt' to whom James V granted privileges in 1540 is recalled in S. R. Crockett's novel *The Raiders*, which is subtitled 'Some Passages in the Life of John Faa, Lord and Earl of Little Egypt'. There would certainly seem to be a strong probability that an 'Egyptian' community existed on the fringes of the Braid Estate.

Littil Egypt, then, was in 1585 a distinct location in the future Morningside district and the first of its Biblical names. Though Canaan does not appear on record until 1661, the name might well have been in use for some years before this date, as the 1661 reference is to 'aikers of the wester commoun mure *commounlie* called Canaan', implying that the use of the name was already well established.

The suggestion that the name Canaan was first applied to the lands adjacent to Littil Egypt a decade before 1661 had the support of William Moir Bryce, the authority on the history of the Burgh Muir, who submitted that 'there can be no question that the name Canaan was first applied during the Covenanting period and in particular during Cromwell's occupation of Edinburgh'.

In 1650, prior to the Battle of Dunbar, Cromwell, with an army of 16,000 men, camped on Galachlaw, a hill which rises above the present-day Princess Margaret Rose Hospital in Frogston Road West. It has been suggested that, during this encampment and his several fruitless invasions of Edinburgh, small bands of Cromwell's soldiers conducted forages in the vicinity of Littil Egypt, then a small community. Here they met with such stiff resistance from the local people that the Puritan troops, who frequently had Biblical phrases on their lips, likened these encounters to 'Joshua against the Canaanites'. This is one theory. Another is simply that Cromwell's men, passing through what they were told was the district of Littil Egypt and being Bible conscious, came to call the adjacent lands by the name of Canaan.

The district of Egypt (the 'Littil' was eventually dropped) remained a distinct location for nearly three centuries. The route taken during the last Riding of the Marches on the Burgh Muir in 1717 included the village of Egypt. Charles Gordon's *Plan of the Barony of Braid*, drawn from a survey made in 1772, shows Egypt Farm occupying a considerable area of land and substantial farm buildings. The site of this farm was the junction of what are now Woodburn Terrace and Nile Grove, just a few yards south of the Jordan Burn. Gordon's plan names various places near the farm and indicates the 'Road to Egypt', now Cluny Avenue. Other maps show Cluny Drive as 'Egypt Avenue'.

In later times it appears that the farmhouse was let to summer visitors, often people from Edinburgh who wished to enjoy a pleasantly rural holiday. Mrs Fletcher, wife of an Edinburgh advocate, records such a stay in 1799:

Mr Fletcher's health as well as my own seeming to require a change of air, we repaired with our children to a very inexpensive cottage in the Morningside district, to the south of Edinburgh, called Egypt, so named in memory of a gypsy colony who, as tradition says, had their headquarters in the immediate neighbourhood.

According to the *Edinburgh Almanack* for 1800, one of the hackney coaches which provided transport to places on the outskirts of the city such as Gorgie, Coltbridge and Canaan also stopped at Egypt, the fare from the Tron Church being two shillings. Egypt is mentioned as a place *en route* until 1802.

In a poem about Carlops written by Robert D. C. Brown in 1793, an interesting description is given of that village. Amongst those who attended the Carlops fairs was, we are told, 'Israel, a man who lived at Canaan, Morningside, near the lands of Egypt and River Jordan in 1792, and whose children were known as "the children of Israel".'

By the 1890s Egypt farmhouse was finally demolished and swept away to permit the building on its site and adjoining lands of the villas of Nile Grove, Braid Avenue and Cluny. Among the last of the farmers of Egypt was a Mr Begbie. There is a Begbie family grave in Grange Cemetery.

We now recross the Jordan Burn from the Braid Estate, in which it was necessary to trace the origins of Morningside's Biblical names. The extensiveness of the land of Canaan, from which we set out, and its many interesting and distinguished people make this chapter the most comprehensive and varied of the chronicles which constitute the history of Morningside.

To continue the account of Canaan, we turn to the south-western corner of the large rectangle formed by these lands, where Morningside Road crossed the Jordan Burn at the Briggs o' Braid, beside which the old Toll House stood. The little row of houses known as the Jordan Burn Cottages, just east of the toll, were razed to permit the building of a modern supermarket, and eventually a modern Post Office, but the original lane from which wicket gates led to the cottages remains, for long giving access to the Morningside Family Laundry, vacated in 1975 and now restored to house 'The Angle Club', which provides billiards and snooker facilities for its members. This house is shown on the 1852 Ordnance Survey Map as 'Elizabethan Cottage'.

On the right as one enters Jordan Lane stands the first tenement block built in Morningside in 1857, replacing the old cottages on this site. When it was built the street which had been called Jordan Bank was re-named Jordan Lane and its houses were renumbered. Continuing along Jordan Lane, we come to Ainslie Cottage on the right, indicated by a name-plate above the entrance. This pleasant little house was one of the original cottages of Morningside village. It takes its name from the Ainslie family, originally farmers and notable sheep-breeders at Oastly near Roslin, the first of whom, John Ainslie, took possession of the cottage in 1827 and whose successors remained here for nearly sixty years.

Some confusion exists over the possible residence in Ainslie Cottage of George Meikle Kemp, architect of the Scott Monument in Princes Street. A number of writers of booklets on Morningside have stated that the public funeral of Kemp took place from the cottage on 22 March 1844. William Mair in *Historic Morningside*, however, states that the celebrated architect's funeral took place from his home at 1 Jordan Bank, and that in the *Edinburgh and Leith Post Office Directory* for 1843-4 he is entered as 'G. M. Kemp, 1 Jordan Lane', his cottage at this address eventually being demolished and replaced by the first Morningside tenements referred to above. In fact, the directory which Mair mentions does not give Kemp as residing at 1 Jordan Lane but simply as at 'Jordan 1' the '1' being an abbreviation for 'Lane'. There is now no evidence of Kemp's precise address. Though the title deeds of Ainslie Cottage bear no reference to him, he might possibly have been a tenant there. He did in fact live for some time at Bloomsberry Cottage in nearby Canaan Lane. Some writers who have stated that he resided in Ainslie Cottage, and in particular Robert Cochrane, were close enough to him in time to have had some traditional, if not recorded, evidence of this.

George Meikle Kemp's life, though relatively short, had certainly been varied before he came to Morningside and died tragically in 1844. He was born in the small village of Moorfoot near Gladhouse Loch, on the border of Midlothian and Peeblesshire. His father was a shepherd who had to move about the district frequently to find employment. Thus young George attended many schools, including West Linton Primary School when he was eight years old, in which a commemorative plaque is treasured. He later went to Penicuik School when his parents moved to Newhall near Carlops. It was while living at Newhall that he was sent on an errand to Edinburgh, returning home by Roslin. There he visited the famous chapel and was overwhelmed by its beauty. This early experience inspired him to become an architect. At the age of fourteen he became an apprentice carpenter at Redscaurhead village, between Peebles and Eddleston. After five years' training, when he was proficient in making sketch plans and drawings, he moved to Galashiels to work as a millwright.

An enthusiastic walker, Kemp set out for Galashiels on foot. *En route* he met for the first time the man whose monument he was to design. As he reached Elibank, a carriage drew up and its occupant offered him a lift, which was gratefully accepted, though he did not recognise his distinguished companion, Sir Walter Scott.

After a year in the border town, Kemp returned to Edinburgh, obtaining a post as a carpenter with John Cousin of Greenhill Gardens, who undertook extensive tenement building in Edinburgh. Kemp's work amounted to ten hours' labour daily, including Saturdays. The potential architect became restless. He left Edinburgh after two years, once again on foot, journeying this time through England, where he was specially impressed by York Minster, and to Europe, where the many famous cathedrals he visited profoundly influenced him. He returned after some time to Glasgow, and then finally to Edinburgh, where he married Elizabeth Bonnar. He found employment with the distinguished architect, William Burn. At this time, Kemp, though not a professional architect, began submitting plans for various restorations, including that of Glasgow Cathedral. For this his plans were seriously considered though not accepted.

In 1836 the committee charged with the erection of a fitting memorial to Sir Walter Scott invited designs, and Kemp's attention was drawn to the advertisement offering a fifty-guinea prize. He submitted his design under the *nom-de-plume* 'John Morvo', a name he had seen inscribed by one of the original stonemasons on Melrose Abbey. His Gothic design was, in fact, the result of a close study of Melrose Abbey, from which, he admitted, 'it was in all its details derived' and not from Antwerp tower as several critics later alleged. Indeed, it was while he was making sketches of Melrose Abbey that his second meeting with Sir Walter Scott took place, Sir Walter looking over Kemp's shoulder to observe and comment upon his work. Neither could then know how their names would eventually be associated. The great novelist could not have imagined that the architectural detail Kemp was so carefully noting would find its place in his memorial.

Kemp's submission, one of fifty entries, was awarded third prize, and he was given fifty guineas, as were the first and second placed entrants. The Scott Monument Committee were, however, not satisfied with the designs and invited further contributions. Kemp, after making some revisions, again submitted his design. This time, on 28 March 1838, the committee adopted his plan. The minute describes it as 'an imposing structure 135 feet in height, its beautiful proportions in strict conformity with the purity of taste and style of Melrose Abbey . . .' He was awarded an initial fee of £100.

For nearly six years, while living at Bloomsberry Cottage in Canaan Lane and, finally, in Jordan Lane, Kemp concentrated on making his architectural dream a reality. Many proposals were made for its site, East Princes Gardens eventually being chosen. The foundations were laid on rock 52 feet below ground level and the height of the monument was increased to two hundred feet and six inches, with two hundred and eighty seven steps. The sandstone used was from Binny Quarry. On 15 August 1840 the foundation stone was laid by another

Morningside resident, Lord Provost Sir James Forrest of Comiston, then Grand Master Mason of Scotland.

The monument's creator was not to witness its completion. For nearly four years he had been laboriously involved in its progress and in discussions over complications concerning costs and the realisation of his design. At the end of one such busy day, Kemp called at the office of the building contractor on the north side of the Union Canal basin near Fountainbridge. His business at last over, he set out on foot for Jordan Lane. Alas, the night was dark: he lost his way and stumbled into the deep water of the canal. Next day his cape and cane were seen floating on the surface, and later his body was recovered. Vast crowds lined the route as the *cortège* of his public funeral proceeded to St Cuthbert's Church burial ground at the west end of Princes Street. His gravestone, within distant sight of the towering pinnacle he designed, is inscribed with lines from the dirge composed by his friend James Ballantyne:

> Art is wrapped in weeds of woe,
> Nature mourns in accent low,
> Scotland sheds a heart-wrung tear
> O'er her son's untimely bier.
> The flowers that blush by mountain rill,
> The flowers that bloom on lonely hill,
> All drooping low their loss deplore
> Alas, their lover comes no more.
> Castled keep and sacred pile,
> Buttressed tower and fretted aisle,
> Wrapt in gloom are left alone,
> Now their worshipper is gone.
> Yet hope still cheers us while we mourn,
> And fame strews laurel o'er his urn.
> Behold that structure cleave the sky!
> And dream not genius e'er can die.

The Scott Monument was completed under the direction of Kemp's brother-in-law, William Bonnar, RSA, on 26 October 1844. His son, Thomas Kemp, was accorded the honour of placing the final coping-stone at the top of his father's masterpiece.

Another Morningside resident is also prominently associated with the monument. The statue, at its base, of Sir Walter Scott and his favourite dog, Maida, was carved from a block of Carrara marble by Sir John Steell of Greenhill Gardens. This was the first marble statue to be commissioned in Scotland.

Kemp's famous monument cost just over £15,000 to build. Reactions to it were mixed; indeed much controversy reigned, in which Kemp was accused of plagiarism and of being 'an obscure man'. Lord Cockburn — not one of Sir Walter Scott's admirers — criticised it strongly. Kemp would, however, have been consoled by the praise of William Burn (the most distinguished Scottish architect of his time), Sir John Britton (the great authority on English cathedrals) and Edinburgh's Town Council and Magistrates whose booklet proclaimed that, 'The Scott Monument is perhaps the finest, as it certainly is the most appropriate, monumental edifice in the Kingdom.' Certainly Edinburgh's Princes Street skyline would be poorer without it.

Another of Morningside's Biblical names was, until recently, to be seen on the gate of 7 Jordan Lane. The originally large villa, of which this is just a part, was known as Salem. Unfortunately, during recent alterations the name-plate was removed. Happily it has been recovered and restored to its original place. Immediately beyond this house, garage premises now occupy what was once the byre of a 'dry dairy' — the cows were never put out to pasture but were always kept indoors. The dairy was acquired by the Paterson family in 1890 and the farmhouse was No. 11 Jordan Lane, now sub-divided. There were normally about 16 cows and the milk was distributed in the district by hand carts. Much of the original byres remain, now accommodating a busy car repair and servicing business. A further reference is made to this farm in *The Living Past*.

A few yards further on, at No. 15, is Jordan Bank Villa: the name is now barely decipherable. This house, along with the adjacent Nos. 14 and 16, was purchased by the notable landscape painter, Sam Bough, RSA, in 1867. Born in Carlisle, Bough was the son of a shoemaker. He worked for some time as a theatrical scenery painter in Manchester, and similarly for seven years in Glasgow. This experience is reflected in the dramatic style of his landscapes, which abound in minute detail.

Sam Bough moved to Edinburgh from Glasgow in 1866, and lived for some time at 5 Malta Terrace before coming to Jordan Lane. The apparent confusion concerning his Morningside address, at first recorded as 7 Jordan Bank, is due to the fact that, when the latter was incorporated into the newly created Jordan Lane, the houses were renumbered, 7 Jordan Bank becoming 15 Jordan Lane.

In February 1867, Bough wrote hastily to a friend: 'Getting newly acquired house in order – place in a mess – plasterers, masons, carpenters, plumbers making house habitable.' A connecting door was made between Nos. 14 and 15 and, in the former, an ornate plaster ceiling was created for the drawing-room and a large glass-enclosed studio built on the stone verandah at the rear. Bough also had studios at 2 Hill Street and 2a George Street.

A reference to the nearby Egypt farm is provided by a neighbour of Bough's. The artist, he recounted, was very fond of mushrooms. When these were in season, the two of them had an arrangement whereby whoever wakened first in the morning knocked at the other's window. Together, the friends then jumped the wall at the foot of their gardens, forded the Jordan Burn, crossed the Egypt Road (now Cluny Avenue) and entered Begbie's, the farmer of Egypt's field, which extended to the boundary of the Hermitage of Braid. Here, apparently, mushrooms abounded.

A man of Bohemian appearance and temperament, capable of great frivolity but also of deep seriousness, Sam Bough was a well-known figure in the still village-like Morningside of his day, especially in the original Volunteers' Rest at the corner of Canaan Lane. As mentioned earlier, the two wooden inn signs he painted are preserved in the present-day Volunteer Arms.

Robert Louis Stevenson in *Edinburgh: Picturesque Notes*

Sam Bough RSA, the notable landscape painter who resided in three adjoining houses in Jordan Lane. *The National Galleries of Scotland.*

describes watching passengers coming aboard the steamer *Clansman* at Portree harbour in 1870. Among them was his friend Sam Bough. It is possible that RLS visited Bough at his house in Jordan Lane. Elected an Associate Member of the

Royal Scottish Academy in 1856, while working in Glasgow, but not a full member until 1875, when he was at the peak of his career, Bough exhibited at the Academy and in various other parts of Britain. His prolific landscapes were mainly of Scottish and North of England scenes. Bustling harbours held a special fascination for him.

The English artist from Carlisle, who became a great lover of Scotland and one of the most distinguished painters of his day, died at Jordan Bank Villa on 19 November 1878, aged fifty-six. He was buried in Dean Cemetery and a special medallion portrait by William Brodie, RSA, is on his gravestone. Sixteen coaches conveyed the principal mourners, including many members of the Royal Scottish Academy, along crowd-lined streets. A contingent of Glasgow artists joined the funeral procession in Lothian Road.

While most of Sam Bough's works are now in private collections, several are in the Glasgow Art Gallery. Two small statues of the artist are in the Scottish National Portrait Gallery.

The predecessor of Sam Bough at 14 Jordan Lane was David Ramsay Hay, a decorative artist and author. Hay, who was responsible for the interior decoration of Holyrood Palace during the reign of George IV was also engaged by Sir Walter Scott at Abbotsford. Since they were friends, Scott may have visited Hay at his Jordan Lane home.

No. 14 Jordan Lane, originally united with Jordan Bank Villa, was the home of the late Wilfred Taylor, the author and columnist, whose *Scot Easy* refers to earlier occupants of this house and provides an interesting account of Jordan Lane in modern times.

At 17 Jordan Lane lived Charles D'Orville Pilkington Jackson (1887-1973), whose sculptures include the Robert the Bruce figure at the Bannockburn National Trust Memorial. The house at No. 20, for long named Braid Hill Cottage, is shown on the Ordnance Survey Map of 1852 as 'Helen's Place'. Returning from the end of Jordan Lane, the secluded modern villa on the right, No. 24, is named Bethel, one of the most recent Biblical names in Canaan, another being referred to later.

Morningside's earliest and tiny St Cuthbert's Cooperative store was at No. 241 Morningside Road. It subsequently became a fish and chip shop and this type of business has continued there for over half a century. The McGillivray family were the long-standing owners, latterly naming their shop 'The Clan Chattan', decorated with impressive Scottish and Jacobite emblems. A serious fire gutted the premises some years ago but it was restored and is now under new ownership. The same popular merchandise remains. Entering Canaan Lane, the little area on the right behind the original village inn, between Canaan Lane and Jordan Lane, was known as 'Paradise'. The 'Paradisers', as they were called, with their small cottages and 'Kailyards' ('the Kailyards of Paradise') formed a small community of their own. Some few yards further along on the right, a small drive leads to the substantial villa built as Morningside's original Police Station. A little beyond this, a small cottage bears a plaque on its west gable-end with the name 'Goshen'. The immediate vicinity is indicated on the earliest Ordnance Survey Map as the district of Goshen, while the large villa standing a short distance back on the right, entered by a little lane, was named Goshen House or Goshen Bank. Here in 1868 resided, for a short time, Henry Kingsley, brother of Charles Kingsley, while editing the *Edinburgh Daily Review*. Before coming to Edinburgh, Henry Kingsley had written many novels and worked as a journalist in Australia. The *Edinburgh Daily Review* was a nonconformist publication most unsuited, one critic felt, to the editorship of Kingsley, who was, he wrote, 'a round man in a square hole, knowing little or nothing about Scottish ecclesiastical history and even less about Edinburgh municipal affairs.' There was considerable consternation over some of his 'rollicking leaders', especially in northern manses, and Henry Kingsley resigned his post after eighteen months. Another quite remarkable man who was born in Goshen Bank is referred to in a later chapter.

We pass the first block of tenements on the right and see yet another Biblical name on the door of No. 32: Hebron. Here for some time resided William Ritchie, co-founder with Charles

McLaren of *The Scotsman* in 1817. McLaren was also a 'Canaanite', living at Morelands, a large villa which is now a part of the Astley Ainslie Hospital. Almost opposite Hebron and immediately beyond the entrance to the modern block of flats, Falcon Court, is a small villa called Stonefield, which has associations with the Misses Balfours, aunts of Robert Louis Stevenson.

The feuing plan of Canaan for 1803 indicates a division into 22 lots. Many of the original purchasers of these built villas in this pleasant rural district, but there were several provisos, one being that villas were not to cost less than £300 to build (in the early nineteenth century this was a fairly substantial sum). When William Mosman had, in 1797, feued one of the lots to Thomas Steel for the building of a small magnesia factory, he laid down the condition: 'So far as the same shall not be a nuisance to the neighbourhood.' Later purchasers of land in Canaan were allowed to build but 'not to establish any trade or manufacture a nuisance to the neighbourhood'. This later proviso seems more restricting than Dr Steel's. Perhaps the magnesia factory, built in what is now Steel's Place, on the western edge of Canaan, was not too popular with local residents. Mosman, in his feuing regulations, also reserved to himself 'the right to the coal mines' on his land. Whether such mines did in fact exist and, if they did, where they were located is now impossible to determine. The original Edinburgh Town Council Charter governing Canaan decrees that, in the event of a brewery being established in the lands, the owner must have the malts and grains milled at the town's mill on the Water of Leith.

The villa is shown on Kirkwood's Map of 1817 as Canaan House, but by 1864 the name had been changed to Streatham House. In 1930 the Roman Catholic Benedictine Order acquired this house and established a day-school for boys, the first enrolment totalling five. Eventually the Priory School, as it was known, took boarding pupils and, by the time that the outbreak of the Second World War forced evacuation to the Abbey School at Fort Augustus, the roll at the Canaan Lane school had reached three figures. In 1945 Streatham House was compulsorily purchased by Edinburgh Corporation for use as a Children's Home and the Benedictine school reopened as Carl Kemp's School at North Berwick. The celebrated broadcasting personality, Gilbert Harding, had been one of the schoolmasters at Canaan Lane. Streatham House, or The Priory, is referred to later.

Canaan Lodge was rebuilt in 1907, the original house of this name having been built on the same site in 1800, but destroyed by fire. Of its many owners, the most distinguished and celebrated was Professor James Gregory, MD, who purchased the house in 1814. The last of 'the Academic Gregories', a remarkable Aberdeenshire family of whom fourteen held university professorial chairs over a period of two centuries, Professor James Gregory graduated from the Edinburgh Medical School in 1774. He then studied further at Leyden with which Edinburgh for a period had close links. When appointed Professor of Medicine at Edinburgh in 1778, he was the fifth member of his family to occupy an Edinburgh University Chair. A brilliant teacher, his personal notes on his classes are still extant and indicate the greatly increased number of students attracted by his lectures.

He was Scotland's leading consultant at a time when, as Professor Christison wrote, 'The Gregorian physic was free blood letting, the cold affusion, tartar emetic and the famous mixture which bears his name.' This for long made Gregory a household name in Scotland, and the means of its manufacture merits a place in the chronicles of Morningside. The prescription required large amounts of magnesia powder, along with pulverised rhubarb and ginger. Dr Thomas Steel had provided the magnesia from his works, and the rhubarb required for Gregory's mixture was grown by Sir Alexander Dick of Prestonfield House. President of the Edinburgh Royal College of Physicians, Dick was an enthusiastic advocate of the health-promoting qualities of rhubarb, and perhaps the first to cultivate it in Scotland. The reason why the gardens at Prestonfield House were particularly suitable for the cultivation of rhubarb was that when Sir Alexander Dick's father, previous owner of the estate, was Lord Provost of Edinburgh in 1680, he had transported to Prestonfield, at his own expense, cartloads of plentiful horse dung which was a feature of the streets of old Edinburgh. It is possible that Professor Gregory and Sir Alexander Dick jointly conceived the composition of the famous mixture, which was in universal demand after its inclusion in the Edinburgh Pharmacopoeia in 1839. It was added to the British Pharmacopoeia in 1885 and may still be obtained.

Professor Gregory was a man of wide cultural interests and one of Scotland's leading Latin scholars of his day. He moved in Edinburgh's highest social circles. He was a deep admirer of 'Fair Burnett', the eccentric judge Lord Monboddo's attractive daughter to whom Robert Burns devoted an elegy. Any hopes Gregory may have had of marrying Elizabeth Burnett were, however, sadly dashed when she died of tuberculosis while still in her early twenties, and while staying at Upper or Nether Braid Farm where it was hoped that rest and fresh air might have brought restored health.

While residing at Canaan Lodge, Professor Gregory's eldest son John, an advocate, built up a large collection of birds. The site of his aviary and eagles' cage in the garden is indicated on the Ordnance Survey Map of 1852. Henry Mackenzie, one of Edinburgh's celebrated literary figures in Gregory's day, was a close friend of the Professor and stayed for some time at Canaan Lodge. Later residents have included Macdonnell of Glengarry. The last occupant of the house before its acquisition by Edinburgh Corporation in 1937 was Dr Thomas G. Nasmyth of the then Scottish Board of Health. After its rebuilding in 1907, however, no traces of the original house remained. Professor Gregory's extensive library, incidentally, was presented to Aberdeen University, while his portrait by Sir Henry Raeburn was bequeathed to Fyvie Castle.

On the wall immediately beyond the gateway to Canaan Lodge are two rectangular stones bearing the numbers 5 and 7. The first denotes the diameter in inches of the pipe laid from Comiston springs in 1681, bringing the 'sweet waters', under-

Canaan Lodge in elegant days. *The Royal Commission on the Ancient and Historical Monuments of Scotland.*

ground at this point, to the reservoir at Castlehill. This was Edinburgh's first piped water supply. The 7 refers to the diameter of the pipe from Swanston, laid in 1790 alongside the original five-inch one. Similarly marked stones, indicating the continuation of the pipes' course, are to be seen on the inside of the south boundary wall of nearby Woodville and on the east wall of Whitehouse Loan, opposite the end of Clinton Road. The notes to the Canaan feuing plan of 1803 assert Edinburgh Town Council's 'liberty of digging for helping or renewing pipes for carrying water to the city'. As the housing estates of Comiston and Oxgangs developed in the 1940s the danger of contamination to the various Comiston springs led to their no longer being used, the considerable supply of water being allowed, instead, to flow into the Braid Burn.

During the demolition of Canaan Lodge in 1991 and the

excavation of the site prior to the building Canaan Lodge and Canaan Home for the Blind, the old water pipes were uncovered and discarded. Water from the important filtration and storage plant at Fairmilehead now flows underground here in a most modern pipe but still following the same route as the original 1681 pipes under neighbouring districts, the Meadows and the Grassmarket up to a supply tank in the Castle with an overflow supply led down to Castlehill Reservoir.

Woodburn House is on the right just beyond the entrance to Canaan Lodge. Adapted in 1966 as the Training Centre for the Scottish Hospital Administrative Staff, it is now occupied by another Scottish Health Service department. This well-preserved elegant and secluded villa stands in pleasant grounds first feued by William Mosman to William Bailie, WS, in 1806. The house was built in 1812 at a cost of £300. The earliest owner of interest was George Ross, advocate, who resided here between 1818 and 1860. Ross was of course the great benefactor, and for long the sole supporter, of the Old Schoolhouse. It is probable that many meetings of the old school's Management Committee took place in Woodburn House.

In 1861 the house passed to D. R. McGregor of the Merchant Shipping Company of Leith. From 1895 until 1921 a succession of medical men, including Dr Bremner (also at one time of nearby Streatham House) resided at Woodburn House. For many years a long wooden pavilion, behind the recently rebuilt high Canaan Lane boundary wall, was a sanatorium. In 1922 the house and the former sanatorium became the Edinburgh Royal Infirmary's Nurses' Home. Many Morningside residents will recall the regular nightly departure of the special bus conveying the red-robed nurses to their night-duty at the Royal Infirmary.

It is possible that the original extremely high boundary wall, recently much reduced in height and moved inwards to widen Canaan Lane at this point, was erected at a time when the building of such walls was undertaken solely to provide employment.

Residents in Woodburn House for some years from 1914 was

Sir Frank Mears, a noted architect and a leading town planner of modern times, much of it heralding a new era. Mears was closely associated with the famous Sir Patrick Geddes, the founder of modern town and country planning. He married Sir Patrick's daughter. During the First World War Sir Frank Mears invented a parachute which was named after him. With Sir Patrick Geddes, he was involved in designing Edinburgh's Zoological Gardens at Corstorphine, creating a quite new concept.

Also resident in Woodburn House for some years was Sir Frank Mears's sister, Dr Isabella (Mary) Mears, the Astley Ainslie Hospital's first Resident Medical Officer from 1923. She also assisted in the tuberculosis sanatorium that was for long in the grounds.

Beyond the southern slope of the pleasant lawn of Woodburn House venerable trees form a glade through which, in a still charmingly rural setting, flows the Jordan Burn. On the high tenement, Woodburn Place, in Canaan Lane, is inscribed the builder's date, 1880.

The gateway to the Astley Ainslie Hospital leads us not only into one of the most pleasant and well preserved areas of modern Canaan but also back in time to an era in Morningside's history which stretches over more than four centuries.

By the beginning of the sixteenth century this had already become one of the less forbidding and more pleasantly cultivated parts of the ancient Burgh Muir. Nevertheless, it was still remote from the town. A short distance eastwards across the Burgh Muir stood the primitive keep or tower of the Grange of St Giles. Beyond this and slightly to the north was the small Chapel of St John the Baptist, built in 1512, and in 1517 the Convent of St Catherine of Sienna. Its site is near the present-day Sciennes House Place, and that of the Convent is the junction of St Catherine's Place and Sciennes Road. A light perpetually burning in the tower of the little chapel guided those bold enough to traverse the Burgh Muir after nightfall.

In the grounds of the Astley Ainslie Hospital today are several early nineteenth-century villas. Once privately owned, they were purchased soon after the establishment of the hospital to accommodate patients. They are now used for administration. One of them is named St Roque after the earliest building erected in this part of the Burgh Muir, the ancient chapel of St Roque or St Roch, the exact site of which is now impossible to determine. The first Ordnance Survey Map of this area (1852) indicates that it stood a little to the north-west of the present-day villa, perhaps on the site of or near to the hospital school. Another possible location is just outwith the southern boundary wall of Southbank Villa, until quite recently the residence of the hospital's Medical Superintendent. In this area there are the remains of an early building and an old draw-well. There is also a traditional belief, for long held by successive hospital gardening staff, that the chapel stood in what became the garden of Canaan Park; here again there are the remains of a very old sunken draw-well. The *Inventory of the Ancient and Historical Monuments of the City of Edinburgh*, published by the Royal Commission on the above, stated that the chapel stood within the grounds of Canaan House, now the hospital's administrative centre.

In the author's booklet *Between the Streamlet and the Town* (1989) a history of the Astley Ainslie Hospital and its historic surroundings, a detailed account of St Roque's chapel will be found and its focal point around which for over nearly two centuries countless victims of the plague or Black Death were quarantined in wooden huts after their having been brought out from the then remote city in wooden carts, some to recover but most to die and be buried in the nearby cemetery or in mass graves. The muster of the Scottish army around St Roque's in 1513 before leaving for the fatal field of Flodden is also described and the account vividly presented in Scott's dramatic poetic work *Marmion*: The booklet may be obtained from the hospital's administrative office; as also a fascinating tape recorded guide to the hospital's historic surroundings for use in a 'walk about', produced by radiographer Gilbert McDonald, and borrowable by individuals or groups.

Since the chapel's disappearance many stones of ecclesiastical origin have been found in the grounds of the Astley Ainslie Hospital and in private gardens in the neighbourhood. A collection of these, some bearing initials and dates, was built into a specially constructed stone panel by Colonel John Fraser, when Medical Superintendent of the Astley Ainslie Hospital, in the southern boundary wall of his residence, South Bank. Also to be seen in the hospital grounds are a draw-well and a font or trough at the foot of the lawn of Morelands, a very old sunken well in what was the garden of Canaan Park, and, just beyond the southern boundary wall of South Bank, the remains of another old draw-well and those of an early building of some kind. To the west of the lean-to greenhouse in what was formerly the garden of Millbank villa, were, embedded in the ground, a row of four large cylindrical stones. Each bears sculpted emblems of the Passion of Christ: the crown of thorns, the nails and a hammer, and an open hand bearing the print of the nails. These are now arranged outside Canaan House, the hospital's administrative centre.

Long before the Astley Ainslie Hospital's first small unit was opened in Canaan Park House in 1923, the ancient medical traditions of this district of Canaan were fittingly continued by the advent of James Syme, who moved into the villa Millbank in 1842. He became Professor of Clinical Surgery in Edinburgh's already world renowned Medical School and became notable throughout Europe as the 'Napoleon of Surgery'.

Early in his career as a medical student, young James Syme distinguished himself as a chemist by making a discovery which, had he patented it and pursued it commercially, might have brought him great wealth and altered the course of his career. At the age of eighteen he had founded a chemical society with some young friends. In the course of his own researches he produced a pure form of naphtha which was capable of dissolving rubber more effectively than any substance then known. He used his discovery to demonstrate that silk cloth could be waterproofed. Syme relinquished the opportunity of exploiting his process commercially, commenting that he was then 'about to commence the study of a profession with which considerations of trade did not seem consistent'. In 1823 Charles Macintosh of Glasgow was credited with the discovery which was rightly Syme's and he not only made a fortune by it but, of course, had his name immortalised as an eponym for a raincoat. Many of Syme's chemistry experiments were carried out in the early University teaching laboratories of John Deuchar at 27 Lothian Street, now the site of the lecture hall of the Royal Scottish Museum. Deuchar was a member of the notable family who for long resided in Morningside House.

Syme was to become involved in an unfortunate controversy and a bitter personal vendetta with his illustrious contemporary Simpson. This aspect of his career and much else of biographical interest is described in *Simpson and Syme of Edinburgh* by John A. Shepherd.

If Syme's relationship with Simpson, pioneer of one of the two revolutionary developments in surgery, anaesthesia, was regretttable, his association with the future Lord Lister, the pioneer of the other great breakthrough, antiseptic surgery, gave Lister both support and inspiration. Having become Professor of Clinical Surgery in the Edinburgh Medical School, Syme invited young Joseph Lister to join his staff for a month. So valuable was their collaboration and so encouraging and beneficial was Syme's influence on his young assistant that Lister remained with his 'Chief' for eight years.

While working with Syme at the Infirmary (which had been established beside the old Edinburgh High School in what is now Infirmary Street in 1832) Lister was a frequent and welcome visitor to Millbank. There he met and fell in love with Syme's daughter, Agnes. They were married in the drawing-room of the villa on 24 April 1856. Lister was later converted from his Quaker beliefs to the Episcopalianism of his wife and father-in-law. A plaque in the present-day Millbank Hospital pavilion commemorates the marriage in the villa on the site of which this ward now stands.

Syme had purchased Millbank, with its extensive and pleasant gardens, meadows and greenhouses, in 1842. It was an ideal retreat from the pressures and harrassing duties of hospital life.

Professor James Syme, in his day 'The Napoleon of Surgery' who resided at 'Millbank', a villa in Canaan Lane where the Astley Ainslie Hospital is today.

His chief joy and relaxation was his garden and the greenhouses in which he cultivated rare plants, fruit trees and shrubs, including, as Dr John Brown records, 'matchless orchids, heaths and azaleas, bananas and grapes and peaches'. Part of the original greenhouse and much of Syme's garden still remain, kept in excellent condition by today's hospital staff.

Millbank was, however, never simply the retreat of a recluse. Here Syme, with the ready help of his second wife, Jemina Burn, entertained many guests. Among the most notable of these was Thomas Carlyle who, during his visit to Edinburgh in 1866 to deliver his University Rectorial address, consulted Syme professionally and underwent a minor operation. After convalescing for two weeks at Millbank, Carlyle was Syme's principal guest at a dinner party which included many distinguished guests, honoured, no doubt, to meet the Sage of Chelsea. After dinner Syme and Carlyle sat on the verandah talking and watching the sunset reflected on Blackford Hill.

Charles Dickens, in Edinburgh in 1869 to give one of his celebrated readings in the Music Hall in George Street, consulted Syme about his lameness.

Perhaps the most scintillating social occasion at Millbank took place during the meeting of the British Association in Edinburgh in 1850, when 'one hundred noblemen and gentlemen including many distinguished foreign scientists were entertained to a sumptuous dinner at Millbank.'

Largely through the encouragement and influence of his father-in-law, Joseph Lister was appointed to the Chair of Surgery at Glasgow University in 1860 and there pioneered and established his techniques in antiseptic surgery. In 1869 he succeeded Syme as Professor of Clinical Surgery at the Edinburgh University Medical School. Eventually he returned to London. Syme was one of the great protagonists for a new Royal Infirmary, at last built at Lauriston Place in 1879. He spent the evening of his life at his beloved Millbank, where he died on 26 June 1870. He was interred in St John's churchyard at the west end of Princes Street.

Millbank witnessed not only the marriage of Joseph Lister to Agnes Syme in 1856 but, 36 years earlier, it had been the scene of another marriage which was something of a sensation at the time. On 28 September 1820, Miss Anne Neilson, fourth daughter of James Neilson of Millbank, married Alexander

Wedding photograph of Joseph Lister and Agnes Syme after their marriage in Millbank villa, 23 April 1856. *By courtesy of Mrs Dowrick, New Zealand, great-great niece of Joseph Lister and the Wellcome Institute for the History of Medicine.*

Ivanovitch, Sultan Katte Gherry Krim. Sultan of the Crimea, Ivanovitch had been converted to Christianity by Scottish missionaries at Carass in the Caucasus. At the expense of Alexander, Czar of Russia, he was sent to Edinburgh to receive further Christian education in the hope that he would return to his country as a missionary. After their wedding, he and Anne settled in Morningside, where the Sultan's wife came to be known in the village as the 'Sultana'. Little is known of her husband's subsequent missionary activities.

The Astley Ainslie Hospital owes its establishment to David Ainslie of Costerton, a village near Crichton Castle in Midlothian. A successful sheep breeder, whose many trophies are preserved in the hospital board-room, Ainslie, a bachelor, willed his considerable estate to a nephew who, however, predeceased his uncle, who then established a trust charged with 'the holding, applying and disposing of his estate for the purpose of erecting and maintaining a hospital or institution to be known as the Astley Ainslie Institution for the relief and behoof of convalescents in the Royal Infirmary of Edinburgh'.

Certain new information has thrown a new light on the David Ainslie Bequest. Certainly Ainslie from his successful sheep farming had gained considerable wealth, and through a fondness for his nephew, John Astley Ainslie, he had decided to bequeath most of his estate to him. The nephew had studied at Harrow and Oxford and had himself inherited substantial wealth. However, he died at Algiers in 1874 aged 26, thus predeceasing his uncle by many years, and leaving him a very large bequest. Was it the circumstances of his nephew's very early death that prompted David Ainslie to bequeath his own estate for the foundation of an, initially, convalescence hospital, specifying that it be named after his nephew?

David Ainslie was a close friend of Gourlay Steell, brother of the famous sculptor whose Edinburgh work included the Wellington Monument at the east end of Princes Street and the figure of Sir Walter Scott and his dog at the base of his great monument. Gourlay Steell himself was a distinguished artist and animal painter to Queen Victoria. The only portrait of John Astley Ainslie that could be traced was one of him as a boy on horseback, the subject of a very large painting by Gourlay Steell fixed to the wall of a room in Canaan House, the Astley Ainslie Hospital's administrative centre.

David Ainslie died on 24 May 1900, but many years elapsed

David Ainslie of Costerton. *Courtesy of Mr. R. Copeland, formerly of the Astley Ainslie Hospital.*

before the accumulated monies of his estate were used. In 1921 a Board of Governors for the projected new institution was established. It was, they specified, 'to deal with patients suffering from curable conditions who have definitely passed the crisis of their illness and who with proper care, sufficiently prolonged, may reasonably be expected to regain normal health and fitness for their usual avocations. The functions of the hospital include the scientific investigation of the process involved in the gradual restoration of health which constitutes rehabilitation.' Such has continued to be the policy of successive hospital boards. Until 1948 and the establishment of the National Health Service, all patients were from the Edinburgh Royal Infirmary. Since that date, however, many have been admitted from different hospitals under the aegis of what was the South East Scotland Regional Hospital Board and, since 1974, has been the Lothian Health Board.

The original site acquired by David Ainslie's trustees included a nine-hole ladies' golf course. One of the holes lay just south of the Jordan Burn which still flows through the hospital grounds.

From its original function as a convalescent hospital, the Astley Ainslie, originally under the inspiration of its first Medical Superintendent, Colonel John Cunningham, became increasingly concerned with and highly skilled in the positive process of rehabilitation by which it has 'worked wonders' for innumerable patients who, often after very serious injuries and other conditions lacked the confidence to believe that they could resume their normal lives. The Day Centre, also named the Cunningham Unit, specialises in the provision of physiotherapy for large numbers of outpatients, especially those with cardiac conditions.

One of the hospital's most notable features is its Occupational Therapy Unit. When first established in 1930 it was staffed by Canadians. The subsequently established training school, the first of its kind in Scotland, has attracted trainee therapists from all over the world. Thus, with the most modern scientific techniques, the hospital proudly maintains the ancient traditions of healing first associated with its district over four centuries ago.

Returning from the pleasant Astley Ainslie Hospital grounds to Canaan Lane and proceeding northwards towards its junction with Newbattle Terrace and Grange Loan, we pass a number of interesting villas. On the north garden wall of one called Bloomfield is a sculptured artist's palette bearing the date 1881, possibly the work of Robert McGregor, RSA, who resided here at that date. In the garden of Norwood now vacated and its future unknown, just within its northern boundary wall at Grange Loan, are the remains of Bloomsberry Cottage, and on the Grange Loan side of this wall may still be seen its long-bricked-up windows. In Bloomsberry Cottage, it will be remembered, lived Gorge Meikle Kemp, architect of the Scott Monument. From the cottage Kemp, in May 1838, wrote to his brother Thomas: 'I am quite satisfied with the change I have made from Stockbridge to the land of Canaan. We have more accommodation for the same rent, a very pleasant little garden enclosed with a high wall, well stocked with flowers and fruit trees, and very few taxes.' This charming rural atmosphere still surrounds the villas beside which Bloomsberry Cottage once stood. For a period prior to its demolition, the cottage was a laundry. Immediately to the east stood, at one time, Canaan Villa, also long since demolished.

In 1821 the remoteness from Edinburgh of Canaan is referred to in an article in *Blackwood's Magazine*, the writer remarking that 'the calls of the fishwives have even reached the lands of Canaan'. Canaan itself he describes as, 'the grounds to the south of the city where a number of snug boxes attest to the taste of the inhabitants for country retirement and the pleasures of rustication'. 'Box' was a term used for 'a small country house or shooting-box'. Of the 'snug boxes', none would then have merited the description more than Woodville, the entrance drive of which is opposite the gates of Norwood. The feu contract for the building of Woodville is dated 1803 and the villa was built soon afterwards.

Of the owners of Woodville, most interesting was James Wilson, FRSE, who came to reside here shortly after his marriage in 1824. A distinguished naturalist and 'a less rollicking blade' than his brother 'Christopher North', the famous literary figure, Wilson wrote at Woodville the whole section on Natural History in the 7th Edition of the *Encyclopaedia Britannica*. It may have been his awareness of failing health which led him to decline the Chair in Natural History at Edinburgh University in 1854. He died two years later.

Something of the atmosphere of Canaan in the early nineteenth century is conveyed by Wilson's biographer, the Rev. James Hamilton, who wrote: 'It would be difficult to find a more charming retreat than, in Mr Wilson's possession, Woodville became. In his domain of two acres, snugly ensconced amidst the groves of Morningside, he caught the whole sunshine of the winter noon, forgetful of biting blasts and easterly fogs.' It has been suggested that this reference to 'the whole sunshine of the winter noon' is a clue to the origin and meaning of the name Morningside. Another, already mentioned, is that the original entrance to East Morningside House faced east — to the 'morning side' of the sun. In recent years the house's original entrance door has been restored.

Apart from his prolific writings on natural history, which included *Illustrations of Zoology* (1826) and the 'Notes of a Naturalist' in Porter's *Illustrations of Scripture*, depicting animals referred to in the Bible, Wilson's other literary works included *A Voyage Round the Coasts of Scotland and the Isles*, illustrated by his versatile neighbour and fellow-voyager, Sir Thomas Dick Lauder of Grange House.

On a window-pane of what was the villa's dining-room, now the study and library, are scratched the initials of James Wilson and his wife, 'J. W. – I. W. 1826'. Mrs Wilson's name before marriage was Isabella Keith. After Wilson's death, soon followed by that of his wife, his niece, Henrietta Wilson, came to reside at Woodville. The house and its attractive garden are described in her book *Chronicles of a Garden: Its Pets and Pleasures*.

Amongst the many distinguished people who called upon James Wilson at Woodville was John James Audubon, famous painter of birds, who came to Edinburgh in 1826 hoping to attract interest to his work. He took rooms in George Street and there had many paintings on show. At first he failed to gain much attention from the prominent Edinburgh people whom he sought to impress. Indeed, he was greatly depressed until he was visited by the noted Edinburgh engraver, W. H. Lizars, who became most enthusiastic and drew the attention of the city's influential people. Then Audubon was invited by many people

John Astley Ainslie, nephew of David Ainslie, whose bequest led to the establishment of the Astley Ainslie Hospital. This is the only traceable portrait and is from a very large wall-sized wall painting by the famous Scottish animal painter, Gourlay Steell, who was a close friend of David Ainslie. The picture is in the Administrative Unit of the Hospital. *Photograph by T. Scott Roxburgh.*

to dinner and to exhibit his work. In his Journal for Friday 3 November 1826, he wrote: 'My birds were visited by many persons this day, among whom were some ladies of fine features and good taste, artists of both ability and taste, and with the numerous gentlemen came Professor James Wilson, a naturalist of pretension, an agreeable man who invited me to dine at his cottage next week.' The Edinburgh portrait painter, John Syme, was commissioned to produce a portrait of Audubon at the request of Lizars and for him to engrave and have distributed in Europe. Syme's portrait hangs in the White House in Washington DC, and there is also a copy in an honoured place in Woodville today. Thomas Campbell, a poet of some achievement, was also a guest at Woodville for some time, at Wilson's invitation.

A later owner of Woodville was Sir James Alexander Russell, MD, Lord Provost of Edinburgh 1891-4. Dr Russell, during his period in office, did much to advance public health, clearing many of Edinburgh's worst slums. In the early 1940s, Thomas Usher, a well-known Edinburgh brewer, added the east wing to the house.

Leaving Canaan Lane and turning westwards along Newbattle Terrace, we notice, on the right-hand side, a wooden door which was once a rear entrance to the grounds of the villa named Woodcroft, now the site of a British Telecom administrative centre. Here begins a fine avenue of beech trees, originally the entrance drive to East Morningside House in Clinton Road. On the left, immediately beyond Woodville, stands another typical red sandstone Canaan villa, of the early nineteenth century, Canaan Grove, now the pavilion for the pleasantly situated municipal tennis courts and bowling greens, previously the recreation grounds for the employees of Martin, the one-time well-known Edinburgh bakers. In the garden of this house are a number of carved ecclesiastical stones similar to those in the Astley Ainslie Hospital grounds.

In the early 1900s Canaan Grove was the family home of William 'Shakespeare' Morrison who became one of the renowned Speakers of the House of Commons. 'Shakes', as he was familiarly known, attended George Watson's College and

James Wilson, a renowned naturalist, who resided in 'Woodville' Canaan Lane.
From the 'Memoirs of the Life of James Wilson, Esq., of Woodville' *by James
Hamilton.*

Edinburgh University where he was much involved in the students' societies, especially in debating. He saw distinguished service in the First World War. Member of Parliament for Cirencester and Tewkesbury for 30 years he held several important Conservative government posts before his appointment as 'Mr Speaker'. He had the task of controlling very lively debates involving such great orators and parliamentarians as Winston Churchill and Aneurin Bevan — rather different from the debating chamber of the Edinburgh Students' Union. The noisy scenes in Parliament during the 1956 Suez crisis presented a challenge to his skill. In 1959, William Morrison was created Viscount Dunrossil. He was finally appointed Governor-General of Australia. He took this responsibility with great dedication but died in Canberra after a year's service in 1961.

Immediately beyond Canaan Grove we come to yet another of Morningside's Biblical names — Eden. Eden Lane leads into one of the quaintest little communities in the district. While the location of Eden appears on the Ordnance Survey Map of 1852, it is not shown in Kirkwood's map of 1817, as the first house was not built here until about 1822. This was Harmony House, named as such by 1852 and still standing today.

In 1816 a small area of land in what came to be called the district of Eden had been disponed to Robert Haxton, whose surname also appears as Halkerston. Whether the house he built in Eden was named Harmony House by him or by a subsequent owner is not known. There are two possible explanations of the name. An owner following Haxton might have been a devotee of Charles Dickens and might have found the name in one of his novels. Alternatively, there is some traditional support for a second theory. Robert Haxton was the Chief Armourer at Edinburgh Castle and it is possible therefore that local people came to call Haxton's house 'the armourer's house', eventually corrupted to Harmony House. The traditional occupations of armourer or gunsmith continued in Haxton's family though they did not long reside in Harmony House. A little to the north of Harmony House, the 1852 Ordnance Survey Map shows Ellen Cottage and Jane Cottage, built by

Robert Haxton for his daughters. Both remain but have been renamed.

Also indicated in the informative 1852 Ordnance Survey Map is Eden Hermitage, a small cell-like building which may still be seen opposite the side entrance to Harmony House. Some part of the little building may have very early origins as the retreat of a hermit, though the cast-iron Celtic cross formerly surmounting it and the apparently antique hinges once on the doorway of the 'cell' were found by an expert to have been relatively modern. In the 1830s a curio dealer lived in Harmony House and it is probable that he was responsible for the Celtic cross and the hinges which perpetuated the belief that a hermit had once lived there. On the lintel above the side entrance to Harmony House are carved the initials 'A.S.L.', which cannot be identified with any previous owner. On the old wall on the left-hand side of Eden Lane are several bricked-up doorways and windows believed to be the remains of cottages once part of the adjacent Canaan Farm. Beyond Eden Lane, in Newbattle Terrace, are a number of pleasant nineteenth-century villas which also formed part of the old Eden community.

Falcon Gardens to the left commemorates one of the largest estates within the lands of Canaan, the Falcon estate, which eventually extended to eighteen acres, from Newbattle Terrace to Canaan Lane in the south, where most of the old boundary wall still remains, and from Morningside Road eastwards to, approximately, the line of the present-day Falcon Gardens. Within its pleasant, tree-shaded confines there came to be created in 1815, by Alexander Falconar, the majestic and ornate mansion, Falcon Hall, from which the streets of today take their names. This part of Morningside is important enough and of such special interest as to merit a separate section.

CHAPTER 5

The Falcon Estate

The site of the house was the junction of Falcon Court and Falcon Road West. The main entrance drive from Morningside Road was half-way between Steel's Place and Falcon Road West, where two short rows of tenements, notably different in design and date, meet above the shops at 193 and 195 Morningside Road. Several writers have stated that the main gateway of the drive leading off Morningside Road to Falcon Hall was at what is now the entrance to Falcon Road West, opposite Morningside Public Library. That this was not so has, however, been revealed by a valuable old photograph kindly provided by a Morningside resident. In fact, the tall stone pillars of the gate, each surmounted by a stone falcon, stood immediately north of what is now 195 Morningside Road. At the time of the photograph, about 1900, only the tenements on the east side of Morningside Road, extending from Steel's Place to No. 195, had been built. Those from No. 193 to Falcon Road West were built after the Falcon Hall gates had been demolished, probably around 1909. The architectural difference between the two blocks of tenements is obvious, especially when studied from the rear. A porter's lodge used to stand just within the gates. Another driveway led from what is now Falcon Avenue, near Falcon Road.

There has been confusion over the origins of Falcon Hall. Mair claims that it was built by Lord Provost William Coulter in 1780, the façade and other embellishments being added by Alexander Falconar in 1815. Grant wrote, in 1880: 'Falcon Hall, eastward of the old village, is an elegant modern villa erected early in the present century by a wealthy Indian civilian named Falconar, but save old Morningside House or Lodge, before that time no other mansion of importance stood there.' Grant, the *Scots Magazine* and the *Edinburgh Evening Courant* also state

Falcon Hall, built for Alexander Falconar in about 1830 by Thomas Hamilton, around the already existing Morningside Lodge, the former residence of Lord Provost William Coulter. Note the 7-feet high statues of Wellington and Nelson at each side of the pillared portico.

that Coulter died at Morningside Lodge on 14 April 1810, but the feu which Coulter held in Morningside was not in the Morningside (originally Wester Morningside) estate on the west side of Morningside, but in Canaan. Furthermore, the sasine records for Edinburgh for the period 1781–1815 reveal that Coulter seised, in 1803, three acres and, in 1806, a further three acres of the lands of Canaan. On 2 February 1814, four years after William Coulter's death, Margaret Thomson, Coulter's widow, purchased a further three-and-a-quarter acres. Fifteen days later, on 17 February 1814, Mrs Coulter disponed to Alexander Falconar her part of the Canaan Estate, approximately nine acres. It may therefore be concluded that the house which Coulter built in his original three acres of Canaan in 1780 was Morningside Lodge and that it was this house which Alexander Falconar purchased with almost nine acres of land in February

1814 and then proceeded to redesign and embellish, naming it, as a play on his surname, Falcon Hall.

William Coulter, head of a large hosiery business in the High Street, became, after many years' service as a Town Councillor, Lord Provost in 1808, but died after only two years in office. He pressed for the foundation of a fever hospital in the City, which was not opened until 1903. He also laid the foundation stone of Edinburgh's 'first proper asylum for the insane', the original East House, completed, on a site between Maxwell Street and Millar Crescent, in 1813. He was a captain in the Edinburgh Volunteers and as such earned a biographical note and sketch in Kay's *Portraits*. Great pride in his 'military' rank led him in an after-dinner speech, when well fortified with port, to remark: 'It is true I have the body of a stocking weaver but I have the soul of a *skyppyo afreekanus*.' His audience were puzzled over his claim until one of the more learned guests suggested that Coulter was comparing himself with the renowned Roman general, Scipio Africanus. In another unhappy speech he expanded upon the progress of history by proclaiming: 'Gentlemen, we live in a great area.' He was honoured by a public funeral from Morningside Lodge, conducted, according to one critic, 'with a parade and show that was gratefully overdone'. The Edinburgh Volunteers preceded the *cortège*; the city bells were tolled and black streamers draped Nelson's Column on Calton Hill. The Coulter monument in Greyfriars churchyard is an altar-tomb supported by six ornamental pillars.

The Falconar family has been the subject of some considerable research. Joe Rock of the Edinburgh University Department of Fine Art, an authority on Thomas Hamilton, the architect who built Falcon Hall for Falconar, has made a special study of the early nineteenth-century Morningside villa and as a result a more complete description of the house and its owner can be presented than previously.

Alexander Falconar (alternatively Falconer) was the eldest son of William Falconer, one-time adjutant of Fort St George, Madras, was born in Nairn. He too had a successful career in Madras, in 1809 becoming Chief Secretary to the Governor. In

1811, having acquired considerable wealth, Falconar retired at the age of 44 and soon afterwards returned to Scotland, settling in Morningside. In 1792, in India, Falconar had married his cousin, Elizabeth Davidson, whose father, a solicitor in the East India Company had come from Cromarty. They had 14 children 12 daughters and two sons, five of the children dying in early childhood. While no portrait of Alexander Falconar could be traced, there is one of his wife, at the age of 16, in the Dulwich Art Gallery.

Provost Coulter's house, Morningside Lodge, which Falconar purchased in 1814, was in itself impressive and in the photograph of Falcon Hall shown on page 136 the bow end at the right side and the rectangular end at the left indicate something of the original house. Thomas Hamilton, whose best known work in Edinburgh is perhaps the former Royal High School below the Calton Hill (note the pillared portico), the Royal College of Physicians premises in Queen Street, and the Dean Orphanage, was commissioned by Falconar to build a façade based on the work of John Nash at Buckingham House in the Mall in London. Hamilton was influenced by Nash in some of his other work and it has been suggested that the portico which he built at Falcon Hall had much in common with Nash's design for Buckingham Palace, which it predated.

Falconar had the impressive pillared portico of his house and other parts decorated with numerous carved stone falcons. Was this simply a play on his name from vanity or does the idea behind it take us from this Morningside house to Rome and the Palazzo Falconieri in the Via Julia where it might have originated? It is believed that Alexander Falconar, while perhaps making the Grand European Tour, which so many of his status did, and which would include Rome, and as suggested by other evidence, being one of the many British people who had sympathies with Napoleon, perhaps led him to visit the Roman villa in the Via Julia, where the French emperor's mother resided, as also Cardinal Fesch his uncle, a great connoisseur of the arts.

The great palazzo of the Falconieri family was not only named

The Palzzo Falconieri in Rome's Via Giulia which Alexander Falconar is believed to have visited. The palace's name, after its owners, the Italian version of his own, and the stone sculpted falcons on its frontage may have influenced Alexander Falconar in the naming and decorating of his Morningside villa. From *Via Giulia, una utopia urbanistica del 500*, Salerno, L., Spezzaferro, L., and Tafuri, M.

after its owners but was also decorated with a number of falcons sculpted on to human torsos.

Was it therefore a visit to Rome and the rather famous villa that inspired Alexander Falconar to name and decorate his Morningside house in similar manner? When it was completed, in about 1830, Falcon Hall had a palatial-like frontage of 12 great pillars of Craigleith stone, flanked by 7-feet tall statues of Wellington and Nelson, the work of the notable sculptor, Robert Forrest. Interiorly, on the upper floor, Thomas Hamilton had designed a magnificent drawing-room of oval shape to suggest the sweep of the Bay of Naples. This room was reached by a great bronze-railed staircase. The room had a domed ceiling, pale blue with gold stars, while the walls were decorated with water-colours of Athens, Venice and Rome, suggested by some writers as being the work of the early nineteenth-century Scottish artist Hugh 'Grecian' Williams.

Whatever the source of inspiration for its design and decoration the Falconar's luxurious family residence was known to the Morningside villagers as 'the big house' and regarded with some awe. The owners had the image of the 'lords of the manor' but theirs was a benevolent feudalism. Alexander Falconar was a generous benefactor of Morningside Parish Church and five of his daughters had headed the list of subscribers towards its establishment in 1838. The village schoolhouse also benefited greatly from his financial support and interest, and two of his daughters made regular donations and presided over the annual prizegiving ceremony. The little school's winter soirées and summer outings also received their generous support. A colourful spectacle in old Morningside village high street was the yellow horse-drawn carriage with two footmen which conveyed five Falconar daughters into town.

Alexander Falconar kept a strict vigil over the affections of his daughters, but one man was to break through the barrier: Henry Craigie, who married Jessie Pigou Falconar. The marriage of Craigie into the Falconar family and his eventual inheritance of Falcon Hall has an interesting and rather dramatic origin. An auction sale of pictures took place in premises at No. 16 Picardy Place on Thursday, 14 March 1833. The saleroom was crowded. Some doubt had been felt as regards the floor's ability to support such a large attendance. The sale proceeded. While a small picture was being displayed and bids invited suddenly there was a grinding tearing sound. The auctioneer's rostrum collapsed and many people near to it were suddenly pitched through a large chasm in the floor. Panic reigned. Though the cavity was very large the carpet which sagged through it saved a complete disaster. Alexander Falconar was amongst those who were heard to groan. He was heard to say: 'Oh lift me gently for I am much hurt'. Many of those notable in the Edinburgh art world were also trapped. About 80 people were injured and two died.

Reputedly Mr Falconar's injuries might have been much worse had it not been for the quick thinking of a young man nearby who drew him back from the broken floor. This was Henry Craigie, a solicitor from Quebec. In gratitude, Falconar invited him to Falcon Hall. There he became friendly with one of the daughters, Jessie Pigou, and married. Unfortunately no biographical details of Craigie could be traced.

After Falconar's death in 1847 Henry Craigie succeeded to Falcon Hall and continued to reside there with his family and four of the Falconar daughters till his own death in 1867. Craigie was also a generous benefactor of the schoolhouse and Parish Church. A memorial stained-glass window in three parts was installed in the latter by his widow. The poor of Morningside also benefited from his kindness. The surviving Falconar daughters continued to live in Falcon Hall, the last dying in 1887, at the age of ninety. It was she who met the cost, some £3,400, of building the chancel and spire of Christ's Episcopal Church at Holy Corner, in memory of her father. She also provided several small stained-glass lights for the five lower windows in the processional aisle behind the altar. The Falconar family tomb, in which are buried also three of Henry Craigie's children, is in the western section of Greyfriars churchyard, not many yards from the grave of William Coulter, first owner of what became Falcon Hall. The Craigie family tomb is in Newington Cemetery, where it was originally marked by a very large stone. This collapsed some years ago.

In 1889 Falcon Hall became a high-class boarding school for boys, the original objective of which was to prepare Edinburgh boys for entry into the Indian Civil Service, Sandhurst and Woolwich — training hitherto available only in England and

John Bartholomew's cartographers' premises in Duncan Street, to which Falcon Hall's pillared frontage was transferred in 1909 by John Bartholomew who was the last to reside in Falcon Hall. *John Batholomew & Son.*

Ireland. The school had first been established as Morningside College in 1883, in the impressive five-storey hydropathic near the junction of Morningside Drive and Morningside Grove. When this building was taken over temporarily by the Royal Hospital for Sick Children, the college moved to Rockville, the renowned baroque villa built by James Gowans in Napier Road in 1858. This eventually became too small and the college moved in 1889 to Falcon Hall, becoming Falcon Hall College. The director was Dr Fearon Ranking and the masters were all ex-Oxford or Cambridge dons. The setting and facilities of the college were unique and especially suitable for outdoor activities and physical training, an important part of the educational programme.

The last owner of Falcon Hall was John George Bartholomew, of the world-renowned Edinburgh cartographic firm. When the mansion-house was demolished in 1909, the regret of many Morningside residents at its disappearance was lessened when the pillared façade was rebuilt to form the main entrance to Bartholomew's premises in Duncan Street where the former Falcon Hall grand staircase was also installed. Neither were the many stone falcons which had dominated the mansion-house and its grounds to be lost: several of these were built on to the frontage of the house at Corstorphine which belonged to Cameron McMillan of Andrew Melrose & Company, the tea merchants. This house, eventually purchased by the Royal Scottish Zoological Society, still displaye its now appropriate falcons. Perhaps with the transference of Falcon Hall's pillared frontage and staircase to Bartholomew's at Duncan Street and some of the stone falcons to the Zoo at Corstorphine, that might have seemed the end of the saga of the great mansion house and its owners. At least certain relics remained.

In recent years, however, further information has come to light. Many people have wondered, after the demolition, what had happened to the 7-feet high statues of Wellington and Nelson that adorned the frontage. It would appear that in 1905, four years before the demolition, they were sold to the owners of Lennel House at Coldstream, where they adorned its Italian garden. The statues were the work of a very notable Scottish sculptor, Robert Forrest, of Lanark. Amongst his better known work, perhaps, is the statue of Sir William Wallace, the great Scottish patriot in Lanark, and the prominent figure of John Knox in Glasgow's Necropolis. Forrest exhibited much of his work in Edinburgh.

The transfer of the statues from Falcon Hall to Lennel House does not seem to have been generally known. In 1987, despite attempts by the Borders local planning officials to serve a listed building enforcement order on the Lennel owners and prevent the statues being sold and removed, Forrest's Lord Nelson and his one-time Falcon Hall companion, the Duke of Wellington, were purchased by a London antique dealer. An appeal by the Borders authorities to a Court of Inquiry failed and the heroic figures and other ornaments remained in London. The Falcon

In 1909 Morningside's 'big house' of the early nineteenth century became a household name. *John Bartholomew and Son.*

Hall exiles are still for sale and perhaps a Morningside resident with a suitable site might bring them back to Morningside.

The Falcon Estate was sold by auction to the Edinburgh Merchant Company in 1889 for £33,000 — £8,000 above the upset price. Among those bidding at Dowell's for the extensive properties was one gentleman who had plans to lay out the estate as a racecourse. Had he been successful the future development of Morningside would have taken a different direction. The playing fields of George Watson's Ladies College for long remained on the Falcon estate. This of course was a Merchant Company School, and the Company owned the land.

St Peter's Roman Catholic Church in Falcon Avenue, built on the Falcon estate in 1907, is notable not only for its architecture. Its first parish priest, Canon John Gray, himself prominent in the world of letters, in association with his close friend André Raffalovitch, who largely financed the building of the church, brought to Morningside many of the country's most distinguished literary figures.

John Gray, the eldest of nine children, was born at Woolwich in 1866, where his father was a carpenter in the dockyard. A scholarship from the local Wesleyan day school took him to Roan Grammar School in Greenwich, which he left at the age of thirteen to become a metal worker in order to supplement the family's meagre income. At evening classes, however, he became proficient in French and Latin, and later entered the Civil Service. After matriculating at London University he became a librarian in the Foreign Office.

For some time young John Gray had cut a dashing figure as a man of fashion, a regular attender at London theatrical first nights, becoming well known in literary and theatrical circles, where he met Oscar Wilde.

Then residing in Park Lane, Gray's articles and poetry began to attract attention. He had come a long way from his humble origins in Woolwich, but the direction of his life was soon to change. In 1888 he had first met young Marc André Raffalovitch in a house in the Temple. Raffalovitch's family, Russian Jews, had fled to Paris in the wake of an anti-Jewish edict in 1863. André's father became a successful international banker and his mother, a lady of great beauty and high intelligence, one of

St Peter's Roman Catholic Church in Falcon Avenue opened in 1907. Sir Robert Lorimer, who designed the Shrine in the Castle, was the architect. Here Canon John Gray was parish priest from 1907 till 1934. *Courtesy of the late Father Walter Glancy.*

Paris's leading hostesses, entertaining distinguished writers, artists, financiers, diplomats and politicians, whose interest she skilfully enlisted in aid of the poor of Paris. When André Raffalovitch came to London, soon enjoying a literary reputation, he and Gray were drawn to each other immediately, and became close and life-long friends.

By 1895 Gray's writing, especially his poetry, became increasingly religious in theme and spirit and, in the autumn of 1898, he resigned from his post in the Foreign Office and entered the Scots College in Rome to study for the Catholic priesthood, having earlier become a convert. On 21 December 1901, he was ordained in Rome, to work in the Archdiocese of St Andrews and Edinburgh. He was appointed curate at St Patrick's Church in the Cowgate, a vicinity then noted for its lodging-houses and slum tenements. In an area in which policemen patrolled in pairs and outbreaks of violence were frequent, young Father Gray, the former social and intellectual dandy, soon impressed people by his willingness to tackle any

Canon John Gray in 1910. *Drawing by Austin Osman Spare. In a private collection.*

situation, to do anything for anyone in the face of the greatest difficulties.

André Raffalovitch regularly came to Edinburgh to meet Father Gray and, finding the climate agreeable to his indifferent health, in 1905 he purchased the large villa at 9 Whitehouse Terrace where he and his housekeeper, Miss Florence Gribbel, took up residence. The same year an important conversation took place in the Scots College vineyard in Marino near Rome between Archbishop James Smith of Edinburgh, Father John

Gray, and others, as a result of which Gray's proposal for the building of St Peter's in Falcon Avenue received support. In May 1905 Sir Robert Lorimer, the leading Scottish architect of the time, especially noted for his creation of the Shrine of the National War Memorial at Edinburgh Castle, was commissioned. In consultation with Father John Gray, the design for the new church was conceived. A site was purchased from the Edinburgh Merchant Company and the foundation stone was blessed by Archbishop James Smith on 17 April 1906; the church was opened a year later, André Raffalovitch, then living at nearby Whitehouse Terrace, bore the major cost of the building. Father Gray was appointed the first parish priest.

Now that his friend was established in nearby St Peter's, Raffalovitch initiated the regular Sunday luncheons and Tuesday dinner parties which were to make his house in Whitehouse Terrace a mecca for men of art, music and literature. With Florence Gribbell's genius for hospitality, Raffalovitch and Father (later Canon) Gray stimulated remarkable dinner conversations. Their guests, it is said, included Henry James, Max Beerbohm, Robert Hugh Benson, Professor Sayce, Lady Margaret Sackville, Eric Gill, Father Bede Jarrett, OP, Gordon Bottomley and, in later days, Compton Mackenzie, Herbert Grierson and Moray McLaren. The celebrated talker Oscar Wilde was, alas, no longer alive.

On 14 February 1934 the long friendship between Raffalovitch and Gray ended: the generous benefactor of St Peter's was found dead when his daily taxi called to take him to Holy Communion. Four months later Canon Gray died. In his latter years he had devoted some time to writing religious articles, poetry for meditation and hymns, while remaining an active mountaineer and an enthusiastic member of the Royal Scottish Zoological Society. Thus ended a great partnership, uniting diverse origins and adding a fascinating chapter to the chronicles of Morningside.

When, in recent times, the interior of St Peter's, a church of unique architectural interest, was radically transformed, reputedly to conform with the spirit of Vatican Council II, there was much adverse criticism. Many of the features which were the subject

André Raffalovich in 1886. *From a painting by A. Dampier May. In a private collection.*

of the late Paul Shillabeer's masterly illustrated brochure, produced for St Peter's Golden Jubilee, have now disappeared or fallen into disuse.

CHAPTER 6

The Jordan Burn

Still murmuring on through Morningside, the Jordan Burn, now largely hidden, is an ancient witness to the development on its banks of a hamlet, later a village, which was to become a populous, bustling suburb. For centuries, and until 1856, the Jordan was Edinburgh's official southern boundary. Many famous men of history have crossed its banks from the south; and there is even evidence that the Romans built a bridge across the Jordan at Morningside.

Early records refer to the 'river', which also features in romantic poetry, while in an important book on Scottish rivers Morningside's own stream enjoys pride of place in the opening chapter. The mushroom growth of Morningside in the late nineteenth century was heralded by 'the builders careering like wild colts' across the Jordan to apply their 'tinkling chisels' to the construction of a modern suburban Promised Land. The frontages of buildings, revealing signs of subsidence, have had to be demolished; building programmes have been delayed — all on account of Morningside's relentlessly flowing stream.

Over many a Morningside dinner table a long controversy, sometimes resulting in the setting up of exploration groups, has raged: where does the Jordan rise? Where may it be seen? What is the course through Morningside on its way to the sea? No chronicle of the district would be adequate without an attempt to answer these questions — hopefully once and for all. These answers are the fruits of a long, careful systematic search through records and in the field.

The first documented reference to the Jordan Burn occurs in the 'Protocol Book of James Young' under the date 23 March 1497. Young was an Edinburgh Notary Public who recorded the principal events in the city, including the transfer of property between its citizens. His entry for the above date describes the

150

disposition of land at Nithirbrad (Netherbraid), within the ancient Barony of Braid. In defining the boundaries of the land in the transaction he refers to 'the Buckstane, Plewlandsike and the Powburne on the north'. The Pow Burn was the name by which the Jordan Burn was known until about 1760, 'pow' being derived from the Scandinavian word for pool or sluggish stream. The name Jordan was later given to the section of the burn between its source (described below) and, approximately, what is now Mayfield Road. This is the part which flowed through Morningside's Biblical area. After that the original name Pow Burn was retained.

While the other documented references to the Jordan Burn do not occur until the late eighteenth and early nineteenth centuries, in *Marmion* Sir Walter Scott describes the Scottish army encamped, in 1513, on the area of the Burgh Muir which today is occupied by the Astley Ainslie Hospital, describing it as 'between the *streamlet* and the town'. Young's reference of 1497 was just sixteen years earlier than the scene Scott describes. In charters of the many feus within the land of Canaan boundaries are frequently defined in terms of 'the straad', 'the streamlet' or 'the burn of Braid'. (This last reference was not to the more southerly Braid Burn; it is simply another title for the Jordan which flowed along and formed the northern boundary of the estate of Braid.) In 1692 there was some damage to property when the then substantial stream overflowed its banks. Edinburgh Town Council, apparently responsible for the burn, paid compensation to James Russell 'tennent in Canaan for the damage caused to his crops'. Russell farmed a substantial area of Canaan for nearly fifty years.

Sir Thomas Dick-Lauder, in his entertaining book, *Scottish Rivers*, written in 1846 and dealing in general with Scotland's mightier rivers, amusingly devotes his first chapter to the Jordan, which skirted his own extensive lands south of Grange House. He describes people and places of interest on the Jordan's then largely unbuilt-upon banks. Certain of his anecdotes are interspersed in the description of the stream which follows.

Apparently even in Sir Thomas's day 'the precise place of the

Jordan's origin was productive of much contradictory speculation'. On one occasion, he recounts, he collected together 'about a round dozen . . . sages of Modern Athens' to impress one of his distinguished friends with their conversational brilliance. The after-dinner talk, however, fell flat; the evening seemed a failure. Then, with a concealed gleam in his eye, their host introduced a subject which, at last, made the dining-room echo with animated conversation. Said Sir Thomas: 'It is a strange thing that, though the little stream of the Jordan runs through our grounds here and within less than half a mile of this house, no-one can tell us where its source is.' The result was sensational: excitement, commotion and a noisy debate ensued as the erudite guests proffered their theories of the Jordan's birth. 'In the Pentland Hills', insisted one; 'at Hunters' Tryst', smugly replied another. Innumerable sources were dogmatically proposed. Sir Thomas Dick-Lauder listened with patience and tolerance, finally suggesting the source described hereafter.

In more recent times, the late Wilfred Taylor of *A Scotsman's Log* had fanned the embers of debate, which continued to smoulder since Sir Thomas Dick-Lauder's day, by raising yet again the same questions. With the object of finally answering them, he entertainingly described the nocturnal researches which he and a friend pursued. They were the two exclusive members of the Morningside Night Exploration Society, the activities of which were frequently conducted by moonlight.

The systematic study of the Jordan Burn now presented takes into account the theories of certain other writers as regards the little stream's source and course. The exploration carried out by William R. Smith in the mid-1970s also the subject of his short documentary film 'Morningside's River: From Source to Sea', began at Craiglockhart Hill above the pond that was for long known as 'The Happy Valley'. A burn, it had been suggested, flowed from the pond's northern end. This was found to be correct. A burn does leave the pond here, flowing parallel to Lockharton Crescent. That this burn proceeded to flow through Morningside was, however, soon proved to be inconsistent with the law of gravity as the level of this stream at Meggetland

Terrace is below that of Myreside. The former was identified as the Stank Burn which flows under the Union Canal to Slateford, past Westfield Avenue and into the Water of Leith at Roseburn.

The next area of investigation was Craighouse Hill above Myreside as it was near here that the Jordan Burn could first be seen. No watercourse could, however, be traced on Craighouse Hill. Myreside, with its ancient village, took its name from the area of 'myre' or marshland in the vicinity referred to in the records as 'the common myre' and shown on old maps as at the western extremity of the Burgh Muir. Other sources refer to a sheet of water at Myreside known as Jordanville Loch, in the vicinity of Morningside and to a water pumping station at Myreside. It now seemed clear that it was within this immediate vicinity that the Jordan Burn arose. On the east side of Craighouse Road entry was made to the allotments beside the former Craighouse Cabinet Works. Slightly to the north of the latter, a few yards east of the railway bridge, in an area overgrown with bushes, the first unimpressive and virtually stagnant source of the Jordan Burn used to be visible. Alongside the north wall of the Cabinet Works, the burn, polluted and unattractive, made its sluggish way. This was the first identifiable source of the Jordan. It may be noted that Sir Thomas Dick-Lauder cited this as the Jordan's source, traced no doubt during his own explorations. Certain early maps also indicate this as the source. The investigations now recorded were, however, uninfluenced by earlier conclusions. Most of this area has now been built on and the original appearance of the burn can no longer be seen.

For some ten or twenty feet here, high up on the southern embankment of the railway line, the burn moved slowly on to a point behind the wall of the then Balfour Kilpatrick works in Balcarres Street. It is interesting that, in this short length of its course, it was contained in an unusual channel with stone slabs on its base and sides. Half-way up the side-slabs were overflow holes — seldom necessary it may be thought, in recent times. This man-made channel then came to a dead end and from this point the meagre flow of water made its way down the railway embankment to the permanent way, where a phenomenon occurred which no-one seemed able to explain. The water which had trickled down from the tiled channel now began to follow the western slope of the permanent way, going back in the opposite direction from which it had come, towards the old Craiglockhart Station. Even more enigmatic — and frustrating for its tracker — it suddenly disappeared down a hole and was lost! When consulted, the Engineer's Department of British Rail pondered this mysterious happening but could offer no explanation or indication of the course the Jordan had now taken.

Morningside's river is not to be written off so easily. Crossing to the north bank of the permanent way, investigation of a very obvious and much reported natural channel at the foot of the northern embankment seemed strongly to indicate that water had flowed there at some time. Excavation at certain points revealed dampness but no significant flow of water. At this point the channel ran parallel to the southern boundary wall of the Royal Edinburgh Hospital. Old plans and descriptions of the hospital grounds indicated that pond-like areas formed there at times. Indeed, curling ponds had once existed within the hospital precincts in this area and these had been the scene of many animated contests.

There is little doubt that the Jordan at one time flowed past the boundary wall of the Royal Edinburgh Hospital. Indeed, Sir Thomas Dick-Lauder's account of the burn's course confirms this.

Where the Jordan once flowed and now trickles past the southern wall of the Royal Edinburgh Hospital, at the point where it is joined by the east wall running downhill from Morningside Terrace, it is still possible to trace the route of the old right-of-way coming down from the ancient village of Tipperlinn, in line with what became Morningside Terrace but now terminating abruptly at the telephone exchange at the end of Maxwell Street. The original reason for the preservation of the ancient right-of-way from Tipperlinn was to give the women of the village access to the Jordan Burn to do their washing, either at the nearest point for them, where today the southern and eastern boundary walls of the Royal Edinburgh Hospital meet, or perhaps, by proceeding further along the right-of-way, where the Jordan was joined by the tributary about to be described. In earlier times there would appear to have been plenty of water in the vicinity of the telephone exchange.

For long the precise course of the Jordan at the foot of the steep pathway which is a continuation of what is now Morningside Terrace, and of the burn which flowed into the Jordan a little east of this point, were difficult to discover. By a stroke of good fortune, at the time that our field studies were being carried out, the preparation of the foundations for the new Maxwell Street telephone exchange revealed invaluable evidence of the waters in this vicinity. To the consternation of the builders and delight of Jordan Burn researchers, the bulldozers brought much of interest to light. The engineers on the site reported that in their excavations, just yards southwards of the old Tipperlinn right-of-way, a very old pipe, approximately nine inches in diameter, was unearthed, in which there was a damp muddy deposit, although certainly no evidence of the steady flow of a burn. This pipe followed what was traditionally believed to be the course of the Jordan coming from Craighouse Hill in the west, as indicated in old maps of the area and in Sir Thomas Dick-Lauder's description. The pipe had obviously been installed to channel the Jordan underground, possibly when the railway goods yard was first laid out on this site.

If no more could now be seen of the Jordan than a damp deposit in an old cracked pipe (duly removed by the site engineers), was it to be concluded that Morningside's ancient river had dried up for ever? Were this so, what was the source of the burn still flowing albeit largely underground, past the back gardens of Nile Grove and Jordan Lane, and surfacing most pleasantly as it passed Woodburn House in Canaan Lane, Blackford, Mayfield and Cameron Toll? The telephone exchange excavations were to confirm the traditional explanation reflected in certain old maps and Sir Thomas Dick-Lauder's book.

The bulldozers literally uncovered a mystery which had long

During the construction of the Post Office telephone building at the end of Maxwell Street, considerable water at this junction of the Jordan and Comiston burns required months of pumping operations. *Photograph by W. R. Smith.*

fascinated Morningside residents, especially those who as children had lived near Maxwell Street and played in the lane climbing from the north side of this street steeply up to Millar Place. Many had placed an ear over an iron grating at the point where the lane was joined by the ancient right-of-way from Tipperlinn: beneath could be heard, sometimes strongly, sometimes faintly, the sound of running water. This, they believed, was the Jordan Burn. The subsequent excavations revealed, however, that it was not the Jordan — now a mere muddy trickle in an old pipe — but a vigorous little tributary, the waters of which meet those of the Jordan under the grating.

Again, over the years, many observers with sharpness of ear had heard the rush of water under another grating, recently covered over, which was on the left as one entered from Balcarres Street the pathway leading over the railway footbridge at Morningside Station. The water sounded deep underground, and beyond the grating its course could not be traced.

Excavations at the old railway goods yard were to solve the mystery, however, bringing to light a strongly flowing stream.

What, then, was the source and the course of this substantial tributary which had for so long been transfusing life into the almost moribund Jordan Burn? Residents on the south side of Comiston Drive have long been proud of the pleasant stream flowing just beyond their garden walls. Many built picturesque little footbridges across it to what was originally the Poorhouse Road. Closed many years ago, it ran closely parallel, on the north, to Greenbank Drive, which leads to the City Hospital. This burn, which tradition and old maps suggested was a tributary of the Jordan, without naming it, was, for the purpose of our research, called the Comiston Burn.

The Comiston Burn flowing past the back gardens on the south side of Comiston Drive may be seen from the railings on the left (where Comiston Drive turns off from Comiston Road), in the back garden of what was once the lodge at the entrance to the former Poorhouse Road, now the site of Greenbank House. It then passes under Comiston Drive and under the rear playgrounds of South Morningside School. At one time, before the adjacent houses in Craiglea Drive were built, the burn might have been visible from the little lane just beyond the row of shops on the south side of Craiglea Drive. It now proceeds downhill on the west side of Comiston Road.

At Morningside Drive, the Comiston Burn passes under the Dunedin Masonic Hall and a shop opposite, then proceeds under Belhaven Terrace. Here it veers slightly westwards and, passing under Balcarres Street, suddenly once revealed itself to the attentive ear, if not the eye, as it flowed under the metal grille to the left of the entrance to the pathway which leads from Balcarres Street over the railway footbridge. That the sound of running water under the grille came from a considerable depth was evidenced by the fact that the ground level of the lane is much higher than that of the railway line, under which the Comiston Burn passes. The burn has been covered in at this point and running water can no longer be heard. The stream then enters the former railway goods yard, now something of a wasteland at this southern point, and makes its way, running parallel to the lane, beyond the footbridge, passing the end of Maxwell Street and the entrance to the grounds of the telephone exchange. At the point already described it flows at right-angles into the now feeble waters of the Jordan Burn and surrenders its identity.

The excavations on the site of the telephone exchange revealed that the Comiston Burn, which enters the former goods yard from under the railway line, had not always flowed in its present direction. An old course was found running in a north-westerly direction towards the Jordan Burn pipeline, near the south-western corner of the Royal Edinburgh Hospital grounds. The first revelation of the Comiston Burn's present course came when a large flagstone was uncovered near the old weigh-bridge hut just inside the entrance of the former goods yard at the end of Maxwell Street. Below lay a channel, the base and sides of which were formed from similar large flagstones some two feet six inches square. Through this the Comiston Burn, once a mere trickle at Greenbank Drive, now flowed strongly. The flagstone channel was replaced by large concrete pipes and the old course to the north-west was filled in. Morningside residents who witnessed the prolonged preparation of the telephone exchange site will remember the veritable underground loch produced by the liberated confluent Jordan and Comiston burns, and the slow but relentless action of the pumps which eventually withdrew their invading waters, until, at last subdued, they were channelled anew, still to ensure the Jordan's ancient onward journey.

Now flowing underground between the very high wall which was originally the southern boundary wall of East House the original asylum, and the low wall and railings of the back greens of the north side of Maxwell Street, the Jordan flows between the shops at 356-8 Morningside Road, above which the original tenements were demolished on account of the burn's erosion of their foundations. There is a narrow concrete channel, revealed some time ago during road repairs at this point, in which the burn passes under Morningside Road and continues beneath the lane at the south wall of the recently built Post Office. This very old lane, once a pathway, and the old toll-house which stood beside it, have been discussed in an earlier chapter. During the building of the former supermarket at the entrance to the lane, considerable delay occurred while the burn was safely confined to a concrete pipe.

Until the end of the last century, when it was covered over for most of its course through Morningside in order to facilitate the great building programme, there were many pleasant open stretches of the Jordan, notably at the point where it now flows under Morningside Road. Here the burn was quite wide, but not too wide to be leapt across by village boys, who preferred this adventurous method of crossing to using the little wooden bridge known as the 'Briggs o' Braid', or simply 'the Briggs'. The Briggs o' Braid is frequently given as a location in old property titles. Some confusion has arisen over the name. It sounds as though it refers to a bridge over the Braid Burn, which is much further to the south, up Comiston Road. The name Braid was applied to the little bridge over the Jordan simply because the land immediately to the south at this point was the beginning of the Braid estate. On the north bank the estates of Morningside proper and Canaan ended. The bridge lay on the ancient Western Hiegait, which skirted the western fringes of the Burgh Muir and was one of the principal routes into Edinburgh from the south. Thus it was across the Briggs o' Braid in its most primitive forms that invaders from the south – the Roman legions, Edward I of England and subsequent English armies – entered Edinburgh. In later times, during the '45 Rebellion, Bonnie Prince Charlie and his Jacobite army, coming by Slateford, Colinton Mains and the path along the Braid Burn, crossed the Briggs o' Braid on their way to Holyrood.

The Jordan Burn, having crossed under Morningside Road, passes the rear of Braid Church, and continues along the natural valley between the back gardens of the houses on the north side of Nile Grove and those on the south side of Jordan Lane. Some years ago when a resident in Jordan Lane was working in her garden the presence of the Jordan Burn was discovered in a dramatic manner. Pulling very hard on a stubborn bush, the lady suddenly disappeared. Fortunately her husband was nearby and rushed to assist his wife. After extricating her from a deep hole it was discovered that a large flagstone had been dislodged, revealing the Jordan Burn below. Further investigation revealed that on the north side of the boundary wall between Jordan Lane and Nile Grove gardens, the burn ran parallel to the wall but was covered over by large flagstones, one end of these resting on a small ledge on the boundary wall and the other end on the soil of the Jordan Lane gardens. It was one of these flagstones that had been dislodged. Fortunately the lady was uninjured.

As a consequence of the incident, the city authorities proceeded to encase the Jordan Burn more securely in this area, an exercise that took many months and much expenditure. It was at this time that the open stretch of the burn in the garden of Braid Hill Cottage was also covered in.

The houses at the far end of Jordan Lane have wooden doors in their back garden walls which once gave entrance from a pathway along the north bank of the Jordan, hence the street's original name, Jordan Bank. These doors, now mostly boarded up or unable to be opened because of the gradual alteration in ground level, today lead into a narrow walled lane directly above the burn. Certain of these Jordan Lane houses have little stone-built sheds at the foot of their gardens, once used as wash-houses, with hand pumps for drawing water from the Jordan. It was here that the first attempts were made to verify, before the telephone exchange excavations provided conclusive evidence, that the Comiston Burn was a tributary of the Jordan. At the point where the Comiston Burn disappears underground below the railings on the left at the entrance to Comiston Drive from Comiston Road, a small amount of innocuous fluorescent dye was added to the stream. An hour later the waters of the Jordan in the garden of Braid Hill Cottage showed the first traces of discolouration.

The Jordan now passes under Woodburn Terrace, where the houses at the gable-end of the flats on the east side seem to have

The author examines an old water suction pump above the Jordan Burn as it runs underground in a back garden in Jordan Lane. *Photograph by W. R. Smith.*

escaped the damage inflicted on other buildings in Morningside built over the Jordan or its tributary. Perhaps the builders of Woodburn Terrace wisely stopped short for this reason. The Jordan emerges from under Woodburn Terrace into the pleasant grounds of Woodburn House, entered from Canaan Lane, and here contributes to a delightfully idyllic rural scene. Two little waterfalls enhance the burn's charm as it murmurs onwards through a glade of tall, venerable trees, the setting signifying the origin of the name Woodburn. It is here that the Jordan may be seen at its best, recalling its charm of earlier days.

The southern slopes of the Astley Ainslie Hospital grounds now accommodate the Jordan as it continues eastwards, close to its early travelling companion, the old suburban railway line. In earlier times the burn formed a natural hazard on the ladies' nine-hole golf course which existed here before the hospital was built. Visible from the road-bridge over the railway line at Oswald Road, the Jordan next flows on through what was formerly the old farm of Blackford, on the site of which the once bustling suburban railway station of this name came to be built. While only a few scattered stones of Blackford House now remain, fortunately the sturdy two-storey farmhouse itself still stands. Long after the farm's disappearance it remained the pleasant home of a family whose lives were spent as farmworkers here. The house, modernised and sub-divided, remains a reminder of past days. In the garden of the farmhouse, the old stone bridge over the Jordan, once a popular subject for photographers, had been carefully and imaginatively preserved and laid out with pleasant flower-beds.

The early days of Blackford House and its pleasant surroundings have been picturesquely described by Sir Thomas Dick-Lauder. He gives a delightful portrait of his friend, Miss Memie Trotter, then in her nineties, last of a branch of the notable family of Mortonhall estate. Perhaps a secret of Miss Trotter's longevity was her daily bathing in the waters of the Jordan, even in advanced years!

There is something of Jekyll and Hyde about the Jordan: its course alternates between calm, pleasant settings and scenes of aggressive destruction, the latter occurring at Blackford as well as Morningside. Immediately beyond its attractive manifestations at Blackford farm, the burn emerges into view just beyond the bridge at the foot of Blackford Avenue and flows onwards in a very narrow channel which is nothing more than a ditch. Yet in this innocent-looking and apparently subdued stretch the Jordan had been secretly taking its toll. A few years ago, as passers-by

The Jordan Burn, once flowing openly as a substantial stream at the Briggs o'
Braid, now runs under Morningside Road near the Post Office. But it still
surfaces, and most pleasantly, in the grounds at the rear of Woodburn House in
Canaan Lane. *Photograph by W. R. Smith.*

noted with some curiosity, teams of workmen were engaged for months on a major and expensive operation. Running parallel to the burn from the old Briggs o' Braid at the foot of Morningside Road is the Powburn sewer, a large concrete pipe nearly five feet in diameter. Just beyond the bridge at Blackford Avenue the Jordan had gradually eroded the soil under a considerable stretch of the unsupported sewer pipe so that it had, at certain points, cracked and collapsed. After months of work the offending Jordan was diverted from the sewer into a new concrete channel.

Once more in safe captivity, 'The little streamlet' which Lord Marmion viewed from Blackford Hill continues along what were the southern fringes of the Grange House estate and onwards to Mayfield Road. On the west side of Mayfield Road, the burn, which for some distance has gone underground, may again be seen emerging from a small tunnel on the north side of the railway embankment. On the banks of the burn, at the point where it reappears from under Mayfield Road, was the ancient village of Powburn. In 1663 Sir James Keith was baronet of Powburn, but this title became extinct. A large villa, Powburn House, in its latter days a favourite summer resort of wealthy Edinburgh citizens, was advertised as vacant in 1773 in the *Edinburgh Advertiser* which described it as, 'A desirable mansion, pleasantly situated from the Grange Toll Bar, with coach-house and four-stalled stable.' This house and the village were eventually swept away as Edinburgh grew southwards.

Just beyond the one-time village of Powburn, the Jordan flows under the now derelict Newington Station, under Mayfield Gardens at the foot of Minto Street, and then washes the southern boundary wall of Newington Cemetery, and presents a pleasing prospect at the allotments situated on its banks. At the foot of Lady Road at Cameron Toll there is a little parapet from which the Jordan may be seen as it leaves the cemetery's precincts.

Now the long persevering flow of Morningside's own river, far from its source, is nearly at an end. Re-appearing from under Lady Road, it compensates for its ignominious and uncomfortable confinement during so much of its travels by enjoying the last luxury of expanding into a new open concrete channel. At times, after heavy rainfall, it has even had the pleasure of welcoming ducks here to its open waters. Its early polluted and sluggish origins at Myreside are long forgotten.

Finally, its end in sight and as if reluctant to accept it, the Jordan once again becomes sluggish and enjoys a last rendezvous with its travelling companion, the suburban railway line. Just south of the University recreation grounds at Peffermill, within the district of Greenend — an area which in ancient days was also a great myre or marshland — the Jordan is at last received by its more southerly Morningside neighbour, the Braid Burn, and carried along by the latter's more powerful waters. If the Jordan's surrender of its proud name to that of Braid is painful, it does not last for long, for soon both streams lose their identity to become the Figgate Burn. Passing through the hinterland of Portobello, the last days of the Jordan and Braid are quickly spent, and skirting the walls of the man-made waters of Edinburgh's former open-air swimming pool, a stone channel under Portobello promenade hastens the death agonies of Morningside's two 'rivers' as, in Swinburne's words, they 'flow somewhere safe to sea'.

CHAPTER 7

Beyond the Jordan:
Morningside Station — Comiston

The first signs of the transition of the village of Morningside into what, in a relatively short time, was to become a rapidly expanding suburb were heralded by Robert Louis Stevenson in *Edinburgh: Picturesque Notes*, published in 1878. Describing the steep descent of Morningside Road from Boroughmuirhead and Churchhill, he notes that at the foot of the hill, just as the road is about to climb again, it passed the toll-bar and then 'issued at once into the open country'. 'Even as I write these words,' Stevenson continued, 'they are being antiquated in the progress of events, and the chisels are tinkling on a new row of houses. The builders have at length adventured beyond the toll which held them in respect so long and proceed to career in these fresh pastures like a herd of colts turned loose.'

This expansion of Morningside beyond the city's ancient southern boundary, the Jordan, roused Stevenson's wrath. He had come to know the old village well in his younger days when walking through it on his way from the city to Swanston Cottage. Recalling how Lord Beaconsfield had once proposed to hang an architect by way of stimulation, he advocated similar measures to save 'these doomed meads from the ravages of the builders . . . It seems as if it must come to an open fight,' he wrote, 'to preserve a corner of green country unbedevilled.'

But, despite Robert Louis Stevenson's words of regret and protest, the march of progress was not to be halted. On the open country beyond the toll a vast residential building programme was soon to begin. The owners of the estate of Braid, the Gordons of Cluny, had feued out extensive lands over an area between what are now Nile Grove in the north and the Hermitage of Braid in the south, Comiston Road in the west and Blackford in the east. Here was to arise the attractive

166

residential district with streets bearing the names of the Gordons' Aberdeenshire estates, Cluny, Midmar and Corrennie, as well as that of their Edinburgh family seat, the Hermitage of Braid. Similarly, on the large Plewlands estate, extending from what is now Maxwell Street and the old village of Myreside southwards to Greenbank Crescent, and from Comiston Road eastwards to Craighouse and the fringes of Meggetland, another vast residential area was to be built. Together, the development of the Braid and Plewlands estates, completed by 1900, resulted in the mushrooming of classical 'villadom' on a scale which even Robert Louis Stevenson's fertile imagination had not conceived. Yet 'the doomed meads' were not entirely obliterated: much pleasant open green space was preserved.

There were other factors which towards the end of the nineteenth century were leading rapidly to Morningside's growth and transformation. The Jordan Burn had ceased to be Edinburgh's southern boundary in 1856. The latter was then extended southwards to a line crossing Comiston Road at Comiston Drive, later to the old Braid Hills tramway terminus and finally, as today, to Hillend Park and along the ridge of Caerketton and the aligning range of the Pentland Hills. Road tolls in Scotland were abolished in 1883, and soon after the old toll-bar at the Briggs o' Braid had, in any case, been swept away and the Jordan Burn covered over by Morningside Road. There was no longer any financial deterrent to those choosing to reside south of the old city boundary. Further, with the gradual extension and improvement of transport facilities from the city, Morningside ceased to be the remote village of earlier days.

While Robert Louis Stevenson does not specify where 'the chisels are tinkling on a new row of houses', Maxwell Street, just beyond the old toll-bar, was built just a year before the publication of *Picturesque Notes*, as the inscription high above the south-east corner of the street indicates, so that it may well have been its construction to which he refers. Writers to the press at the turn of the century have described Maxwell Street as the first scene of new building across the Jordan. It is probable that Maxwell Street takes its name from Herbert Maxwell, a member of Edinburgh Town Council in 1591 and the owner of land in this area. On the wall at the south-east corner of Maxwell Street is the inscription 'Watt Terrace'. This may have been the original name of the short stretch of Morningside Road from this point up to Morningside Station. As was often done, it might have been given the name of its builder.

Before Maxwell Street was built, the area was apparently grassy parkland which in winter was frequently flooded and frozen over, providing a popular resort for skaters. The street has earned a place in Edinburgh's early annals of tele-communications. Alexander Graham Bell, inventor of the telephone, was born at South Charlotte Street in 1847. The Scottish Telephonic Exchange Limited was established in the city in 1879. Morningside's first telephone exchange (comprising two fifty-line units) was installed in 1893 in the house of a family named Swanson at 8 Maxwell Street. It is interesting that not many yards from this first Morningside exchange a modern British Telecom telephone exchange was established in the former railway goods yard in 1974.

Ten years after the completion of Maxwell Street, the chisels began tinkling on the construction of Braid Church, opened in 1887. It was built only a few yards from the toll-house which, a year later, was dismantled stone by stone and rebuilt as the entrance lodge to the Hermitage of Braid. The site of the toll-house became part of the church's surrounding lawn. The history of Braid Church forms an interesting part of the annals of Morningside and reveals a number of sidelights on the general growth and development of the district itself. Braid was the first church to be built in Morningside after the establishment of the Parish Church at Churchhill fifty years before. While St Matthew's Parish Church, opened a few months after Braid, was established and fostered by the original Parish Church, Braid has always been proud of its independent origins.

Braid Church had its beginnings in a little iron church built in January 1883 on the site of the present-day junction of Braid Road and Comiston Road. The generous benefactor who

The Braid iron church built at the corner of Braid Road and Cluny Gardens in 1884. *Water-colour by Frederick Dove Ogilvie. Photograph by W. R. Smith. By courtesy of Morningside Braid Church.*

provided £500 for the purchase of the iron church for long remained anonymous. He was, in fact, Dr John Kerr. The original congregation of seventy 'adherents' were of the United Presbyterian Church (similar to but independent of the original congregation of North Morningside Church at Holy Corner). As its site was within the estate of Braid, the church adopted that name.

The little iron church of Braid soon proved too small for the rapidly growing congregation built up by the first minister, the Rev. Walter Brown, called from Galashiels. Proposals were made and funds gathered to build a new church. The site at the north-west corner of Nile Grove was acquired and plans were drawn up by George Washington Browne, who later became the leading Scottish architect of his time, for a church which would accommodate seven hundred and fifty people. The estimated cost was £5,000. This was George Washington Browne's first public building in Edinburgh. His later achievements were to include Edinburgh's Central Public Library on George IV Bridge, the Royal Hospital for Sick Children on Sciennes Road and the Scottish National Memorial to King Edward VII at Holyrood.

The foundation stone was laid on 9 October 1886 and, after only nine months, the church was opened on 10 July 1887. The final cost was only £500 above the original quotation.

A Braid Home Mission Station had been established at Swanston, meeting in the village schoolroom. It had the active support of the farmer, Mr Finnie, and later of his widow. For a time, services were conducted on the village green, worshippers being summoned by hand-bell.

By the early 1900s Morningside had begun to take on the features of a modern suburb offering attractive housing. At this time the Braid records throw light on prevailing health problems. An entry for 1907, for example, reports regular services conducted in the crowded tuberculosis wards of the City Fever Hospital at Greenbank, opened four years before.

Morningside Station was opened for passenger traffic in 1884. The story of the construction of the Edinburgh Suburban and South Side Junction Railway, as it was originally named, is linked with one of the most tragic events in the history of Scottish railways, the Tay Bridge disaster of 28 December 1879. The Tay Bridge had been designed by Thomas Bouch of Comely Bank, whose workmanship, along with other circumstances of the tragedy, was later the subject of a Board of Trade Court of Inquiry. Proceedings opened in Dundee in January 1880 and were concluded in May of that year.

While Bouch awaited the Court's findings, he did not, as some reports related, retire into obscurity, dreading the verdict. He firmly believed that his design was without defect and, retaining his confidence, he meanwhile undertook other assignments. One of these was the preparation of plans for submission to Parliament in order to seek permission to proceed

Braid Church (from 1991 Morningside Braid Church) opened in 1887. The octagonal design and the interior 'auditorium' by Architect Sir George Washington Browne was considered unique. *Photograph by W. R. Smith.*

with the construction of Edinburgh's suburban railway.

The conclusions of the Tay Bridge Disaster Court of Inquiry had been equivocal, and not unanimous. Bouch regarded himself as having been exonerated but certain press reports took the opposite view: the Court's verdict resulted in controversy.

The new suburban stations were at Haymarket, Gorgie, Morningside Road, Blackford, Newington, Duddingston, Portobello and Abbeyhill, and trains travelled regularly in both directions. Craiglockhart station was opened three years after the others, in 1887. The line from Gorgie to Morningside followed a gradual uphill gradient until the summit was reached just west of Morningside Road Station. At a number of points cuttings had to be made for the track, most notably through deep rock east of Craiglockhart, which meant that the station

Thomas Bouch, who planned the Edinburgh Suburban Railway, opened in 1884, while he awaited the verdict of inquiries into the Tay Bridge disaster. The ill-fated bridge had been his creation. *National Library of Scotland.*

offices there had to be built on the street bridge level, as also at Morningside Road and Newington. As mentioned elsewhere, a footbridge had to be built at Morningside Station to ensure the old right-of-way from the village of Tipperlinn, although by 1884 the village had long since disappeared.

A year after the inauguration of the railway, the Edinburgh Suburban and South Side Junction Railway Company amalgamated with its parent company, the North British Railway Company. The establishment of the suburban railway encouraged increasing numbers of people to take up residence in Morningside, a trend particularly evident in the 1930s, when, perhaps, the railway was at its peak, having trains arriving at Waverley Station every ten minutes during peak hours.

The opening of the railway goods yard and coal depot at the end of Maxwell Street proved invaluable to the farmers of Comiston, Hunter's Tryst and Swanston, and many older Morningside residents will recall the bustle there as farm carts went to and fro' loaded with cows, sheep, potatoes and turnips. In the days before electricity and gas were used for heating, the constant stream of carts and lorries from the important coal depot added to the bustle.

Soon after the opening of Morningside Station the spacious crossroads area comprising Morningside Road, Balcarres Street, Comiston Road, Braid Road and Cluny Gardens became the hub of Morningside. Morningside Station was the terminus of the horse-drawn trams. Here the horses were changed and rested before the steep pull to Churchill. Here, too, was the stance of the horse-cabs, the cabbies' shelter being just round the corner in Balcarres Street. The cabs, which included brakes and pair and four-in-hand coaches, operated from 8.45 a.m. until 10 p.m. The cab fare to Waverley Station in about 1900 was 1/6d. Near the station, telegraph boys waited until hailed by the postmistress of Plewlands Post Office at the beginning of Comiston Road, then set out on foot or bicycle with their urgent messages for the important people in the 'big houses' then rapidly being built.

To complete the services which centred on Morningside Station, a group of enterprising Morningside businessmen, of

'Murray's Edinburgh Diary' cover, 1916.

opposite:

The Suburban Railway timetable published in the then popular 'Murray's Diary' for 1916. Price one penny! Most people carried one. Trains to and from the Waverley Station and the suburbs were frequent at peak times.

132 EDINBURGH SUBURBAN AND SOUTHSIDE RAILWAY

‡ Passengers for Edinburgh from Duddingston and other Stations change at Portobello.

INNER CIRCLE	am	am	am	am	a.m	a.m	a.m	r.m	p.m	p.m	pm	pm	pm	p.m	p.m	p.m	p.m	p.m	p.m	pm	pm	p.m	Sat	Sat
Leith (Cent.) lev	530	8 8	830	9 33	1034			1135	1235	1 5	1 35	2	3 34	355	4 35	4 45	5 5	5 35	6 55	734	8 33	9 33	5 55	1051
Abbeyhill	555	811	833	9 36	1037			1138	1238	1 8	1 38	2 38	3 38	438	5 38	4 9	5 8	5 38	6 58	737	8 36	9 38	5 55	1034
Edinburgh arr	537	815	837	9 40	1041			1142	1242	112	1 42	2 42	3 42	442	5 42	6 15	5 12	5 42	741	8 40	9 42	1058
Edinburgh lev	545	825	845	9 45	1047		1145	1245	115	145	2 45	3 45	445	5 45	6 45	645	5 15	7 45	8 45	9 45	1045
Haymarket	549	829	849	9 49	1051		1152	1249	119	149	2 49	3 49	449	5 49	6 49	6 19	5 19	749	8 49	9 50	1049
Gorgie	552	832	852	9 53	1054	1 2	1155	1252	122	152	2 52	3 52	452	5 52	6 52	6 22	5 25	752	8 52	9 53	1052
Craiglockhart	555	835	855	9 56	1057		1158	1255	125	155	2 55	3 55	455	5 55	6 55	6 25	5 28	755	8 55	9 56	1055
Morningside Rd	558	838	858	9 59	11 0		12 1	1258	128	158	2 58	3 58	458	5 58	6 58	5 86	758	8 58	9 59	1058
Blackford Hill	6 1	841	9 1	10 2	11 3		12 4				3 1	4 1		6 1		16 3	8 1	3 10	1058		2 14	4 11	3
Newington	6 3	843	9 3	10 4	11 5	1 3	12 6		131	2 3	3 4	4 3	5 1	5 86	7 18	8 39	3 10	10 5	4 13	14
Duddingston	6 7	847	9 8	10 10	11 9	3 13	1210		132	2 7	3 5	4 35	5 33	6 37	7 38	8 39	7	14
Portobello	613		914	1017	1115	137	1216		135	213	5 13	4 15	5 37	6 18	714	8139	14	1055
‡ EDINBURGH arr	635		937	1038	1137		1228	1 24	225	3658	424	552		6 35	753	851	734	1026
Piershill	617		918	1021	1119		1220	1 17	217	3 73	17417	518		6 21	717	8179	1024
Leith (Cent.) arr	620		921	1024	1122		1223	1 20	220	3 20	20420	521		6 24	720	8209	1022

OUTER CIRCLE	am	am	am	am	am	am	p.m	p.m	pm	pm	p.m	p.m	p.m	pm	pm	p.m	p.m	pm	pm	p.m
Leith (Cent.) lev	651	814		917	1117	1048	1217	1 10	2 22	317	4 17	512	5 14	616 7	17		9 16	924	9 31
Piershill	655	818		921	1121		1221	1 22	2 25	321	4 21	518	620 7	20		9 2	935	951
§EDINBURGH lev	613	810		915	1048	1212	1 26	2 30	325	4 25	522	6 36	6 24 7	1	9 55	937
Portobello lev	659	822		925	1125	1132	1225	1 33	2 37	331	4 38	529	5 36	637 7	13	955	943
Duddingston	710	853	859	3 940	1135	1239	1 37	2 41	336	4 41	536	18	657 7	18	9 57
Newington	712	836	9 943	1138	1241	1 40	2 42	338	4 42	538	639 7	21	4	943
Blackford Hill	716	830	840	9 947	1144	1245	1 42	2 47	342	4 44	540	643 7	23	4 3	946
Morningside Rd	718		842	911	1919	1144	1247	1 46	2 49	344	4 48	542	645 7	24	950
Craiglockhart	721	833	845	914	1952	1147	1250	1 49	2 52	347	4 55	546	647 7	26	953
Gorgie	721	833	845	914	1952	1147	1250	1 49	2 52	347	4 55	546	647 7	26	953
Haymarket	725	838	850	918	100	1152	1254	1 52	2 56	351	4 59	550	654 7	35	956
Edinburgh arr	729	842	851	922	1003	1155	1258	2 2	3 0	355	5 4	554	658 7	39	959
Abbeyhill lev	734		858	922		1924	103	157	2	5	2 25	283	3 6	6 37 7	41	1 45
Leith (Cent.) arr	740		9 4	930		12 3	109	12 3	1	8	2 62	3 15	6 43 7	8	102

§ Passengers from Edinburgh for Duddingston & other Stations change at Portobello

b Saturdays 2-24 p.m.
c Saturdays 2-5 p.m.
h Saturdays 7-26 p.m.
‡ Wednesdays 9-25 p.m.

Morningside Road Station on the Suburban Railway. A typical scene at the peak period when trams were frequent. The commuters could be at Waverley Station in 12 minutes. *Edinburgh Evening News.*

whom Colonel Trotter of Mortonhall was chairman, decided to build a hotel. Thus at the corner of Braid and Comiston Roads a substantial five-storey building arose in 1884, the year the station was opened. It was designed to provide ample accommodation for short-term visitors to Morningside. Colonel Trotter proposed that this new creation be named the Pentland Hotel, while some partners preferred the Belhaven Hotel (nearby Belhaven Terrace had then just recently been built). The need for a decision did not arise. When the building was completed, financial resources to continue the enterprise were not forthcoming and the scheme was abandoned. The prospective hotel was sub-divided into the comfortable flats of today. The two small sculpted animal figures which still surmount the stone balustrade above the corner premises at 1 Comiston Road

One of Morningside's best known family businesses. Above Torrance's bakers shop here at No. 1 Comiston Road were tea rooms where many Morningside organisations and enterprises were first planned.

were placed there during the occupancy of the British Linen Bank, whose insignia they represented.

What has become a cherished landmark, the station clock, was installed in 1910. It was the gift of three Morningside Town Councillors, R. K. Inches, William Inman and William Torrance. During the construction of a new traffic control system in the Morningside Station area in 1968, the clock was removed and, when some considerable time passed with no sign of its replacement, many residents made inquiries in official quarters. All was well. The clock was duly re-sited, a new electrical mechanism having been installed. The station area regained its traditional appearance.

Another pleasant feature of the area were the tea-rooms above Torrance's bakery at the corner of Belhaven Terrace and Comiston Road. Owned by Councillor William Torrance, one of the donors of the clock, the premises were a popular

A South Morningside School group of pretty girls in about 1900.

rendezvous and no doubt many important discussions took place over Torrance's tea-cups. One, recalled by an elderly Morningside resident, occurred on 7 October 1894 when the pioneers of Morningside's Baptist Church at Churchhill held their informal initial meeting here.

A century ago this year an important event took place in Comiston Road. This was the opening of South Morningside Primary School, which signified the rapid development that the district had undergone. From 1823 until 1891, the Old Schoolhouse had been Morningside's principal educational establishment and was free, compared with a small number of privately run house-schools. Its tiny classroom catered for about 100 children attending from 'far and wide'. Two teachers coped with a wide age range. With the passing of the Education (Scotland) Act of 1872, making education compulsory for the first time, the old village school naturally became quite inadequate. While not officially opened until 2 October 1892,

South Morningside School had in fact admitted pupils from the previous year. On the first day, the headmaster had been presented with an expected roll of 522 names. In fact 344 appeared on the first day but by four days later 572 had been enrolled. Amongst the distinguished guests at the official opening ceremony was Andrew Carnegie, who spoke briefly. When South Morningside School opened the Old Schoolhouse closed, bringing to an end nearly seventy years of service. The centenary of the school in Comiston Road will be marked by many celebrations including the publication of a book to relate a proud story. This publication should have appeared before the completion of this book and recounting of any further detail here would be an unnecessary duplication.

Blackford — Braid

The Blackford Hill Station staff in about 1923. In the back row the two signalmen. Mr J. Laurie is on the right. Sitting are the stationmaster (his name could not be traced), and on each side the booking clerks. *Photograph by courtesy of Mr R. Lawrie, Bruce Street.*

Cluny Parish Church, opened as St Matthew's Parish Church in 1890 at the corner of Braid Road and Cluny Gardens. Entered into union with the former South Morningside Parish Church in 1974 to become Cluny Parish Church. *By courtesy of Cluny Parish Church.*

The sign above the Hermitage Bar in Comiston proclaims its association in name with the Hermitage of Braid. *Photograph by W. R. Smith.*

CHAPTER 8

Plewlands — Craighouse — Greenbank

Plewlands

The lands of Plewlands or Ploughlands are referred to as 'Plewlandsike' in the Protocol Book of James Young under the date 23 March 1497. For long they were part of the extensive adjacent lands of Braid which comprised 412 acres. Plewlands as such extended from what is now Maxwell Street and the southern boundary wall of the Royal Edinburgh Hospital (following the line of the western stretch of the Jordan Burn) southwards to what I have called the Comiston Burn, flowing behind the south side of Comiston Drive. What is now Comiston Road formed the eastern boundary, while on the west the frontiers were the ancient village of Myreside and the nearer fringes of Meggetland.

A large dairy farm with a tannery was established in Plewlands in the early 1800s. The farmhouse and extensive byres and steadings were situated close to the site of the present-day Morningside Park, entered from Morningside Drive and Balcarres Street. The farm is indicated and named in Edinburgh Post Office Directory maps until 1908. The following year its ruins are indicated but no longer named. Soon after this date these were swept away as the present-day residential district of Plewlands was gradually extended.

In the 1820s, immediately beyond and westward of the Briggs o' Braid, a farm-cart track led to Plewlands Farm, crossing the Comiston Burn near the point where today this little stream flows underground beside the railway footbridge at Balcarres Street. The farmhouse was a much-sought-after retreat for many notable Edinburgh citizens. One such who came to reside here in 1823 was the Rev. Robert Morehead, DD, at one time Episcopalian Dean of Edinburgh. Dr Morehead wrote of his

Plewlands stay with some enthusiasm, describing the farmhouse as, 'A most beautiful summer residence near Braid where I am alone with my daughter, Isabella. In the mornings, I study Hebrew,' he wrote. 'I sometimes think of writing my journal here in blank verse. There is a great deal of poetry scattered about me if I could catch it, and it is a pity to lose the power of versification. The poetry of life is the only poetry worth preserving. But I shall not strike it out from prose this morning.'

In 1882 a feuing plan for the lands of Plewlands was published by the Scottish Heritages Company which had acquired superiority. Illustrated in colour, this showed that a fair degree of building of detached and semi-detached villas had already taken place on the south side of what was then, and for years remained, South Morningside Drive, later coming to be named simply Morningside Drive. Ethel Terrace, Dalhousie Terrace, the east side of St Ronan's Terrace and a short length of Craiglea Drive (on the north between Dalhousie Terrace and St Ronan's Terrace) had, by 1882, already been built. The considerable building programme proposed for the remainder of the Plewlands estate is indicated and the plan shows the different architectural styles of the houses and what accommodation they would offer prospective purchasers. In addition to proposed new streets which have since been built and named as planned, others are indicated which were either never constructed or else given different names. North Morningside Crescent and South Morningside Crescent are illustrated as little semicircular streets near the west side of Comiston Road (then Penicuick Road). North Morningside Crescent was to have extended from South Morningside Drive to Craiglea Drive and South Morningside Crescent from Craiglea Drive to what became Comiston Drive, which is shown but not named in the 1882 plan. What today is Plewlands Terrace was proposed, rather strangely, as Lancaster Road. St Clair Terrace and Morningside Grove were not then envisaged. According to Charles Boog-Watson's *History and Derivation of Edinburgh Street Names*, Ethel Terrace was named after its builder's daughter, Ethel Clark, while Dalhousie

An important unexpected discovery by Joe Rock in Norwich Castle Museum of a painting by Hugh William Williams (1773–1829) of 'Ploughlands Cottage, near Edinburgh 1813'. No illustration of this house had previously been known to exist. Here, in 1823, resided the Rev. Dr Robert Morehead, then Episcopal Dean of Edinburgh. *Norfolk Museum Service.*

Terrace and other streets bearing saints' names are ascribed to 'baseless fancy'.

The Plewlands feu plan of 1882 also indicates other points of interest. The tramway terminus (a single line with a car turning) is shown at the Comiston Road end of Morningside Drive. Morningside Station is indicated in anticipation of its opening two years later in 1884. The Morningside toll-bar also appears. A year after the plan's publication, tolls in Scotland were abolished and the toll-house was dismantled.

What became Braid Road is shown as the Old Penicuick Road. Belhaven Terrace is also indicated as already built at the entrance to what is described as the Metropolitan Cemetery.

While the origin of its name is not on record, Belhaven Terrace may have had some association with the little place of that name near Dunbar.

The construction of Balcarres Street was begun by 1884 and completed in stages over a period of 15 years. The first part to be built, originally named Balcarres Terrace, commenced at Morningside Station, opposite Belhaven Terrace. Its south side consisted of the short row of tenements extending from the small triangle of ground on the right of the entrance gates to the cemetery to what was, in more recent times, George Horne's mission hall above two shops, now 8-10 Balcarres Street. After this the cemetery wall began.

On the opposite side of the street, in what was originally Balcarres Terrace was a small builder's yard. In about 1900 this became a blacksmith's shop and very much part of the scene at this point. Mr James Moyes, who established the blacksmith's business here some years previously had operated in premises beside the city refuse department yard further westwards in Balcarres Street, just beyond No. 38. Here at a railway siding were delivered iron and other metals for the making of railings and gates, much in demand for many of Morningside's houses. When James Moyes subsequently transferred his business to the blacksmith's yard of today, he built beside it a house for his family. This long ago passed into another ownership.

Mr Tom Moyes, who succeeded his father in the business, was a pupil at the Old Schoolhouse in Morningside Road. In time, his son James worked with him for some years but he gave the family tradition another dimension by qualifying as a technical teacher in metalwork and woodwork. In 1955 the Moyes blacksmith's shop of three generations was acquired by Mr James Anderson, who, after nearly 30 years' service to the people of Morningside and beyond in a now specialised trade, retired in 1982. The premises are now owned by Mr Kenny Donaldson of Currie. The resident blacksmith is Mr Iain Thomson whose work is mainly on gates and railings, with a much-in-demand additional skill in the restoration of metal Victorian fireplaces.

Morningside grew up round its smiddies where the public library now stands. The tradition was continued when James Moyes (centre) opened his blacksmith's shop in Balcarres Street around 1900. A proud family group! Back row, left, Tom Moyes who later took over. *Courtesy Mrs J. McKean.*

By 1900 the north side of Balcarres Street, from the blacksmith's premises to those of Messrs McKenzie and Moncur had been completed. At this time Balcarres Terrace ceased to appear on the Post Office Directory maps and the whole length from Morningside Station to the beginning of what is now Craighouse Gardens became Balcarres Street.

It is possible that Balcarres Street was given its name by Bailie McKenzie, a heating engineer who, with his partner, Mr Moncur, owned much of this part of the old Plewlands estate. McKenzie had built Appin Terrace in Edinburgh, naming it after his birthplace in Fife. He may have named Balcarres Street after Balcarres House, a notable residence in Fife with which he also had connections.

For some time before building extended beyond what is now 36 Balcarres Street, the road was a *cul-de-sac*, sealed off by a

The village blacksmith! Iain Thomson, blacksmith at the long-established 'shop' in Balcarres Street. The forge, anvil and the skilled touch are still basic requirements. *Photograph by W. R. Smith.*

wall of railway sleepers. Beyond were the pleasant lower slopes of Plewlands farm and the Craighouse estate. In this area a nine-hole golf course was laid out and here two young Morningside residents who were to earn a place amongst the world's most celebrated golfers first learned the royal and ancient game. These were Tommy Armour and Bobby Cruickshank.

Tommy Armour's family lived in a cottage within the Craighouse grounds, his father being on the maintenance staff of the asylum. Born in Edinburgh in 1896, Armour's early promise first became obvious when, at the age of fourteen, he played with his brother Sandy in the winning team of the Edinburgh Western Club's Dispatch Trophy contests. His subsequent achievements are legendary. He was a member of the British Walker Cup team in 1922. After leaving for the United States in 1926 and becoming an American citizen, he was in the American Ryder Cup team that same year. He went

on to win the United States Open Championship in 1927, the
P.G.A. Tournament in 1930 and the British Open Championship in 1931 – three of the world's four supreme golfing
accolades. Tommy Armour was also the author of several best-
selling books on golf. When his playing days were over he
turned to coaching in Florida, his pupils including USA
President Richard M. Nixon and many millionaires. Armour
was the first recipient of the Frank Moran Trophy awarded
annually to a Scot who has gained golfing distinction. His son
became a leading surgeon in the United States and his grandson
a professional golfer who has taken part in a number of British
tournaments in recent years.

Bobby Cruickshank, born at Grantown-on-Spey, also played
his early golf at the short Balcarres Street course. A prisoner of
war during the First World War, he later became a professional
golfer and also went to the United States, where he was regarded
as one of that country's best professionals in the 1920s and 30s.
On account of the brilliance of Bobby Jones, Cruickshank found
himself runner-up in many a championship he might otherwise
have won. While his achievements were not so numerous or
spectacular as Tommy Armour's, Cruickshank nevertheless
became one of the world's most celebrated golfers.

Morningside Cemetery, opened in 1878 and orginally entered
by an impressive gateway at Belhaven Terrace, closed some
years ago when modern houses were built within the cemetery
precincts, is now entered some distance up Morningside Drive
on its north side. The cemetery is the resting place of many
famous and interesting people amongst the humbler folk of
Morningside and others from outside the district. It is perhaps
not widely known that a memorial to all those from Morningside
who died in the First World War is here. Nearby is a quite
considerable area of ground devoid of any headstones to mark
the graves of innumerable people who died in the City
Poorhouse at Greenbank, the Edinburgh Asylum as it was then
known, off Morningside Park, and for a brief period from the
old Royal Infirmary at Infirmary Street.

In 1981, Mrs Sheila Durham of Comiston Drive, who had

Alexander Low Bruce, married Agnes, daughter of the famous explorer, Dr David Livingstone, also commemorated on the stone. Bruce, a director of Younger's brewery at Holyrood, was instrumental in persuading Louis Pasteur to attend Edinburgh University's tercentenary celebrations in 1884. The famous French scientist's meeting with Low influenced him to bequeath money to help found the Usher Institute of Public Health, originally in Warrender Park Road. *Photograph by W. R. Smith.*

carried out much personal research with a team of members of the Morningside Association made a detailed survey of the monumental inscriptions in Morningside Cemetery. This considerable piece of valuable genealogical research, published and lodged in the National Library of Scotland and in the Edinburgh Central Library, lists all headstones of between 1878 and 1981. These are indexed and classified according to qualifications, occupations, type of headstones etc. This is the most significant work of its kind since the classical study of certain famous Edinburgh graveyards by William Pitcairn Anderson many years ago.

IN MEMORIAM
THOMAS EDWARD CARLYLE
BORN 2 JUNE 1880
DIED 17 DECEMBER 1903
OLIVER CARLYLE
BORN 27 NOVEMBER 1881
DIED 31 MAY 1929
LILIAS MacVICAR
SECOND WIFE OF ALEXANDER CARLYLE
BORN 21 JANUARY 1854
DIED 24 FEBRUARY 1929
ALSO THE SAID
ALEXANDER CARLYLE
BORN 29 APRIL 1843
DIED 30 NOVEMBER 1931

MARY CARLYLE AITKEN
FIRST WIFE OF ALEXANDER CARLYLE
AND MOTHER OF THE ABOVE
THOMAS EDWARD AND OLIVER CARLYLE
BORN 20 APRIL 1848
DIED 30 MAY 1895
SHE LIES BURIED WITH HER KINDRED
IN ST. MARY'S CHURCHYARD DUMFRIES

UNTIL THE DAY DAWN

The Carlyle grave. *Photograph by W. R. Smith.*

On one gravestone, simple but significant words recall 'Cummy', Alison Cunningham, the 'dear old nurse' of Robert

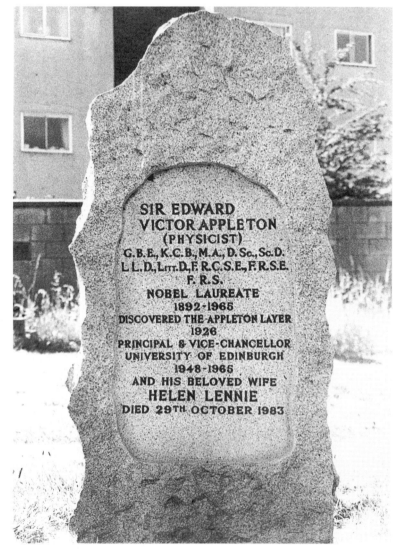

Sir Edward Appleton, one of the world's greatest scientists of recent times. *Photograph by W. R. Smith.*

'Cummy' — Alison Cunningham, Robert Louis Stevenson's beloved childhood nurse, in her home after he and she had left Swanston Cottage. 'Her laddie's' picture is just visible on left. *Edinburgh City Museums*.

Louis Stevenson's early childhood, of his sleepless, illness-plagued nights at Heriot Row, and his dear friend until his death far from Scotland. Miss Cunningham spent the evening of her life in Morningside, leaving Swanston Cottage when Stevenson had finally set out for the South Seas in 1880, where he spent the remainder of his life after his marriage in the United States. She resided for some years alone at No. 23 Balcarres Street and then, requiring some attention and companionship, went to live with her maternal cousin, Mrs Murdoch, at No. 1 Comiston Place. Here she died in her ninety-second year. Only Cummy's relatives and members of the Stevenson family attended her funeral to Morningside Cemetery and the only floral tribute placed on her grave was a posy of wild flowers from Swanston.

Part of the open area beside what for long has been a city refuse depot, situated here beside the old suburban railway line to permit transport of material, was the site of the busy Buchan family dairy farm. Mrs Elizabeth Notman, who still resides in Balcarres Street not far from the little farm where she worked as a girl, recalled its early beginnings. Her grandparents had come to Edinburgh from Freuchie in Fife in the late 1800s, living first at Gorgie. It was her grandmother, Helen Buchan, who saw the advert for tenancy of the little farm and who was most anxious to acquire it. This she did and the family moved to the farmhouse, No. 36 Balcarres Street, still to be seen. Her first cow cost £10!

While Mrs Notman's grandfather continued his trade as a stonemason, her grandmother ran the dairy, enlisting the help of her own family and her grandchildren. Mrs Norman herself was born in a cottage on the old Plewlands farmland, opposite where she lives today. She acted as cowherd, taking the cows in summer to pasture on the Plewlands fields. There could be as many as 36 cows. Herding them was not always without incident when occasionally a cow would break off and enter a tenement stair, climbing to the top flat. There were byres and stables reached through a pend which still remains beside No. 36 Balcarres Street. There were dairies in Comiston Road and

Mrs Helen Buchan, who started the family dairy farm at 36 Balcarres Street just before 1900 and worked there till the farmhouse was taken over by the city authorities in 1921. *By courtesy of her grand-daughter, Mrs Elizabeth Notman.*

Millar Crescent. Milk was delivered in the Morningside district in metal pitchers. Mrs Helen Buchan who had started it all died in 1921 but the remaining family kept the farm going. In 1968, Edinburgh Corporation withdrew the tenancy of the farmhouse and occupancy was given to a refuse department official. Thus came to an end the Buchan farm which for over 80 years had brought something of country life into Balcarres Street.

Morningside Drive, immediately south of Belhaven Terrace and originally named South Morningside Drive, leads into a district with a variety of fine houses. At the beginning of the south side of Morningside Drive is Dunedin Hall, now the well-appointed premises of the Masonic Lodge Dunedin. Built soon after the feuing of the Plewlands estate began in 1882, this ornate red sandstone building was originally known as Morningside Hall or simply 'The Hall'. In addition to being used for social events in winter, it was also the meeting place of at least two embryonic church congregations. The pioneers of South Morningside Free Church, later built in Braid Road, first met here in 1889, while in 1893 Episcopalians from south of the Suburban Railway, outwith the parish bounds of Christ Church (Scottish Episcopalian) at Holy Corner, held their first meeting here.

The hall later served the social needs of many Morningside organisations. For a period it was the property of the Morningside Unionist Club. In 1926 it was purchased by the Lodge Dunedin, which had originally met in a warehouse in Clyde Street and later in the hall of the Lodge Abbotsford at Churchhill. What had been known from its establishment as Morningside Hall then came to be known as Dunedin Hall.

A feature of Morningside Drive is its stately procession of venerable trees growing up through the narrow pavement on the north side. Morningside Recreational Park entered on the right half-way up the street just where the trees end, and extending down to Balcarres Street, was opened in 1913. The park was laid out on land once part of Plewlands farm, the ruins of which remained close by until the 1920s. For long the park was very popular with children and young people. In addition to its tennis courts, the bowling green was particularly popular and most evenings and weekends was crowded. In recent years the park has become run down and not so attractive. As a result of the dedicated interest and efforts of the Morningside Association, £7,000 was raised by many enterprises. The remainder of the cost of refurbishing has been met by the Edinburgh District Council Recreation Department. The latest safety playing surfacing has been installed. After a survey conducted by the Morningside Community Council it was found that there was no significant demand by local people for the restoration of the former bowling green. Very many people now belong to private clubs.

A short distance uphill on the west side of Morningside Grove, on the site of the semi-detached villas between 28 and 38 Morningside Grove, once stood an impressive five-storey building, the Morningside Hydropathic. It is shown as already in existence in the Plewlands feuing plan of 1882 although the precise date of its establishment is not on record. Surrounded by thirteen acres of pleasant grounds, the Hydropathic was built at a cost of £20,000. It had over one hundred bedrooms and one of its corridors was a hundred and forty feet long by twelve feet wide. An attractive feature of the establishment was its heated indoor swimming pool.

As a result of much research by Mr I. Beveridge, it has been established that once completed, Morningside Hydropathic never in fact opened as such. Morningside College was able to obtain early occupation.

By early 1882 the Morningside Hydropathic had closed, re-opening later that year, after alterations, as the well-appointed Morningside College (or Academy) for Boys. The windows in the long corridor had stained-glass panes depicting the College arms, those of the City of Edinburgh and various Scottish symbols. Cricket and football pitches, tennis courts and a cycling track were laid out in the extensive grounds. All resident masters were either Oxford or Cambridge Honours graduates. The course of studies was wide, ranging from the classics to carpentry and metalwork, and scholarships were available to both residential and day pupils. The College moved in 1889 to Rockville in Napier Road and later to Falcon Hall. A considerable amount of information regarding Morningside College is on file in the Edinburgh Room of the Central Public Library.

This removal proved fortuitous for the development of one of the city's great hospitals — the Edinburgh Royal Hospital for Sick Children. In 1848 two Edinburgh doctors, Dr Charles Wilson and the famous Dr Henry Littlejohn (14 years later Edinburgh's first Medical Officer of Health) visited Paris, where they were most impressed by *L'Hôpital des Enfants Malades*, the first hospital in the world to be devoted entirely to children, established in 1802. After visiting various other European capitals to study similar hospitals, they returned to Edinburgh and campaigned for the foundation of a children's hospital here. The need was certainly great. In 1860 the first Sick Children's Hospital was opened in a house at 7 Lauriston Lane (now Lauriston Terrace), immediately beyond what became the mortuary of the Edinburgh Royal Infirmary.

In 1865 Dr Henry Littlejohn published a report on the health of Edinburgh's population for the year 1863. The census of 1861 had recorded the population as numbering 170,444. In 1863 the total number of deaths in the city was 4,412, including 2,010 children under the age of ten years. Children's deaths thus accounted for 45.5 per cent of the death rate, and just under half of the children who died were under one year.

Such children as were hospitalised were admitted to Edinburgh's only such establishment in the mid-nineteenth century, the old Royal Infirmary in Infirmary Street. The opening of the little hospital in Lauriston Lane was a beginning, but the need for increased facilities was urgent. Amongst those who supported Dr Henry Littlejohn's campaign was Charles Dickens, who had written much in support of proper medical care for children. In 1857, speaking at a dinner in London in aid of funds for the Sick Children's Hospital in Great Ormond Street, Dickens described a pathetic scene he had witnessed in one of Edinburgh's congested, overcrowded closes: a sick child lying in an old wooden egg box. The famous novelist wrote in 1864: 'We want to move Johnny to a place where there are none but children; where the good doctors and nurses pass their lives with children, talk to none but children, touch none but children.' This was also the plea of the pioneers of Edinburgh's Sick Children's Hospital.

Eventually it became impossible to deal with the vast number of children suffering from infectious diseases. A much larger building was acquired — the four-storey Meadowside House at the foot of Lauriston Lane, facing southwards across the Meadows.

In 1890 there was an outbreak of typhoid fever amongst the children in Meadowside House and it was decided to evacuate and demolish this building and erect a new children's hospital on the same site. Temporary premises had to be found. The annals of the hospital record: 'A conveniently sized building was found in the Morningside Academy. The Sick Children's Hospital was transferred to it in 1890. The annual rent was £500 and the building was re-named Plewlands House.'

The Sick Children's Hospital was to remain within the precincts of Morningside for five years. The present-day Royal Hospital for Sick Children in Sciennes Road was opened in October 1895, at a cost of £40,000. The architect was George Washington Browne.

While it was temporarily located at Plewlands House, the name most closely associated with the Sick Children's Hospital was its first Ordinary Surgeon, Dr Joseph Bell, great-grandson of Dr Benjamin Bell. One of Edinburgh's earliest and most distinguished surgeons, and one of Professor James Symes's 'two bright boys', Dr Joseph Bell was also perhaps the source of a wider fame. He is traditionally believed to have been the prototype for Conan Doyle's immortal detective, Sherlock Holmes. Conan Doyle had studied medicine in Edinburgh under Dr Bell, for whom he developed a deep admiration. It was the surgeon's great gift of quick perception and rapid deductive reasoning, displayed in the diagnosis of cases, which, it was believed, was the inspiration for Sherlock Holmes.

Whether or not Dr Joseph Bell was the prototype of Conan Doyle's Sherlock Holmes there was certainly a similarity in their acute powers of observation. An example of this was Bell's keen perception of the fact that often children under his care in the Plewlands House wards when suffering from certain enteric conditions seemed to have a desire to eat green mouldy cheese — a very early anticipation of Sir Alexander Fleming's discovery of the fungus penicillin's antibiotic effect. Dr Joseph Bell's arrival each morning at Plewlands House in his horse-drawn Victoria was eagerly awaited: he endeared himself to children and staff alike on account of his great kindness and generosity. A man of deep religious conviction, he also served as a 'father confessor'.

A few years after the departure of the Sick Children's Hospital to its new premises in Sciennes Road in 1895, Plewlands House, which in short succession had housed an intended Hydropathic, an expensive boys' college and one of Edinburgh's great hospitals, was demolished. Much of its stonework was used to build the villas between 28 and 38 Morningside Grove which now occupy its site.

Craighouse

At the top of Morningside Drive, Craighouse Road turns northwards. On the left are the venerable stone pillars at the entrance to the driveway leading up to the ancient mansion of Craighouse. The great avenue of trees which once enhanced the approach has largely gone. Behind the sixteenth-century mansion-house, now known as Old Craig, on the slopes of Easter Craiglockhart Hill, towers the administrative block of this part of the Royal Edinburgh Hospital, one of the great landmarks of Edinburgh when approaching from the north-west.

The lands of Craighouse appear in the Scottish Records as early as the reign of David II. There is some evidence that they belonged to the Abbey of Newbattle, as there is a charter by Edward, 'Abbot of Newbottle', dated 1528, which refers to a land transaction with Hugh Douglas, burgess of Edinburgh,

Dr Joseph Bell, visiting surgeon at The Royal Hospital for Sick Children, while temporarily at Plewlands House. Dr Bell, with keen powers of diagnostic observation, is said to have been the prototype of medical student Conan Doyle's Sherlock Holmes.

and Mariota Brown, spouse, who owned the 'lands commonly called Craighouse, between the lands of the Laird of Braid called the Plewlands . . .'

As several other ancient mansion-houses on the Burgh Muir still remain, restored and serving modern purposes, so too does Craighouse. Bruntsfield House, the old Whitehouse and Merchiston Tower have been integrated into modern educational establishments; the Old Craig has provided comfortable accommodation for patients of the Royal Edinburgh Hospital, at the Thomas Clouston Clinic.

MacGibbon and Ross, in *Castellated and Domestic Architecture of Scotland*, describe the architecture 'of this old-fashioned mansion-house' and provide a sketch plan indicating its two portions, one nearly 150 years older than the other. The original portion is a long narrow structure, approximately 72 by 26 feet, which faces south. It has a projecting tower near its west end, at the base of which is the entrance doorway and a wheel-staircase leading to the first and second floors. Because of the peculiar position of the tower, MacGibbon and Ross found it difficult to decide whether the house had been built to an 'L' or 'T' plan. In this original part of the mansion-house, the whole ground floor is vaulted. The kitchen is at the west end, well illuminated by two large windows. There is also a cellar with small windows or slits. In certain sections of the vaulted ground floor the walls are ten feet thick. Much of the original corbie-stepped gabling has been rendered flat during repairs and restorations.

Visitors to the Old Craig may pause at the old doorway which gives entrance to the wheel-stair. On the stone lintel above the door are carved the initials, 'L.S. C.P. 1565'. These are of Laurence Symson (or Simpson) and his wife Catherine Pringle who came to reside at the old mansion at this date. It seems from records that they may possibly have inherited or purchased the house from their parents or grandparents, which suggests that it was built prior to 1565.

Much has been written about Craighouse and its successive

owners or tenants, of which a great deal appears more legendary and romantic than factual, including the ghostly green lady.

In 1861 Craighouse came to be associated with two of Scotland's most distinguished historians. In that year Dr John Hill Burton presented to his wife, Katherine Innes, as a birthday present, the keys of the dream home of her childhood, the old mansion of Craighouse. Katherine Innes was the daughter of Professor Cosmo Innes, one of the great source writers of Scottish history.

Dr Hill Burton was a native of Aberdeen who, after graduating at Marischal College, took up law and became an advocate. Seeing little prospect of progress in this profession, he turned to the study of history and political economy. Best known for his standard work on Scottish history, written at Craighouse, he also wrote lives of David Hume, Lord Lovat and Duncan Forbes of Culloden. He was appointed the Queen's Historiographer Royal for Scotland.

Burton wrote much of his own work at Craighouse and was also visited there by many other writers seeking advice. One of these was Captain Speke, who, while a guest at Craighouse, worked on the outline of *The Discovery of the Source of the Nile*.

The library which Burton built up at Craighouse numbered some ten thousand volumes, for which he himself constructed all the shelving. One of many anecdotes concerning the historian related that, so well was his library organised, he could find any book within minutes, even in the dark.

Dr Hill Burton, during his 17 years at Craighouse, became a well-known 'character' in Morningside, seen walking daily to the offices of the Prison Board in George Street, of which he was a member. One Morningside resident recalled that he was 'a bent figure clad in rusty black, his large pockets stuffed with books and papers'. Burton's son William was also well known in the district. Familiarly referred to as 'Little Willie Burton', he had long flaxen hair falling over his shoulders. He travelled to and from Craighouse in a carriage drawn by a very small pony,

Dr John Hill Burton, a noted Scottish author, the last private tenant of Old Craig, 1861–78. His library there housed 10,000 books. Here he is adding to them from the one-time old bookshop beside Greyfriars Bobby on George IV Bridge. *Portrait by W. B. Hole.*

driven by his sister Mattie. William Burton eventually became a consultant engineer to the Japanese government and died in Japan. He was said to have contributed considerably to the technical skill of the Japanese.

The advent of a new era brough Dr Hill Burton's attachment to Craighouse to a deeply regretted end. The old mansion-house and surrounding estate was sold in 1878 to the Commissioners of the Edinburgh Lunatic Asylum, who planned to develop the slopes of Craighouse Hill. Burton's tenancy ended suddenly, and, it seems, unexpectedly. The distinguished historian moved to Morton House in the village of Winton near Fairmilehead, where he died in 1881.

Morningside's tradition of attracting historians to its quiet seclusion was to continue into recent times. Professor P. Hume Brown, Queen's Historiographer Royal for Scotland, lived at Corrennie Gardens, while, until his death in 1958, Dr Henry Meikle, Historiographer Royal for 18 years, also resided in Morningside.

The man responsible for Dr Hill Burton's departure from Craighouse was Dr (later Sir) Thomas Clouston, who has a prominent place in the annals of the study and treatment of mental disorders. He was appointed Physician Superintendent of the Edinburgh Asylum at Morningside Park in 1873 and held the office for 35 years. Five years after his appointment he became disturbed by the inadequate facilities offered at East House and West House and turned his eyes towards the 60 acres of pleasant woodland on Craighouse Hill. He eventually persuaded the Board of Directors to purchase the property, which he described as being 'on the most beautiful site in Edinburgh', and, with the help of an architect patient prepared sketch plans from which Sydney Mitchell, the architect eventually engaged, created the massive complex that came to be known as Craighouse Asylum.

Before completing his plans, Dr Clouston had toured the United States and Europe to study the design of similar institutions in those countries. The foundation stone of the administrative block of Craighouse Asylum was laid by the 10th Earl of Stair, the Deputy Governor, on 16 July 1890, and new premises were opened by the Duke of Buccleuch, the Governor, on 26 October 1894. The total cost of the buildings, which offered unique facilities, was more than £150,000, considered a large sum at that time.

As a result of his study tour Dr Clouston had decided to plan the new asylum as a series of separate villas: Queen's Craig, East and South Craig, Bevan Villa and the restored mansion-house of Old Craig. From its establishment Craighouse was exclusively for private paying patients. It attempted to offer surroundings of the utmost comfort to patients, who were wealthy and often of aristocratic background. Some paid as much as £1,000 per annum for treatment and accommodation, which frequently included a suite of rooms, with personal servants and a carriage to convey them into the city. Each detached villa was to be a little community. Decor was of the brightest, in conformity with Dr Clouston's often expressed belief that 'Truly the light is sweet'. Sunlight and cheerful colours, he sensibly believed, were therapeutic. The present-day Thomas Clouston Clinic at Craighouse commemorates his long and distinguished direction for over 35 years.

Dominating the skyline above Craighouse, the administrative block, with its great tower, is one of Edinburgh's most prominent and pleasant landmarks. Entering this building, the original grandiose conception of Dr Clouston is sensed immediately. The wide marble staircase seems to lead back to days when life was lived in the grand manner. On the oak-panelled wall above the first steps of the staircase is a carved plaque which fittingly commemorates the man to whose concern and tenacity of purpose the hospital owes its origins, Dr Andrew Duncan. Added to this tribute is one to the generous support of an early patron of the hospital, Elizabeth Bevan, after whom one of the villas is named. On the left at the top of the staircase is the magnificent oak-panelled Grand Hall, in Tudor baronial style, eloquently exemplifying Dr Clouston's grand design. Among the most notable features of the hall are the large canopied twin

Dr Thomas Clouston (left) with his colleague the notable physician, Dr Argyll Robertson.

fireplaces, one of which is surmounted by Dr Andrew Duncan's Coat of Arms and the other by those of Dr Thomas Clouston. Several portraits of those prominent in the history of the hospital include one of Dr Andrew Duncan by a pupil of Sir Henry Raeburn. The fine barrel-vaulted ceiling may be studied more closely from the Minstrel Gallery, from which, in the hospital's earlier days, musicians played during grand balls, graced by the noble surroundings. Orchestral recitals were also once a regular feature of the patients' entertainment. Today the Grand Hall recaptures some of its former atmosphere during the medical staff's annual dinner-dance and the staff-patients' Hallowe'en parties. Adjoining the hall is a very fine drawing-room with period furniture where patients met regularly for group therapy.

Dr Hill Burton, during his long occupancy of Old Craig, firmly believed that part of the house dated back to Roman times. He also noted an underground passage leading from the thick-walled basement and believed that this eventually emerged at Edinburgh Castle. Various opinions as to the ultimate destination of this tunnel were expressed. In fact, foundation excavations many years ago revealed that the tunnel, now largely blocked up, emerged only a short distance from the old mansion-house, in the overgrown northern slope of the grounds. The chronicles of Craighouse have been so colourfully and enthusiastically embroidered with legends that the task of presenting authentic historical fact is no easy one.

The magnificent panoramic view from the Craighouse administrative block tower, encompassing Edinburgh and far beyond, reveals one place in the foreground which merits reference. At the foot of the north-east slope of the hill, just beyond the point where the railway lines are bridged by Myreside Road and just within the boundary wall of the Royal Edinburgh Hospital, was the ancient village of Myreside, the name of which was derived from the considerable expanse of marshland which in early centuries existed at this western fringe of the Burgh Muir. It is in this once waterlogged area that, as already related, the Jordan Burn has its origin. Myreside Cottage, the last remains of the old village, became the property of the Royal Edinburgh Hospital in the 1860s and was used as a hospital annexe until its destruction by fire a century later.

Greenbank

The top of East Craiglockhart Hill (or Craighouse Hill) above the fine buildings of the Royal Edinburgh Hospital is a convenient and indeed picturesque setting from which to view the southerly districts of Greenbank, Comiston, Oxgangs, Firrhill and finally towards Swanston and Robert Louis Stevenson's beloved 'Hills of Home'.

If nearmost Greenbank may seem on the fringes of Morningside nevertheless some mention may be made of it, for here were established two of Morningside's important 'institutions', built out here purposely when the area was remote from the city and surrounded by pleasant farmland.

In the mid distance there still remains, although recently considerably and impressively altered, interiorly and exteriorly, of the large, sturdy building which for 50 years was the City Poorhouse. Prior to 1870 when it was opened, Edinburgh's workhouse straddled what is now Forrest Road from Greyfriars to Bristo Port and the vicinity of Teviot Row. So numerous were the city's paupers that accommodation at the Workhouse was never adequate, nor as might be said, entirely congenial.

The move to a purpose-built Poorhouse at the Greenbank, Craiglockhart site took place in 1870. At first providing for 600 inmates – men, women, children, 'lunatic paupers' and destitute sick, this was a mere fraction of the 3,454 people who had applied for admission. By 1894, there were 950 inmates, thus so coldly described. Males and females were strictly segregated and further divisions were made based on 'good character', 'dissolute', 'doubtful' etc. . .

The institution operated on the motto proclaimed by the builder, George Beattie: 'Comfort for the Poor and care for the Ratepayer'. The régime was strict, almost prison-like. Many inmates who had once lived, however poorly, in the bustle of the old town found the remoteness intolerable. Many absconded back to the poverty but congeniality of their former haunts. Should they be compelled by circumstances to return to the poorhouse, they were punished by reduced food and other

The City Poorhouse main building of 1870. After successive changes and improvements it finally became Greenlea Old People's Home. The buildings were sold in 1987. Amidst a complex of modern flats this original building, impressively modernised, remains the centrepiece. *Photograph by W. R. Smith.*

amenities and confined strictly to the premises.

It was an era immortalised by the pen of Charles Dickens. Prevalent philosophies portrayed the poor as having earned the displeasure of God by their sloth, crime and other faults. To be comfortably off and secure was a sign of God's blessing. At any rate the way of life at the poorhouse continued for many decades until new ideas prevailed and conditions became more humanitarian.

The poorhouse had its own infirmary and tuberculosis wards, these buildings being demolished only in recent times. Morningside's more elderly residents will remember 'the men from the poorhouse' coming into the district with their hand carts selling firewood which they had chopped up in the poorhouse grounds. They wore the characteristic thick grey herring-bone 'institution suits'. Those who thus supplemented the poorhouse's funds and kept themselves 'usefully occupied' were rewarded with extra tobacco and other 'perks'.

In 1944 after the passing of the National Assistance Act, reflecting changes in social philosophy and social care, poorhouses were of course no longer designated as such, and their grim days were but a memory; a new era had begun.

After the Second World War the former City Poorhouse, much refurbished, became Glenlockhart Old People's Home, although the old structure still remained with large hospital-style dormitories, considered unsuitable. Further improvements were made and in the 1960s when the Home was renamed Greenlea. In 1987 Greenlea closed and in accordance with new social work policy, residents were transferred to various purpose-built homes in the city. The modern well-appointed 'Oaklands' in Canaan Lane in Morningside is a fine example of modern provision. After the closure of Greenlea in 1987 an exhibition was held in the premises which included relics and reminders of the grim life once endured by many in the City Poorhouse.

The City Hospital

Just across the last stretch of Greenbank Drive and facing the former City Poorhouse of 1870 is the spacious red sandstone complex of the City Hospital built just over 30 years later. Originally the City Fever Hospital, opened in May 1903, its eventual establishment signified the triumph of a long hard campaign by two prominent men to see proper provision made for the very large number of cases of various and serious infectious diseases which frequently ravaged the city, and affected children in epidemic severity. The two men of foresight and dedication were Dr Henry Littlejohn and Bailie James Pollard. Littlejohn was appointed Edinburgh's first Medical Officer of Health in 1862, and held the post for 50 years. During that period, through his dedication and great ability the state of Edinburgh's public health improved most dramatically. Dr Littlejohn's ardent supporter in the city's political area was Bailie Pollard, an orphan from a very poor social background who, possibly from his own experience, had seen the need for a proper fever hospital. Pollard, when Chairman of the city's

Dr Henry Littlejohn, Edinburgh's famous first Medical Officer of Health, who campaigned for a purpose-built fever hospital. *From John Comrie's* 'History of Scottish Medicine'.

Public Health Committee, had favoured the building of the new hospital in Drummond Street on the site of the former Royal Infirmary, but after studying fever hospitals abroad and through the influence of Dr Littlejohn, he was persuaded to support the Greenbank site.

In the sixteenth and seventeenth centuries, the countless people in Edinburgh who fell victims to the plague or 'Black Death', mostly fatally, were quarantined in primitive wooden huts out on the remote, desolate Burgh Muir where the Astley Ainslie Hospital stands today. In later times, other 'plagues' such as smallpox, typhus fever, cholera, typhoid and scarlet fevers, along with diphtheria and venereal disease were at first isolated and treated in the first Royal Infirmary at Infirmary Street, and when the Infirmary moved to Lauriston, admitted there, but especially to the city's first Fever Hospital in part of the vacated buildings at Drummond Street. Children were amongst these many admissions.

In these early hospitals, on account of the large number of cases requiring admission, facilities became quite inadequate. Further, before the historic discovery of bacteria by Louis Pasteur as the cause of infectious disease, treatment had been rudimentary and often ineffective. By the end of the nineteenth century the need for a proper and large fever hospital was urgent as also was the need for the training of doctors and nurses in the new understanding of disease.

At last, after many controversies concerning a suitable site, many people, including doctors, feared that a large fever hospital built at Drummond Street in the heart of the city could be the source of bacteria escaping into the atmosphere etc., the proposal of Dr Henry Littlejohn and Bailie Pollard for a new purpose-built hospital outwith the city was approved. Colinton Mains farm of 72 acres was purchased for £20,000 and the great new City Hospital (or Colinton Hospital as it was alternatively known), designed by Robert Morham, the City Architect, arose.

The plan by Morham shows the symmetry of the hospital, the unity of the plan, a tower above the entrance at Greenbank Drive that was never built, and the large nurses' home in the foreground providing separate bedrooms for 150 nurses. Something of the then only partially built Morningside may be seen and opposite, the buildings of the City Poorhouse. While access to the new hospital could have been available part of the way, using the Poorhouse Drive from Comiston Road, the management committee regarded this route as having a social stigma attached to it and insisted that the separate Greenbank Drive be built.

The buildings were of a warm red sandstone. The wards, peninsular in shape and running north and south were designed so to ensure maximum sunshine. Toilets were at the south ends to attract sunlight for hygienic reasons. An early report stated: 'There are no buildings of any kind at present to intercept the space between the grounds and the Pentland Hills. Great stress was placed on fresh air. There was for long an avenue of pine trees, thought to provide a health-promoting walk for those with chest diseases'.

The very impressively designed wards were to allow for the admission of 750 patients. It was estimated that the number of infectious diseases cases in the city at any given time averaged 600. The wards were allocated and designated for the various types of cases e.g., 7 large two-storey wards for the then almost endemic scarlet fever; 4 wards for diphtheria; and others according to the estimated admissions for typhoid and other enteric diseases; erisipelas; measles; whooping cough etc. . . The estimated admissions were mostly accurate. The wards were normally full. At times during epidemics they were over-crowded. There were special wards for tuberculosis; small cottage-like units for the isolation of dangerous infectious cases; and during smallpox outbreaks, wooden pavilions were built on the lower slope of West Craiglockhart Hill rising above the hospital and these were often burned down after an outbreak had ceased.

The great new City Fever Hospital, built at a cost of £350,000 and one of the best of its kind in Britain, was officially opened on 3 May 1903 by King Edward VII accompanied by Queen Alexandra. From Tollcross out to Morningside grandstands were erected to enable the great crowds to glimpse the Royal carriage on its drive out to Greenbank. Comiston Road witnessed a great mass of Morningside people who were much aware of the great event about to take place on the fringes of the district. One anecdote of the occasion has been passed down. It was a memorable scene outside the new Fever Hospital main entrance, watched from the grandstands. The cavalcade of Life Guards which had escorted the Royal Procession southwards was drawn up outside the gates. The platform reception party, which would certainly have included Dr Henry Littlejohn witnessing his dream become reality, was led by Lord Provost James Steel. Steel was noted for his broad Scots tongue. Reputedly when the great moment was reached and Steel presented Edward VII with the golden key to ceremonially open the main doorway, there was a slight hesitation as regards who should enter first. The king invited the Lord Provost to precede him. Steel deferred to His Majesty. The delay might have been prolonged until James Steel was heard to say to Edward: 'Hoots, man, we'll baith gang in thegither!'

The City Fever Hospital was to continue admitting, isolating and treating a high and constant level of cases for many years after its opening. On account of its deliberate remoteness from the city, relatives of patients who did not have telephones and did not always find it easy to come out by tramcar then had a special hospital bus along Greenbank Drive. Many people may still remember the communications system by which in the *Edinburgh Evening News* and *Evening Dispatch*, there was a small boxed notice giving the allocated hospital reference numbers of the patients and wording such as 'Critically ill: relatives please come out': 'Seriously ill: no immediate danger'; or 'Ill: making satisfactory progress'. Many children with various infections could not be visited but were only allowed to be seen through the ward's glass doors.

Over the years as a result of better housing and improved social conditions and the advent of antibiotics etc., the whole scene has changed dramatically. For long, the one-time Fever Hospital has simply become the City Hospital, still specialising in chest infections but now with a wide range of other admissions. In 1991, despite much local opposition by residents in the vicinity of the City Hospital, apprehensive concerning the possible leakage of infection from the premises, the Milestone House for the care of HIV/AIDS patients was opened within the hospital complex.

While some reference to the former City Poorhouse and the City Hospital at Greenbank seemed relevant to the history of Morningside, space prevents a comprehensive study of this pleasant district. However, two other features merit inclusion.

Greenbank Parish Church

For many people resident in the district and indeed beyond, Greenbank Parish Church is the focal point of their worship and fellowship. Such it has been for just over 90 years.

One of Morningside's more modern churches, its opening in October 1927 signified the steady expansion of Morningside to the south. While St Matthew's Parish Church was originally an extension of Morningside Parish Church at the corner of Newbattle Terrace, the establishment of the original Greenbank United Presbyterian Church was fostered by Braid Church which was of the same denomination. The first worshippers met in the hall, opened on 13 May 1900. In July of that year the 35 Greenbank members were formally declared a congregation. The first Kirk Session included Joseph Bennet and William Forrest, two elders from Braid Church who had been appointed to take charge and act as founder elders of Greenbank. Two years after the union of the United Presbyterian Church and the Free Church of Scotland in 1900, the Reverend Norman Fraser, BD of Hamilton was appointed the first minister of Greenbank United Free Church. Under his charge the congregation steadily increased until his departure for Liverpool in 1913.

In January 1914 the new minister inducted was the Rev. T. Ratcliffe Barnett, called from St Andrew's Church, Bo'ness. Dr Barnett was to earn a high reputation not only as a powerful preacher and devoted parish minister but also as a distinguished and prolific author of a long series of scholarly and entertaining books on various parts of Scotland, from the Borders to the

Greenbank Parish Church. Its original establishment as Greenbank United Free Presbyterian Church in 1900, fostered by Braid Church, then of the same denomination, signified the steady growth of Morningside to the south. The present church opened in October 1927 under the ministry of the notable Dr Ratcliffe Barnett, at a cost of £518,000. The architect was Lorne Campbell. *By courtesy of Greenbank Parish Church.*

Western Isles. He was awarded a Doctor of Philosophy degree by Edinburgh University. Soon after his appointment, Dr Barnett began pressing for the building of a church. The Great War, however, intervened. During the war years and in the period immediately afterwards, the congregation contributed to a building fund and, when the foundation stone was laid on 24 April 1926, £11,000 was already available. The final cost of the church was £18,000, the additional amount being raised by further generous gifts. The architect, Lorne Campbell, designed the church in simple style but with an impressive dignity. Seating was for 600. The opening service of dedication took place on 8 October 1927.

After a ministry of nearly 25 years, Dr Ratcliffe Barnett resigned in 1938 to make way for a younger successor. He died in 1946. Under his vigorous pastoral ministry, the original congregation of 35 in 1900 had become 800.

Perhaps it is not so widely known as it should be that the important Princess Margaret Rose Orthopaedic Hospital at Fairmilehead was opened very much through the tireless efforts of Dr T. Ratcliffe Barnett, who, despite his very busy ministry at Greenbank and his prodigious publication of books, still found time one evening per week to assist in a club for crippled young people in George Street. As a result of his effective efforts in fund raising, in 1933 'The Edinburgh Hospital for Crippled Children' was opened, later to become the 'PMR' so widely known today and now caring for adult cases. The man who had shared Barnett's aim from an early stage and collaborated in his efforts, also becoming the original hospital's first surgeon, was Mr William A. Cochrane, FRCS (Edin.).

Another notable name in the succession of ministers of Greenbank Church is the Rev. David Reid who was mobilised as a chaplain in the Second World War almost immediately after his call to Greenbank. After being a prisoner in Germany for five years, he returned to his ministry at Greenbank in September 1945, where one of the first of his many enterprises was the foundation of 'Quest', a challenging and stimulating organisation for the young people of the parish, inspired by a discussion group he had formed in the German prisoner-of-war camp. The well-presented annual Quest entertainments in the Churchill Theatre drew large audiences. The organisation has inspired a wide variety of service by its young members. The Rev. David Reid left Greenbank in 1949 to become Chaplain at Edinburgh University, and a few years later he became minister of the notable Madison Avenue Presbyterian Church in New York.

The Rev. Donald G. M. Mackay who was called to Greenbank in 1950 served until his retirement in 1982. Sadly for so many people to whom he had endeared himself, the Rev. Donald Mackay died on 26 July 1991.

A native of Glasgow, Donald Mackay was related to a succession of notable ministers, one of whom, his uncle, was

This photograph of the Greenbank area was taken about 1930, before the bungalows were built. The fields were part of Greenbank Farm. *Photograph by W. R. Smith.*

one of the first to translate the Bible into modern English. A distinguished academic career, including studies in the United States, was followed by an appointment in Glasgow, missionary work in India and service as an army chaplain in India and Burma during the Second World War.

The Rev. Donald Mackay came from Aberdeen to Greenbank in 1950. From the outset he enthused the parish in its worship and service in many spheres, continuing the activities of 'Quest' for some considerable time and establishing much else which gave Greenbank the reputation of being 'one of the liveliest parishes in Edinburgh'. In these days of falling church membership a very large congregation were inspired by his preaching and encouraged by his practical parish ministry. Mr Mackay died soon after he had completed a valuable historical account of the parish. In another earlier publication he described the very fine stained glass in the church. When the

Through the Braidburn Valley to Stevenson's 'Hills of Home' – the Pentland Hills. The open air theatre can be seen *Photograph by W. R. Smith.*

Rev. Donald Mackay retired in 1982, he was succeeded in January 1983 by the Rev. Ian G. Scott, BSc., BD, STM, from Holborn Central Parish Church, Aberdeen.

Braidburn Valley Park

The other most pleasant feature of Greenbank, a quite unique 'green space' and considered to be the common heritage of Morningside is the picturesque Braidburn Valley, extending to 31 acres, purchased by Edinburgh Corporation from the Mortonhall estate in 1937 for the nominal sum of £2,000. It was at once laid out as a public park and the open-air theatre was constructed which could hols an audience of two and a half thousand. The stage on the east bank of the burn is enclosed by trees and a little orchestral pit has been carved out on the water's edge. The floral surround to the steep, tiered auditorium, in the form of a crown to mark the Coronation of 1937, was executed by the late John T. Jeffrey, then City Gardener. In 1935, 400 cherry trees were planted by five thousand Guides, Rangers and Brownies of Edinburgh in honour of the Silver Jubilee of the late King George V. This imaginative project has, now that the trees have reached maturity, provided most pleasant colourful avenues. To mark the completion of the open-air theatre in 1937 a dancing display was given by a thousand school children. The special wooden stage, which was not always used and could be stored in sections was 150 feet long. Occasional performances were held in the theatre, even during the Second World War, but it was not until 1945 that there were regular productions, notably of several Shakespearian plays by the Phillip Barrett Company in June of that year, which series of performances attracted a total audience of ten thousand in one week. Another series in the same year played to twenty thousand people. *Rob Roy* was presented by the Scottish Community Drama Association in July 1946. However, due perhaps to the problem of inclement weather, the use of the open-air theatre gradually declined, although sheepdog trials were occasionally arranged there.

At the time of writing there have been signs of a revived interest in making more use of this beautiful park's facilities, including the open air theatre. During the summer of 1991, Edinburgh District Council provided puppet shows for children on the bank of the Braid Burn.

CHAPTER 9

The Living Past

Over many years much information on Morningside's past has been obtained from the recollections of elderly residents. Indeed such contributions are invaluable in the compilation of local history. In addition new developments take place or research brings further information to light. Such is reason and basis for this chapter.

East Morningside House in Clinton Road has become something of a mecca for Susan Ferrier admirers — and there do seem to be signs of a revived interest in her work. Through the kind hospitality of the present owner members of further education classes have been able to visit the house and see the oak-panelled study in which Susan Ferrier did much of her writing. On certain occasions Dr Margaret Oliver, attired in appropriate costume, plays the part of Susan Ferrier, gives a brief description of the history of the house, reading excerpts from her writings and mounting a small exhibition. A play on the East Morningside author's life written by Morar Kennedy, a cousin of Ludovic Kennedy has been performed at Windsor. In 1984, 160 years after its first publication, Susan Ferrier's second novel *The Inheritance* was reprinted in attractive modern format and with an introduction by Judge James Irvine, an authority on the author.

There are Morningside residents who can still recall the 'dry dairy' which once existed in Jordan Lane on the site of what is now a motor mechanic and repair firm. From about 1890 the dairy was owned and managed by the Paterson family of Jordan Lane. To commemorate this interesting chapter in the annals of Morningside, the grandchildren of the family installed in Cluny Parish Church a stained glass window. The window depicts St Francis, one of the best loved saints of all time, surrounded here

The fine stained glass window installed in Cluny Parish Church in March 1989 to commemorate the Paterson family's 'dry dairy', at one time in Jordan Lane. The theme is St Francis of Assisi surrounded by the various animals that once enjoyed the country amenities of the dairy farm. The window was the gift of the grandchildren. *Courtesy of Mrs M. Dickson.*

by the animals of the dairy — cows, a horse, duck, dog, cat and hen, with the saint himself holding a dove. Legend has it that the birds often gathered to listen to him preaching. Apart from its fine coloured glass, the window has a special lightness and freshness which adds to its attraction. The dedication reads: 'To the Glory of God and in memory of the Paterson family, The Dairy, Jordan Lane, Morningside. Gifted by the Grandchildren. 26th March 1989.'

Turning to Morningside's sporting history, Mr Gilmour Main recalled two once thriving football teams, Morningside Primrose and the Southern Hearts. Due to the kind assistance of Mr J. Chisholm and Mr C. Moar, both former players, I was able to obtain a photograph of the Morningside Victoria football team — 'The Vic', as it was known. Unfortunately the names of all the players could not be recalled except those above, along with Mr J. Moyes, the team treasurer. Mr Moar signed for Leeds United and for some time played for the reserve team. In the days before most players were full-time professionals, Mr Moar travelled to the Leeds game each weekend and returned for work on Monday mornings. There was also the Cluny Rugby Club, playing in the early 1900s, at Myreside, and Salmond's Sons, another early Rugby team which took its name from the Rev. Charles Salmond, first minister of South Morningside Free Church in Braid Road.

Of Morningside's 'characters' of early days Mr Main recalled one whom several other residents I had spoken to had also vaguely remembered, and who is referred to by Mr Andrew Patterson in his article in Volume XXXII the *Book of the Old Edinburgh Club*. This was Theodore Napier, who lived in Merchiston but was regularly to be seen in Morningside. Although an Australian, he habitually wore the full regalia of an eighteenth-century Highland chieftain and was an ardent Jacobite, being a strong upholder of a German prince who claimed descent from the House of Stuart and, therefore, the British throne. At dinners, Mr Napier would give the Jacobite toast, raising his glass across a bowl of water to signify his loyalty to 'the King across the water'. Each year on the anniversary of

Morningside Victoria Football Club – 'the Vic' – around 1940. Mr Cecil Moar, goalkeeper, and Mr S. Chisholm, (3rd from right, centre row) both kindly supplied information about this team and the photograph. Mr James Moyes, a member of the one-time well-known Balcarres Street blacksmith family, club treasurer, on extreme left, back row.

the execution of Mary Queen of Scots at Fotheringhay in 1587, he travelled there to place a wreath at the scene of her death.

Lastly we talked of old street-sellers and their cries, a familiar and tuneful feature of Morningside in times before the present-day roar of traffic. One dealer with a horse and cart – and powerful lungs – proclaimed that he was selling: 'Jeely rhubarb . . . jeely rhubarb! . . . three ha' pence a bunch!' Another, seated on his horse-drawn cart, announced: 'Briquettes! . . . Eglinton briquettes! . . . a shillin' a dozen.' Then there was the rag and bone man, who would arrive with a sack slung over his shoulder and place a large wicker basket on the pavement. He would tunefully announce himself in each street with a few blasts from a bugle. Children seeing his basketful of balloons, cheap toys and imitation canaries on sticks would hurry up their tenement

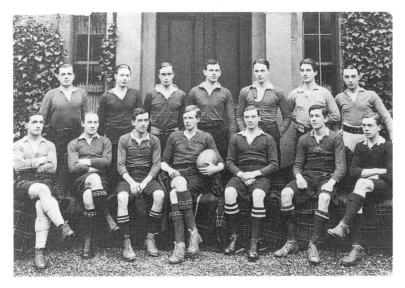

'Cluny Football Fifteen'. A Morningside rugby club that played at Myreside. Photograph dated 1912–13.

stairs and beg their mothers to look out old woollen rags to exchange for these glittering offerings. On Saturdays an old Italian woman with a pony-drawn barrel-organ would visit Morningside; a little monkey performing tricks on top of the organ would be rewarded with titbits from passers-by. The 'Ingin Johnnies' from Brittany were also regular visitors who brought an international dimension to the scene; attired in black berets they had strings of onions draped over their bicycle wheels. The back-green singers were also recalled, and their rendering of songs, often sad, such as 'The Old Rugged Cross'. Their begging eyes would look up to the kitchen windows at the back of the tenements, some of whose residents, either in appreciation or to encourage the singer to move on, would throw down a penny wrapped in newspaper, which was gratefully acknowledged by a glance up to the window and a touch of the singer's hat.

A well-known figure in the Merchiston and Morningside districts was Theodore Napier of West Castle Road. An ardent Jacobite, he made an annual pilgrimage to Fotheringhay, where Mary Queen of Scots was beheaded. Died 1900.
Courtesy Mr Gilmour Main

One of the largest and oldest institutions in Morningside is the Royal Edinburgh Hospital founded over 160 years ago as 'an Asylum for the cure and relief of mental derangement'. In his office off one of the busy main corridors some years ago, I had talked to Dr J. W. Affleck, the late Physician Superintendent. I discussed with Dr Affleck the short note which appeared in a biography of Robert Fergusson, published in 1952 and edited by Sydney Goodsir Smith, in which Dr Chalmers Watson presented a retrospective medical history of the poet. This suggested that Fergusson was a manic depressive and that, had modern treatments been available to him, he would probably have recovered. Dr Affleck felt that, despite the lack of precise case notes available to Dr Chalmers Watson, his observations were probably valid.

In 1990 Dr Alan Beveridge, a psychiatrist at Dunfermline, who has made a special study of Robert Fergusson's life and fatal illness, published a paper throwing new light on the subject. Dr Beveridge with Dr Mike Barfoot, Lothian Health Archivist, also published a paper about a very articulate and notable patient, John Home, who was a patient in the Royal Edinburgh Asylum during 1886–7. The history of the Morningside hospital's treatment of mental illness remains a subject of ongoing study.

When I commented that it was incredible that Dr Andrew Duncan had had to campaign for over thirty years to establish the original asylum, Dr Affleck drew attention to present-day situations in which obviously urgent projects to improve hospital conditions could still be delayed for many years, not only through the lack of financial support but also through having to await the decisions of innumerable committees.

Turning my attention to the 'Land of Canaan', I found a number of links between past and present, and some features of the changing scene which merit comment. Recently in one of the three villas in which Sam Bough resided in Jordan Lane, two important artistic discoveries were made. On the sitting room ceiling, at the intersections of diagonal decorative moulding, the monograms of Sam Bough's and his wife's initials were discovered. On the ceiling itself, after expert stripping of the overlaid paint, artistic work was brought to light. It is hoped that the completion of the treatment of the whole ceiling will be possible. In the back garden of the house a further important 'artistic treasure' was identified. This was a terracotta model by the famous sculptor Roubilliac embedded in a rear wall. Expert study revealed that the sculpture was Roubilliac's rejected proposal for a monument to Henry Petty, 1st Earl of Shelburn (1675–1751). The work is therefore of the mid-eighteenth century. It is not known how it came to be in the garden. It may have been placed there by David R. Hay, a notable artist and 'the first intellectual house-painter' who lived and died in the house in 1866; or the sculpture may have been installed by Sam Bough, the landscape painter, who purchased the house soon after Hay's death. The valuable piece was skilfully removed and is now in the European Art Room in the Royal Museum of Scotland in Chambers Street.

The small area behind the Volunteer Arms between Canaan Lane and Jordan Lane, was in early times known as 'Paradise'. Little information about this area was to be found in booklets or on old maps, but the photograph of the cottages at Paradise in 1865, taken by W. E. Evans and loaned to me by Mr George Anderson, threw valuable new light on this little district and is the only known illustration. The cottages had their own small vegetable gardens known as the 'Kailyards of Paradise', and their owners were known locally as the 'Paradisers'.

On the right, just after entering Canaan Lane, and immediately beyond the entrance to the old police station, is a row of old cottages, the first of which for long had an old metal plate at the corner of its west gable-end bearing the name 'Goshen'. When this disappeared mysteriously some years ago, the only visible reminder to passers-by in Canaan Lane that the tiny district of this name had once existed just eastwards of 'Paradise', Morningside Association, a local organisation with a strong pride in the area's heritage met the cost of a replacement

The Roubilliac sculpture is skilfully removed from the wall in a garden in Jordan Lane. *By courtesy of the Royal Museums of Scotland.*

plaque. Some of the last cottages of Goshen were demolished, making way for a small block of modern flats named 'The Hamlet'.

Immediately beyond these cottages, and just before the tenements on the right, a lane leads up to the tall, austere villa, shown on early maps as Goshen Bank or Goshen House, which presided over the humbler cottages of Goshen. In this house, for a short period from 1868, resided Henry Kingsley, brother of the celebrated Charles, when editor of the *Edinburgh Daily Review*. My nearby neighbour, Mr Wilfred Taylor, *The Scotsman* columnist and an author, received a telephone call, a few years ago, from Professor Stanton Mellick of the Department of Literature at the University of Queensland in Australia, who was writing a biography of Henry Kingsley. When visiting Edinburgh he wished to see and photograph Goshen Bank. Mr Taylor contacted me and I duly met Professor Mellick, to whom I was able to confirm Henry Kingsley's occupation of the house.

Together we studied its exterior, deciding that the best place from which to take a photograph would be one of the rear windows of the tenements on the north side of Jordan Lane. This meant disturbing residents at a relatively early hour, but they were most interested and cooperative. Eventually a suitable window was selected. Thus a living link with Henry Kingsley and Morningside's old Biblical district of Goshen had interestingly arisen from a quite unexpected quarter.

In 1989, Goshen House again became of special interest. The present writer was telephoned by a London newspaper inquiring if he knew the location of Goshen House; could it be photographed; could it be confirmed in Edinburgh's Register House that a certain Reginald Johnston had been born in the house in about 1870; where was the private school nearby, that he had attended, called Falcon Hall? The writer was able to confirm that Reginald Johnston had been born in Goshen Bank House (its proper name) on 31 October 1874, and that Falcon Hall, which had for some time been a school, had stood near Goshen Bank House but had been long since demolished. The reason for the inquiries (soon directed to the writer by several other national newspapers) was that a new film was being completed in Hollywood entitled *The Last Emperor*. It presented the story of the last Boy Emperor of China prior to the communist revolution there. In real life, Reginald Johnston, after a short period at Edinburgh University and the School of Oriental Studies in London, had been appointed tutor to the Boy Emperor and had lived in his palace. He would be portrayed in the film and Peter O'Toole would play the part. In accordance with the practice of certain film producers and principal actors, they had wished to learn as much as possible about Reginald Johnston, especially O'Toole. After his retirement from China, Johnston had bought an island in Loch Craignish, Argyllshire. Here he built himself an impressive house in Chinese style. Here he became ill and was taken to a nursing home in Edinburgh where he died in March 1938.

Pausing at the corner of Canaan Lane and Woodburn Terrace and looking towards the junction of Nile Grove and Braid

Reginald Johnston, who was born in Goshen Bank House in Canaan Lane in 1874, became the tutor to the last Emperor of China. He was portrayed in the film 'The Last Emperor' by the actor Peter O'Toole. Johnston, who as a boy attended the then nearby Falcon Hall school, is seen dressed as he was in China. *Sunday Express Magazine.*

Avenue, it may be recalled that here stood Egypt farm. The name 'Littil Egypt' first appeared in the city records in 1585, and

THERE'S SO MUCH MORE IN TOMORROW'S

News

Weekend

A LEGEND IN DARKEST MORNINGSIDE

A CHINESE legend lurks in darkest Morningside ... and Peter O'Toole plays the man who became tutor, confidant and close friend to the boy emperor in a new film The Last Emperor, which opens with a charity Royal premiere next month. Find out about his fascinating background.

Preview to an article by the author on Reginald Johnston which appeared in the Edinburgh *Evening News*. *Edinburgh Evening News*.

it seems that a gypsy colony once existed here. During a visit to Kirk Yetholm in the Borders (from early times the gypsies' 'capital' in Scotland), where there is still a house known as the Gipsy Palace, I obtained some interesting information about Scottish gypsies of more recent days. I met Mr Gordon Townsend, Squadron Leader, RAF (retired), proprietor of the Border Hotel, who directed me to a local joiner's shop where the owner was in the process of re-framing two old photographs

Morningside's latest house nameplate in Canaan Lane to commemorate the district nearby once known as 'Littil Egypt'. *Photograph by W. R. Smith.*

for the hotel. One was of Charles Faa Blyth, the Gypsy King, taken at his coronation in Kirk Yetholm in 1898; the other showed the coronation of the Gypsy Queen. The present King of the Scottish Gypsies is Mr Charles Douglas, who lives with his family in a large caravan at Larkhall in Lanarkshire. A few years ago he was awarded the MBE for his services 'to the Gypsy Groups in Scotland', now known as 'the travelling people'.

On the left, at the top of Canaan Lane, just before it joins Newbattle Terrace, is the drive leading to Woodville, a most pleasant secluded villa built in 1804, a typical early nineteenth-century country residence such as many wealthy Edinburgh citizens built in rural Canaan. One writer described those early residents of the 'Biblical' land of Canaan as being 'ensconced in snug boxes' probably a play on the words from the Book of Amos, 'Woe to those ensconced so snugly in Zion'. A distinguished recent owner of Woodville was the late Rt. Hon. Lord Strachan, a former Scottish judge, in whose day the house

The author meets Charles Douglas, Scottish 'King of the Gypsies' at Larkhall in 1979. The possible origins of Morningside's Biblical names—associated with sixteenth-century gypsies—and the life of the travelling people' in Scotland were discussed.

became a port of call for adult education summer-term walks around South Edinburgh.

Something of the past has been brought to life as regards the visit to Woodville in November 1826 of the famous American artist, John James Audubon, as it is now learned that a copy of his *Birds of America* was, until recently, in the possession of Edinburgh University, one of the original subscribers.

Round the corner, at 9 Whitehouse Terrace, is the very fine villa purchased in 1905 by André Raffalovitch, the friend of Canon John Gray, parish priest of St Peter's Roman Catholic Church in Falcon Avenue. Here Raffalovitch held his celebrated lunch and dinner parties for many great authors of his day. Father Brocard Sewell, the biographer of Raffalovitch and Canon Gray, telephoned me some years ago to say that, although his books had contained detailed references to 9 Whitehouse Terrace and St Peter's Church, he had not seen either. I had the pleasure of taking him to visit them. At St Peter's we were hospitably received by one of Canon Gray's present-day successors, the late Rev. Walter Glancy, who talked to us in what had been Canon Gray's study, which retains much of his extensive library. Father Sewell was then shown the foundation stone of the church, built in 1907, on which was a sculpted portrait of Canon Gray. At 9 Whitehouse Terrace we were kindly welcomed by the present owners, Mr and Mrs Massie, who are greatly interested in the period when Raffalovitch resided in their house. We talked of the literary lunches and dinners in the dining-room in which they had taken place and enjoyed a glass of wine made from the still flourishing vine Raffalovitch planted in the greenhouse. Mr Massie, an advocate, was for some time Solicitor-General of Malaysia.

At Craighouse, two links with the Royal Edinburgh Hospital's past deserve mention. One of the most interesting features of the 'huge chateau' as the building has been described, in recent times commemoratively named the Thomas Clouston Clinic, is the Grand Hall, oak-panelled and with valuable historical portraits of people associated with the foundation's history, interesting fireplaces, coats of arms and other memorabilia. This was part of the original private asylum's — as one writer put it — palatial facilities to allow wealthy and often aristocratic patients to continue to live in the grand manner to which they

John James Audubon, the famous American painter of birds, who was the
dinner guest of James Wilson of Woodville, Canaan Lane, in November 1826.
Audubon's *Birds of America*, in four volumes was until recently in the possession
of Edinburgh University which was one of the original subscribers to this very
valuable publication. *The Curator, The White House, Washington, D. C.*

The villa at No.9 Whitehouse Terrace was the home of André Raffalovitch from 1907 until his death in 1934. Many famous British literary figures and artists were guests here. Raffallovitch and Canon Gray were the hosts at the regular lunch and dinner parties. *By courtesy of the present owners, Mr and Mrs L. A. Massie.*

William 'Shakespeare' Morrison, one of the most notable Speakers of the House of Commons. A former pupil of George Watson's College and brought up in Canaan Grove, Newbattle Terrace, he became Lord Dunrossil and ultimately Governor-General of Australia. *By courtesy of* 'The Watsonian' *and Mr James C. Allan.*

had been accustomed. Here banquets were held. Some years ago an Edinburgh University extra-mural studies class held an end-of-term social evening with a small group of musicians playing period music in the Minstrels' Gallery. Again, in recent times, Morningside Association, in fund-raising for local community needs has organised buffet evenings with musical entertainment in the Grand Hall.

Also some time ago, on the roof outside the large north window of the Grand Hall, metal rails leading to a wooden hut were discovered. It was found that the hut enclosed a very large and quite antique film projector. This could be wheeled to the window and the projector lens pointed through a removable window pane.

CHAPTER 10

Morningside Today

Defining Morningside's geographical boundaries is simple enough. Edinburgh District Council has done this in relation to its Community Council. Defining its identity or special character is a more difficult task. This several writers have attempted to do.

The late Forbes Macgregor, noted educationalist and local historian, contributed the section on South Edinburgh in the 1966 Third Statistical Account of Scotland. In this he suggested that Morningside had contributed significantly to the unique character of the city's southern area and outlined its historical development. He described Morningside not only as a distinct geographical location but also as 'a frame of mind, a social attitude, a form of speech'. He had much else to say about the district's lifestyle and he traced how the city's people of means dwelling in the Old Town had escaped from its overcrowding and decay across the new North Bridge to the famous New Town; but many after some time, finding this not entirely a 'Promised Land', sought the pleasant rural seclusion of such southward districts as the Grange and Canaan in Morningside.

But the significant development which was to lead in due course to the rapid growth of Morningside, which was to become 'a frame of mind' and to develop other characteristics was greatly improved transport, especially the suburban railway of 1884, resulting in virtually an overnight mushroom growth of what Robert Louis Stevenson, not a little disparagingly, called 'villadom', and this notably in the districts of Cluny, Braid, Midmar and Corrennie, all taking their names from the north of Scotland estates of Charles Gordon of Cluny who in 1772 acquired the Braid estate including the Hermitage.

Life Style of Villadom

It was in this most pleasant area of finely built 'villadom' as also in Morningside Drive, Craiglea Drive and Comiston Drive, with the linking terraces, that Morningside's 'frame of mind' and 'social attitude' and perhaps 'form of speech' developed. If these districts were unique, something of their alleged manner of speech was not unknown to music-hall comedians who often enjoyed introducing a reference to 'Morning*sade*'.

That a distinct way of life did develop in Morningside around 1900 and was still to be found until the late 1930s was undoubtedly the case. Perhaps since most of the residents of 'villadom' were from the professions, academic life, or successful businessmen and merchants, there may have been a similarity between 'Morning*sade*' and Glasgow's district similarly mimicked, 'Kelvin*sade*'.

At any rate, in the high residential density of the districts described, life took on a distinctive pattern. Families were often large. Mothers seldom worked outside the home and if they did so, most houses had their complement of 'servants', house-keepers, tablemaids, nannies, ladies' companions, all in residence, the design and size of the house providing appropriate accommodation 'upstairs or below stairs'. So numerous were the loyal devoted servants that in the census returns for this particular era, Morningside's unusually large percentage of female population was to some extent explained by the large number of resident servants. In St Matthew's Parish Church, opened in 1890 (now Cluny Parish Church as from 1974), the marble steps to this cathedral-like church's chancel were gifted by the many domestic servants who were members of the congregation. Indeed, the church held weekly short services followed by a social evening for these important residents of Morningside.

Domestically, the lady of the house or the kitchen staff could telephone the local grocer, dairy, bakery or fish shops and requests would be delivered promptly. Several shops sent a horse-drawn van or message boy on a bike to seek orders, and these were often delivered within a short time. Before and after school hours message boys (few girls) abounded. Morning rolls were on the doorstep with the newspaper and that morning's freshly bottled or pitchered milk or cream.

In a pre-DIY era, tradesmen were in constant demand. Jobbing gardeners were often essential for the very large gardens. Outwith the lifestyle of 'villadom', the great 'canyon-like row of tenements' in Morningside Road (as one writer has described them) and in the side streets, all arising between the 1880s and the early 1900s, attracted many people of more modest means to migrate from other parts of the city. Life in the flats, often with 16 families to a stair, developed a character and community sense of its own.

Church Centred Life

The Sunday morning and evening carillon of church bells brought a large response. Well-attended churches were a feature of Morningside of the early 1900s. Sunday schools had large rolls. Annual sales of work reflected industrious winter evenings in a pre-television era. Stalls at the sales were often elaborate and imaginative. As an early specially published booklet for the former St Matthew's Church indicated, the parish 'bazaar' was a highlight of the year. Again in the absence of the small flickering screen, the church halls were the main centres of leisure activities, with various guilds and youth organisations.

Outdoors, leisure-wise, Morningside had several soccer and a few rugby teams. The Braids' two public golf courses were highly popular for those who could not afford or did not wish to join private clubs. There were private and public tennis courts, and the nightly often crowded bowling green at Morningside Park off Morningside Drive and Balcarres Street was a most lively community scene. The billiard saloon in Millar Crescent (then little snooker was played) produced several players who became prominent in Edinburgh competitive circles.

Thus something of Morningside's early days of 'villadom' and in other areas of its life, up until the outbreak of the Second

Weekly for 6 months, around twenty Morningside 'senior citizens' met to tape their early reminiscences of the district. In this group, at the book launch of *Morningside Memories*, published in March 1988, are (left to right): Margaret Cantley, Mary Peter, Robert Prentice and Elizabeth Notman. The booklet, edited by Miss Margaret Jeff and published jointly by the Morningside Association and the Morningside Heritage Association, was a bestseller. *Edinburgh Evening News*.

World War. Many recollections of former days have been recorded in first-hand accounts by those who have lived in the district during the last half century or longer, in *Morningside Memories*, published in 1988 by Morningside Association and the Morningside Heritage Association, and based on tape-recorded reminiscences of a group of about 20 residents who met weekly for six months.

The Changing Scene

Perhaps the significant changes in the pattern of life in Morningside may be traced to the end of the Second World

War. With the upheaval experienced throughout the country perhaps change was bound to come. What happened to 'the frame of mind', 'the social attitude' . . . ? Many people unfamiliar with Morningside's earlier days will not be aware of any special change. John Macleod, a journalist who came to reside in the district in 1982, in an interesting article in *The Scotsman* in May 1991, entitled 'Organic Meat and Soor Plums', reviewed many of the legends and myths which over the years have been associated with Morningside. Of Morningside's reputation as 'the high temple of privilege, prejudice and pretension' the writer questioned how far this was deserved. The introduction to his article claimed that he laid bare this myth. And others, such as 'a form of speech': all received analysis. He wrote: 'It is predominantly a proletarian area these days, with a substantial student and "working class" (a bad phrase but better than the alternatives) population'. The more southerly part of the district, the writer remarked, was still largely the preserve of professional people.

While some people might no doubt insist sadly that 'Morningside is no longer the place that it was', with its turn-of-the-century life style gone, others, and perhaps they are many, see and rejoice in a new kind of uniqueness in the district's make-up, namely, a wide mix of social classes living in a wide variety of housing, yet all simply different facets of what is still one identifiable community. Another new feature of Morningside today is the considerable number of families from many parts of the world who have made their homes in the district and are to be found in the city's professional and business worlds, while others render valuable service to the community by a chain of late closing 'corner shops' and restaurants.

'These Doomed Meads'

Although already quoted in earlier chapters, Stevenson's words in his classic work, which is especially graphic and relevant to this district: 'Edinburgh: Picturesque Notes' are still so relevant today that they must again be recalled. Writing of the route he

Departed glory. 'Rubislaw' in Braid Avenue: once a most impressive villa. For long vacated, then derelict and demolished. The site awaits planning permission. *Photograph by W. R. Smith.*

knew so well on foot on his way out to his familiar summer house at Swanston Cottage, as he reaches the old toll house at the foot of Morningside Road and relates how for long enough the road had continued onwards and 'issued at once into open country' but then, he wrote (1878) 'chisels are tinkling on a new row of houses' beyond the toll; and he recalls with some apparent indignation and perhaps glee, how a famous judge, Lord Beaconsfield, had once proposed to hang an architect . . . and he advocated similar measures 'to save these doomed meads from the ravages of the builders'. 'It seems it must come to an open fight', he continued, 'to preserve a corner of green country unbedevilled'.

Over a century after they were written, Stevenson's words, if not precisely, certainly in spirit, have had their echoes in public meetings called to save — if not 'these doomed meads' — certainly other areas of pleasant and valuable green space in the district constantly under threat by speculative builders. Residents with large garden ground are frequently approached to sell house and garden, or the latter, for single or multiple house building.

In Morningside in recent years concern about and resistance to threats to the district's amenities and heritage have found organised and constructive expression. This great new area of development had its origins in the first public meeting of *The Morningside Association* held in February 1981. The original initiative was to come primarily from a small group of Morningside Drive residents but very soon the Association was enrolling members from various parts of Morningside. The agreed aims and objects of the Association were to promote and represent the interests of residents of the Morningside area and to protect and improve the amenities thereof.

Amongst many issues to receive early attention through collective concern was the threat to graves and to the sensitivities of the relatives of those buried in Morningside Cemetery by a programme of house building which had begun there. The Association took every possible step, including representation at all political levels, to have further building prevented, and although in the end the ombudsman ruled in favour of the Association's views and deep concern, it was by this time too late, and other houses were built in very close and disturbing proximity to graves. One positive outcome was the valuable study survey carried out by a group of Association members led by Mrs Sheila Durham of the headstones of those buried in the cemetery. This study carried out in consultation with the Scottish Genealogical Society, was published, and copies are lodged in Morningside Public Library and the Central Public Library.

Lest anyone might think that the activities of the Morningside Association have been primarily negative and obstructive, in fact regular meetings have been held during a decade on a wide range of topics and issues of local and wider interest, providing a platform for interesting and qualified guest speakers. Events in aid of various charities have been held and of other local needs. Most notable as regards the latter has been the fund-

The Grand Hall of the Thomas Clouston Clinic at Craighouse in which Morningside Association have organised buffet/musical evenings in aid of local needs. *Royal Edinburgh Hospital.*

raising campaign over four years resulting in a sum of £7,500 contributed towards Edinburgh District Council's refurbishment of Morningside Park at a total cost of £40,000. Amongst the enterprising and enjoyable events in aid of the Park Fund which also brought an aspect of Morningside's history alive was the holding of a number of musical evenings with buffet, held in the magnificent Grand Hall built in 1894 and remaining a most interesting feature of the Thomas Clouston Clinic of the Royal Edinburgh Hospital at Craighouse. The Association has contributed towards the social fund for patients in the Clinic and this and enjoying the use of the Hall signifies that the patients here and at the other part of the hospital at Morningside Place are members of the Morningside Community. The Morningside Association in collaboration with the Morningside Heritage Association has published a number of booklets.

Morningside's Heritage

Chronologically the next local organisation to be founded, also in 1981, was one concerned specifically with the district's history and heritage, *The Morningside Heritage Association*. Its winter programmes of illustrated talks by many speakers, authorities on the area or on other parts of Edinburgh have attracted large and appreciative audiences. Spring and summer outdoor visits locally and further afield have been highly popular. *Morningside Memories* (1988) and *Morningside Walks* (1990) published jointly with Morningside Association were soon sold out and have done much to advance the aims of the Association and have given much pleasure.

Morningside's sense of identity as a community and the district's statutory right to be officially represented before the District and Regional Councils was greatly strengthened when, in 1981, the *Morningside Community Council* was established. Morningside Association and Morningside Heritage Association were spontaneous developments to meet local needs. The Community Council was set up on a more formalised basis and in accordance with the Local Government (Scotland) Act 1973 (familiarly known as the implementation of the Wheatley Report). This Act, in addition to bringing into being Regional and District Councils, also provided for the establishment of Community Councils as the 'grassroots' structures for the two-way communication between the above Councils and members of the community within defined areas. Community Councils, however, were not immediately set up 'from the top' but brought into being when a specified number of voters in a district expressed a desire for such a Council. Morningside's request was made by a large number of signatories at a Morningside Association meeting.

As mentioned in the Introduction to this book, for the purposes of the Community Council Morningside was defined within certain boundaries by Edinburgh District Council. The approximate population within the area was 17,600. Morningside is one of the most densely populated communities in Edinburgh.

The Council membership consists of 14 publicly elected members (by ballot on a rotational basis) and 7 members nominated by recognised 'local interest groups'. There is also provision for representation of the main political parties at local level.

The Council meets as such and also calls public meetings. Its activities are financed by a standard lump sum from the District Council and also a *per capita* payment based on the total electorate in the area. Since its establishment, the Community Council has collaborated closely on issues of common interest with the Morningside Asssociation, such as planning permission applications locally that might not be considered satisfactory in terms of amenity and infringement of green space; traffic safety problems etc. An outstanding success was the Council's organisation of the 'Morningside Saturday' held in the eminently suitable Cluny Church Centre in October 1983. In this memorable full-day event many local organisations and charity agencies took stalls to display and talk of their activities while children's groups presented stage shows. A 'Meet the Authors' session at a bookstall revealed just how many notable writers in many fields are resident in Morningside.

A stimulating and enjoyable feature of Morningside's cultural life are the annual exhibitions of paintings, photography and crafts and hobbies, held in the halls of what is now Morningside Braid Church at Nile Grove organised by the Community Council. The Council has also been involved in the provision of leisure activities for the district's more senior citizens.

'Maisie Comes to Morningside'

Of the very large number of authors, on a wide range of subjects who now reside or at some time have done so in Morningside, none has made the name of the district more widely known among children – and their bed time reading parents! – than Aileen Paterson, creator of Scotland's best known and loved cat, Maisie, heroine of one of Ms Paterson's best-selling and beautifully illustrated stories: *Maisie Comes to*

Morningside; once in the 'Top Ten' of a leading Edinburgh bookshop and for a Morningside shop also a bestseller.

Maisie, coming to Morningside from the quiet north-east of Scotland, finds the bustle of its main street, especially on a Saturday morning, rather overwhelming. The characters she meets, all cats differing from each other, in the author-artist's fascinating illustration of an easily recognisable busy part of Morningside Road are almost human! The neighbours in the stair in which she lives are also uncannily realistic, especially the forbidding Mrs McKitty. Indeed many people have written to the author asking to know the original character! A mixture of grimness and kindness, Mrs McKitty would personify a certain type of Morningside resident who not a few writers have suggested as typical. In fact, perhaps the social comment in the Morningside 'Maisie' story is as penetrating as any learned social study.

Maisie's creator for some time lived in Jordan Lane and the impressions that she absorbed of the Morningside of her time are cleverly conveyed. The portrayal of Edinburgh's Royal Hospital for Sick Children — in which Maisie becomes a patient — is born of the author's sad experience: for here her son, Max, died of leukaemia. So real has Maisie become that groups of children living far from Morningside come here specially to view the actual scenes of their beloved Maisie's adventures. Success indeed! And this is only one of Ms Paterson's beautifully illustrated stories.

The Canaan Project

As already related and a recall of the same situation in Robert Louis Stevenson's day, threats to Morningside's green open spaces from speculative house building have caused many residents much concern, but happily also led to the development of a strong sense of community and of the need to safeguard the district's heritage. The future of two particular areas, both most pleasantly situated and of considerable historical interest, has been the subject of public meetings and strong representation

The hub of bustling Morningside Road, from *Maisie Comes To Morningside* by
Aileen Paterson. Courtesy of the author.

to the appropriate authorities. First, the possible loss to many
young people in the district of the long enjoyed playing field at
Craighouse. This facility was made possible by permission of
the Royal Edinburgh Hospital whose ground it is. Now with the
changing plans for the future of the hospital and the need for
the latter to draw upon its financial assets there has been a
protracted 'stop-go' situation at this site as regards the sale of the
land for the building of houses. At the time of writing, the field
in question, and indeed the great towering Thomas Clouston
above it, faced an uncertain future.

Some time ago this was also the situation concerning a very
pleasant part of 'the Land of Canaan' one of Morningside's most
historic areas. Here the nineteenth-century villas known as the

Priory (originally Streatham House), and Canaan Lodge, built on the site of the earlier villa of that name, had for long been children's homes owned by Lothian Regional Council. They were eventually vacated and became derelict. Their future, and indeed that of the pleasant surrounding grounds, with many venerable and fine trees, was uncertain. Largely attended public meetings were held to propose a solution and to avoid indiscriminate building. The local councillors made representations in various quarters. Happily in due course a plan was drawn up which must have given rise to wide satisfaction.

This most pleasant part of Canaan will provide ideal surroundings for two admirable charitable enterprises. On 16 April 1991, *The Canaan Project* was officially opened by the President of the Royal Blind Asylum and School and his wife, together with the Duke and Duchess of Buccleuch, in the beautiful tree-shaded grounds of the former Canaan Lodge. This project is the name for two establishments adjoining each other. Canaan Lodge, situated immediately inside the new gateway and drive off Canaan Lane, housing five family units, providing for 30 multi-handicapped blind children. Teaching staff are provided by Lothian Regional Council. This children's unit has every modern facility, including a swimming pool and high-tech computerised equipment for education and training in various skills. There is a resident staff.

Further up the driveway is Canaan Home for the elderly blind, housing 72 residents, male and female, and a large nursing and domestic staff. This has succeeded the former Thomas Burns Home at Newington, as a plaque inside the new building indicates. Canaan Home also has every modern facility, including hydraulic lifts. It has a hotel-like atmosphere. Apart from the care provided, Morningside residents who call here will be most impressed, for at the entrance block to the Home, the original Canaan Lodge villa which had fallen into advanced disrepair has been skilfully replicated in simulated stone, produced at Plean in Stirlingshire. While the Edinburgh District Council Planning Committee and the architectural heritage 'watchdog' body, Historic Scotland, were concerned that the

The derelict front entrance to the original Canaan Lodge before demolition and replacement by the fine new traditional building, Canaan Home. *Courtesy of Mr Forbes Sinclair, architect of* 'The Canaan Project'.

Canaan Project, and especially Canaan Home, should retain some traditional features in design and building materials, credit for this excellent piece of 'conservationism' and the project's surrounding environment of gardens and fine venerable trees must go to the architect, Mr Forbes Sinclair, and his colleagues at Cluny Gardens. Sean Connery, in Edinburgh to be made a Freeman of the City, spent over an hour visiting The Canaan Project on 11 June 1991.

The Priory Saved

Just westwards of Canaan Lodge and Canaan Home is the former Benedictine Priory School which, until some years ago, was a Lothian Region home for children. After being vacated the future of this fine early nineteenth-century villa originally named Streatham, had greatly deteriorated and lay dejectedly

The traditionally designed Canaan Home for the Elderly Blind which, with Canaan Lodge, a residential school for multi-handicapped blind children, forms the 'Canaan Project' of the Royal Blind Asylum and School in Canaan Lane. Opened in April 1991 at a cost of nearly £7 million, this house replicates the original Canaan Lodge which was demolished. *Photograph by W. R. Smith.*

with its windows boarded up. Happily, as with the Canaan Project, the house will enjoy a new lease of life, having been acquired by the Ark Housing Association whose work runs parallel to the nearby Canaan Project, being concerned with the housing of adults with mental handicap. This Association has pioneered such supported housing in Scotland.

The Ark Housing Association was founded by a group of members of Morningside Baptist Church at 'Holy Corner' in 1977. Their practical concern for the homeless, and particularly the helplessness of the physically and mentally handicapped was stimulated by an actual 'case' that they encountered. Their first small-scale project led to their founding the Association which now has supported housing units throughout Scotland. Those who reside in the housing provided are encouraged to integrate themselves into the local community where they live. The Ark Housing Association's Scottish headquarters are in

Sean Connery, in Edinburgh to be created a Freeman of the City, took time to visit the Canaan Project in June 1991, where he spent over an hour with the elderly and young residents. He is seen with Mrs Marion Smith, Matron. *Courtesy Edinburgh Evening News.*

Balcarres Street, and after the refurbishment of the former Priory they will be transferred to these new commodious premises. The other well-appointed establishment in this part of Canaan is 'Oaklands', opened here some years ago after the closure of 'Greenlea', and is a comfortable Lothian Region residential home for the elderly. Within the precincts of this thoughtfully restored area a playing field for the use of nearby St Peter's School will remain, as will also the children's play park.

Chosen Area for Many Hospitals

As related in earlier chapters, on account of its one-time remoteness from the city and its reputedly healthy atmosphere,

The Priory, formerly Streatham House, built in about 1820, became a children's home. After this closed the house began to deteriorate and was put up for sale. Happily it is to become the Scottish Headquarters of the Ark Housing Association. *Photograph by W. R. Smith.*

Morningside was chosen for the establishment of many hospitals. The earliest was Edinburgh's first 'ane proper asylum for the insane' in the heart of what was still Morningside village in 1813, now long since renamed the Royal Edinburgh Hospital with its Andrew Duncan and Thomas Clouston Clinics and McKinnon House; the then City Fever Hospital (1903); the Astley Ainslie Hospital (1923); and the more distant Princess Margaret Rose Hospital at Fairmilehead (1933). While the work of these hospitals and types of cases admitted or seen as outpatients have undergone various changes to meet the various health problems of today, the Royal Edinburgh Hospital, established nearly 180 years ago, is one of the leading hospitals in Britain for the treatment of mental illness, a branch of medicine in which new challenges and new approaches to treatment are now of quite considerable public interest.

A brief update concerning the Royal Edinburgh Hospital was kindly provided by Dr Andrew Zealley, its Physician Super-intendent and Consultant Psychiatrist. While on average there is still an admission rate of 2,000 patients per year and around 60,000 out-patient consultations, there have been changes in the management of patients and of the hospital itself. Now the trend is to avoid admission to hospital if at all possible. Patients who are admitted are often discharged after quite a short stay of a few weeks' duration. More and more psychiatric consultation with out-patients takes place at out-reach clinics nearer to the person's home. Long-term patients with severe psychiatric disability tend to be treated more and more in private nursing homes or in supported accommodation run by voluntary organisations such as Penumbria. This practice would increase if more facilities were available.

The Alcohol Problems Clinic is an important feature of the hospital's services. The only new building in recent times has been the Jardine Clinic for elderly people with psychiatric disorders. Happily, many are enabled to return home. Almost a century since it was built on Craighouse Hill, the Thomas Clouston Clinic is being phased out. For some time it has not been entirely suitable for modern clinical treatment. Two centuries after Robert Fergusson's tragic death in the grim City Bedlam, the treatment of mental illness has undergone profound change.

Historic Church Developments

If Morningside does not quite have its own 'Holy Corner', the well-known location at the beginning of Morningside Road where three (originally four) churches face each other, neverthe-less it does have as many churches, for over a century a traditional feature of the district. Indeed the writer referred to earlier who identified as the district's special characteristics 'a frame of mind . . . a social attitude . . .' might also have added, for the early 1900s '. . . and large church attendance'.

Of considerable historic importance was the union between

Morningside's first village church of 1838, Morningside Parish Church, at the corner of Newbattle Terrace and Braid Church which was opened at Nile Grove just over half a century later as the district's second church. In the latter part of the 1980s the falling roll of Morningside Parish Church resulted in the Church of Scotland's Union and Readjustments Committee studying this situation. In 1989, the Rev. Angus Morrison left Braid Church for a charge at Port Ellen in Islay. While Braid was without a minister discussions took place between Morningside Parish Church, Braid Church and Cluny Parish Church concerning rationalisation of church provision in Morningside. Cluny Parish, with a congregation of 900, was not readily able to absorb the congregations of Morningside Parish Church and Braid. It was therefore agreed that these two churches would unite with effect from 12 May 1990, to become Morningside Braid. On Sunday 6 May 1990, the minister of Morningside Parish Church, the Rev. Dr John Kirk, who had served this church for 20 years, preached his last sermon there and thus brought to an end the witness of this church in Morningside for just over 150 years, and in which the famous Dr Thomas Chalmers had preached the inaugural sermon in July 1838.

It was agreed that the church at Newbattle Terrace should close and that the new congregation meet in Morningside Braid Church. On 29 January 1991, the Rev. John R. Wells became the first minister of the new congregation.

Morningside Christian Council

The other important development in the life of the churches in Morningside also has some historical significance. It is a sign of the modern times and it would hardly have been considered possible, or perhaps even desirable, say fifty years ago. This is the closer understanding and practical cooperation between the many Christian denominations in the district, finding expression in the formation of the Morningside Christian Council.

The Council acts as a clearing house for promoting, coordinating and publicising ecumenical activities. These have

In May 1990 Morningside Parish Church at Churchhill, which opened in 1838, united with Braid Church to form Morningside Braid Church at Nile Grove. In front of the new notice board is a stone mounted plaque commemorating the centenary of the then Braid Church opened here in 1887, and with an illustration of the original Braid iron church built at the corner of Braid Road and Comiston Road in 1883. *Photograph by W. R. Smith.*

included house study groups, processions of witness in Morningside, Holy Week services in various churches. Perhaps the origins of ecumenical activity in Morningside may be traced to an inter-denominational service held in 1969 in the then St Matthew's Parish Church (since 1974, Cluny Parish Church) when the special preacher was the Right Reverend Columban Mulcahy, OCR, Abbot of Nunraw, near Haddington.

The Open Door

A most admirable, and for many people now a quite indispensable joint Christian enterprise in the heart of Morningside is 'The Open Door', at No. 420 Morningside Road, close to the one-time Morningside Station. Described as a

Christian Community Centre and Good Neighbourhood Service, it was opened in 1982, the originator being Miss Peggy Hunter of Greenbank Parish Church, who found herself challenged to found this basic 'market place' Christian centre of service by a sermon that impressed her deeply. Miss Hunter was joined in the initial stages by Mrs Margaret Gibbins of the Society of Friends.

Situated in the commodious premises at street level and below of a former well-known Morningside provisions and wine merchant, 'The Open Door' is true to its name. It is open from Tuesdays to Fridays from 10 a.m. till 4.30 p.m. At street level, the spacious café, retaining the interesting decor of the earlier shop, provides beverages and light snacks at minimal cost. This service is much appreciated and used especially by many elderly people who live alone, and by mothers with young families new to the district who enjoy meeting other similar people here. People who have spent some time in the nearby Royal Edinburgh Hospital find 'The Open Door' a most helpful stepping stone amongst caring people as they seek rehabilitation and reintegration into the wider community.

Another day, a lunch club for the frail, confused elderly, giving their carers an opportunity to go shopping or visit friends. Suitable outings are arranged, in summer with a meal en route. Back indoors, the Friday Club for those with special needs and an opportunity to learn new skills and make friends. A Mother and First Baby Group meets weekly, and a health visitor is present. Voluntary transport is provided for those attending groups and who are not so fit. In the café area, helpful leaflets and other information are available. A most valuable service and a sign of the times is the help provided in form filling for various benefits etc. 'The Open Door' is one of the most important developments in Morningside today.

Epilogue

This brief account of some of the new developments in Morningside's churches and the Christian community has been

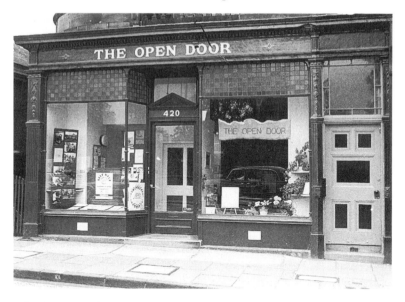

'The Open Door' at No.420 Morningside Road is greatly used as a hospitable Christian Community Centre and Good Neighbourhood Service. Its trustees are representatives of the various Morningside Churches and the Society of Friends. *Photograph by W. R. Smith.*

kept till the end, since many of Morningside's developments came about through their influence, and they preserve a continuing link with the district's earliest days. With so many changes having taken place in Morningside – as elsewhere – since its origins as a village two centuries ago, apart from the first smiddy which has long since gone, the early inn at the corner of Canaan Lane which was the forerunner of today's hostelry and still there, the village's other treasured 'institution', the Old Schoolhouse of 1823, remains well-preserved; and indeed through the care and generous attention of the Christian Brethren who have been the custodians for over 80 years, the little historic building has been greatly enhanced and its original appearance conserved. This small Christian community has had an important influence both in Morningside, in the city, and in the missions abroad.

Here in the Old Schoolhouse, while Morningside was but a relatively remote 'row of thatched cottages and a blacksmith's forge', with its future still to unfold, ministers came out faithfully on foot or on horseback from the relatively distant St Cuthbert's church at the West End to hold weekly evening services in the village school, until 1838, when Morningside Parish Church further up the hill was opened. Now the latter is no more. Its tall stout gates are closed and padlocked, but happily it has been acquired by Napier Polytechnic, who will doubtless ensure its future. One of Morningside's oldest and most cherished landmarks will remain.

As one of several signs of the continuity of the life of the parish church within the new Morningside Braid, the bell from its little steeple at Newbattle Terrace was transferred to the north tower of Morningside Braid Church from which its peals were heard across Morningside on Sunday, 29 September 1991, 153 years after it had been made at Whitechapel in London as its inscription tells, for its long service from the Parish Church steeple at Churchhill. While on weekdays the bell is silent, the floodlit tower of Morningside Braid keeps alive Morningside's past.

From the steeple of Cluny Church Centre in Braid Road (seen in the cover photograph) the illuminated cross has become an integral feature of Morningside's Christmas skyline.

CHAPTER 11

Morningside's Changing Face

While there was gradual change in the buildings of Morningside during the last thirty years, more rapid transformation has taken place in certain areas during the last decade. It is hoped that the illustrations and their captions tell their own story.

The modern flats of Clinton House in Whitehouse Loan encircle the early nineteenth-century villa of the same name. *Photograph by W. R. Smith.*

At the west end of Albert Terrace the new flats of Dove Court recall in their name the ancient Doo Loan, derived from its being the resort of many pigeons from the doocot of nearby Merchiston Tower. *Photographs by W. R. Smith.*

Albert Terrace, off Morningside Road at Churchhill. (*See also* p. 41).

Above: the waste ground at the north-east corner of Falcon Avenue had at one time been allotments and then became overgrown and a rubbish tip. The crow-stepped roof of Bank House is seen in the background. *Below*: the architect's sketch of Falcon House which has recently arisen on the site. *Photographs by W. R. Smith.*

Above: the little bungalow, No. 2 Morningside Place, for a short time the temporary residence of the famous Dr Thomas Chalmers while he awaited the completion of his fine villa at Churchill. *Below:* a doctors' surgery now occupies the site. *Photographs by W. R. Smith.*

Above: the well-known and popular dance hall, the Plaza, later became Jones' Motor House, then the firm as seen today; Safeway. *Photographs by W. R. Smith.*

Originally in the days of Morningside village, the lower part of the not very elegant building (above) was Dick Wright's smiddy; then the Blackford Press and William Cheyne's joiner's shop. Long since gone, the modern 'Merlin' lounge bar and function suite leave no recollection of earlier days. *Photographs by W. R. Smith.*

Above: Morningside Road in about the year 1900, or perhaps earlier. The walls of Morningside House are to be seen to the left; and the gates of Falcon Hall, two stone pillars on the right. Not much traffic! *Below*: Morningside Road today. *Old picture, courtesy of Miss Jean Campbell. Today's picture by W. R. Smith.*

Above: Morningside Station about the year 1900. Considerable horse drawn traffic! *Below*: The same area today New Year's Day 1991. Little traffic! *Photographs by W. R. Smith.*

The longstanding Craighouse Cabinet Works gives way to new flats.
Photographs by W. R. Smith.

The old entrance lodge at the beginning of the Poorhouse Drive (long since closed) was replaced by Greenbank House, modern flats. *Photographs by W. R. Smith.*

Suggested Further Reading

R = Reference libraries only: Central Public Library; National Library of Scotland; University Library.

General

Anderson, W. P., *Silences that speak* (R), 1931

Bryce, W. M., *Book of the Old Edinburgh Club* (OEC), Vol. 10, 1918

Edinburgh and Leith Street Directories (R), 1773–1976

Grant, J., *Old and New Edinburgh*, 3 vols. (R), 1882

Hunter, D. L. G., *Edinburgh's Transport* (R), 1964

Kay, J., *A Series of Original Edinburgh Portraits*, 2 vols. (R), 1837

Smith, J. S., *The Grange of St Giles* (R), 1898

Mair, W., *Historic Morningside*, 1947

Wilson, Sir D., *Memorials of Edinburgh in the Olden Time*, 2 vols. (R), 1891

Keir, D., ed., *The Third Statistical Account of Scotland, City of Edinburgh*, 1966

Gifford, J., McWilliam, C., Walker, D., Wilson, C., *The Buildings of Scotland Edinburgh* (R), 1984

Chapter 1

Harris, S., 'The Tower of Merchiston', *Book of the Old Edinburgh Club*, Vols. 31, 33, 1962, 1969

Napier, M., *Memoirs of John Napier of Merchiston* (R), 1834

Napier Polytechnic: various booklets, leaflets, with outline history of College

Brown, T., *Annals of the Disruption* (R), 1893

Stevenson, R. L., *Edinburgh: Picturesque Notes*, 1878

Various, *Life of Dr Thomas Chalmers*.

Davidson, D., *Memories of a Long Life* (R), 1890

Doyle, J. A., *Susan Edmonstone Ferrier: Memoir and Correspondence of*, 1782-1854 (R), 1889

National Library of Scotland, *Catalogue of Exhibition on Susan Ferrier* (available at National Library), 1982

Ferrier, S., *The Inheritance*. New edition with Note by Judge Irvine, 1984

Wilson, J. A., *Memoir of George Wilson* (R), 1860

Hanson, L. & E. M., *Necessary Evil* (Letters of Jane Welsh Carlyle) (R), 1952

Chapter 2

Brown, Dr John, *Rab and His Friends* (illustrated by Hannah Preston McGoun)

Caw, J. L., *Scottish Painting Past and Present* (ref. H. P. McGoun) (R), 1908

Gowans, J. S., *Morningside Parish Church* (R), 1912

Mair, W., *History of Morningside Parish Church*. *Book of O.E.C.*, Vol. 24, 1942

Westminster Gazette, *Homes and Haunts of Thomas Carlyle* (re Mary Aitken Carlyle) (R), 1893

Mackenzie, Alexander, 'Mr Speaker'. *The Watsonian*, May 1952, 1952

Campbell, N., 'William Shepherd Morrison'. *University of Edinburgh Journal*, Vol. XXXI, No. 1 (R), 1983

Lockhart, J. G., *Cosmo Gordon Lang* (R), 1949

Chapter 3

Mair, W., *Historic Morningside*, 1947

Cochrane, R., 'Memories of Morningside', in *About St Matthew's, Morningside* (R), 1908

Cochrane, R., *Pentland Walks, with their Literary and Historical Associations* (R), 1920

Cant, M., *Villages of Edinburgh*, Vol. 2, Chapter 7, 'Morningside', 1987

Edinburgh Room, Central Public Library, Press cuttings on Morningside from early times.

Morningside Association and Morningside Heritage Association, *Morningside Memories*, 1988

Morningside Association and Morningside Heritage Association, *Morningside Walks*, 1990

Chapter 4

Bonnar, T., *Biographical Sketch of George Meikle Kemp* (R), 1892

Gilpin, S., *Sam Bough RSA* (R), 1905

Fletcher, E., *Autobiography with letters etc.* (R), 1875

Glasgow Herald, 'From Morningside to the Court of the Manchus', Ref. Reginald Johnston, February 13, 1988

Shepherd, J. A., *Simpson and Syme of Edinburgh*, 1969

Fisher, R. B., *Joseph Lister*, 1977

Smith, Charles J., *Between the Streamlet and the Town. History of Astley Ainslie Hospital*, 1989

Hamilton, J., *Memoirs of the Life of James Wilson of Woodville* (R), 1859

Various, Biographies of John James Audubon.

Royal Blind Asylum and School, Various booklets on the Canaan Project. Available at Gillespie Crescent

Taylor, W., *Scot Easy* and *Scot Free*, 1953–1955

Chapter 5

Anderson, J., *Falcon Hall College*. In Illustrations. Edinburgh Room (R), 1889

Gordon, E., The Royal Scottish Academy, Ref. Alexander Falconar in saleroom accident (R), 1976

Rock, J., Thomas Hamilton, Architect 1784–1858 (R), 1984

Sewell, B., *Two Friends* and *In the Dorian Mode* (Canon Gray and Raffalovitch) (R), 1963–1983

Note: The information relating to the Palazzo Falconieri in Rome and the photograph of the Palazzo were obtained from: Portoghesi, P., *Francesco Boromini*, Milan, Electe Editrice, 1984 (R) Salerno, L., Spezzaferro, L., and Tafuri, M., *Via Giulia, una utopia urbanistica del 500*, Rome, Casa Editrice Stabilimento Aristide Staderini, 1973 (R)

Chapter 6

Lauder, Sir Thomas Dick, *Scottish Rivers* (R), 1890

Chapter 7

Mitchell, A., *The Story of Braid Church 1883–1933*. Revised (R), 1933

Stevenson, R. L., *Edinburgh Picturesque Notes*, 1878

Chapter 8

Guthrie, D., *The Royal Edinburgh Hospital for Sick Children, 1860–1960* (R), 1960

Guthrie, Lord Charles, *Cummy: the Nurse of Robert Louis Stevenson* (R), 1913

Beattie, G., *The New City Poorhouse at Craiglockhart* (R), 1865

Pollard, J., *Care of Public Health and the New Fever Hospital in Edinburgh* (R), 1898

Burton, J. H., *The Bookhunter 1882* (R)

Mackay, Rev. D. G. M., *The Story of Greenbank* (Church) (Available from church), 1990

Durham, S. *et al.*, *A Survey of Monumental Inscriptions in Morningside Cemetery* (R), 1981

St Matthew's Church, *About St Matthew's Church*, Morningside (R), 1908

Chapter 9

Beveridge, A., 'Edinburgh's Poet Laureate: Robert Fergusson's Illness Reconsidered', *History of Psychiatry* 1, 1990 (R)

Chapter 10

MacLeod, J., 'Organic Meat and Soor Plooms', *The Scotsman*, 11 May 1991

Index

Ainslie Cottage 104
Ainslie, David, of Costerton 125
Ainslie, John Astley 125
Aitken, Mary Carlyle 56
Albert Terrace 40, 62
Angle Club 104
Astley Ainslie Hospital 118, 119, 120,
    125, 127
Ark Housing Association 253
Armour, Tommy 186, 187
Audubon, John James 129, 233, 234
Avalon 30, 31

Baillie's School 10
Balcarres Street 184
Bank House 58, 59, 61
Barnett, Dr T, Ratcliffe 214, 215, 216
Bartholomew, John George 142
Begbie, Mr, of Egypt Farm 103
Beilby, Dr George 96
Belhaven Hotel 176
Bell, Dr Benjamin 197, 198
Bevan, Elizabeth 204
Biblical names 98, 99, 112
Blackford House 162
Blacksmith's shop 184
Bloomsbury Cottage 128
Bore stone 46, 47, 48, 56
Bouch, Thomas 170
Bough, Sam 94, 109-111
Braid Church 168-170, 257
Braid iron church 168
Braidburn Valley Park 218, 219
Briggs o' Braid 62, 159
Buchan's dairy 192, 194
Burghmuirhead House see Grangebank
    House
Burgh Muir 1, 8, 62, 63, 79
Burton, Dr Hill 201, 203

Cable cars, 36
Canaan Grove 131
Canaan Lodge 114, 115, 251

Canaan Project 249-252
Canny Man's see Volunteers Rest
Cant's Loan 27, 45, 54, 88
Carlyle, Jane Welsh 29, 37, 38, 39, 56
Carlyle, Thomas 37-40, 56, 123
Carmen's shelter 35, 36
Chalmers, Dr Thomas 11-21
Church of Scotland, Disruption 11-18
Churchhill 11, 13, 17, 18
Churchhill Theatre 10, 11
City Hospital 209-214
Clinton House 32
Clouston, Dr Thomas 203, 204
Cluny Church Centre 248, 261
Cluny Parish Church 53, 220, 222
Cockburn, Andrew Myrtle 69
Comiston Burn 157, 158, 160
Comiston Springs, water supply 115,
    116, 117
Connery, Sean 252
Coulter, Lord Provost William 135,
    136, 137
Craigenvilla 37, 38, 39
Craigie, Henry 140, 141
Craighouse, 198, 199
Craighouse, Grand Hall 204, 205, 206,
    234, 238, 246
Craiglockhart Hydropathic 4
Craiglockhart Poorhouse 207, 208, 209
Cromwell, Oliver 102
Cruickshank, Bobby 187
Cuddy Lane 70, 73, 74
Cunningham, Alison ('Cummy') 189

Davidson, Col. Sir, David 28, 29
Denholm's Smiddy 76, 77
Deuchar, David 81, 84
Doo Loan see Albert Terrace
Dunedin Hall 194

East House 87
East Morningside House 21, 26, 27, 28, 220
Eden Hermitage 134

Eden Lane 133
Edinburgh Street Directories 7, 64
Edinburgh Suburban and South Side
  Junction Railway 63, 65, 170, 173
Egypt Farm 102, 230
Elm Cottage 32, 33
The Elms 31, 32

Falcon Hall 135, 138, 139, 142, 143
Falcon Hall College 142
Falcon Hall, statues 140, 143, 144
Falconar, Alexander 135-142
Falconar, Jessie Pigou 141
Fergusson, Robert 226
Ferrier, Susan Edmonstone 22-26, 220
Flodden, Battle of 119
Forbes, Sir John Stuart 19, 21, 49

Gardenstone, Lord 79-81
Gordon, Charles of Cluny and Braid 239
Goshen House (or Bank) 112, 228, 229
Grangebank House 5, 6, 8
Grant, James 62, 74
Gray, Canon John 145-148, 234
Green, Charles Edward 30, 31
Greenbank Parish Church 214-218
Gregory, Professor James 114, 115
Gypsies 100, 101, 231, 232

Hamilton, Thomas, architect 138
Harmony House 133
Hay, David Ramsay 111
Henderson, John, architect 37, 51
Hill, David Octavius 16
Horse-drawn trap 33-35

Jackson, Charles D'Orville
  Pilkington 111
Johnston, Reginald 229
Jordan Bank Villa 108
Jordan Burn 118, 150-165

Kemp, George Meikle 104-107
Kerr, James 91-93
Kingsley, Henry 112, 228

Lang, Cosmo Gordon, Archbishop of
  Canterbury 58, 59, 61
Lang, Rev John Marshall 59-61
Lang, Dr Marshall B 58-60
Lauder, Sir Thomas Dick 151, 152, 162
Lennel House 143, 144
Lister, Joseph, 1st Baron Lister 121, 123

Littil Egypt 101
Littlejohn, Dr Henry 209, 210

McGibbon and Ross architects 18, 200
Macgoun, Hannah P. 54
McGregor, Forbes 239
McLaren, Charles 112, 113
Merchiston Tower 1, 40
Morningside vii, 1, 21, 45, 62
Morningside Association 227, 245, 246
Morningside Cemetary 187, 188
Morningside College 195, 196
Morningside House 79-84
Morningside Hydropathic 195
Morningside Liberal Club (Morningside
  Club) 85, 86
Morningside Lodge 135, 136, 138
Morningside Parish Church 48-54
Morningside Public Library 77
Morningside Public Park 194, 195
Morningside Road 1, 9, 39, 64
Morningside Road Station 171, 173
Morningside Station Clock 177
Morningside Victoria Football Team 222
Murray's Edinburgh Diary 174, 175
Myreside Cottage 206

Napier College (Polytechnic) 1-4, 261
Napier, John 1, 2, 27
Napier, Theodore 222
Newbattle House 56

Oaklands 209, 254
Ogilvie, Frederick Dove 92-93
Old Craig 200
Old Schoolhouse 52, 66, 68-72, 260

Palazzo Falconiari 138, 139
Paradise 112
Paterson's Dairy 108, 220, 221, 222
Peddie and Kinnear, architects 4
Pitsligo House 56
Plewlands 181
Plewlands Cottage 181, 182
Plewlands Farm 181
Plewlands feuing plan 182
Plewlands House 197
Pollard, Bailie James 209, 210
Powburn Village 164
Princess Margaret Rose Hospital 216, 255

Raeburn, Henry 81, 84
Raffalovitch, André 145-148, 234

Recreational facilities 241
Reid's Dairy 78, 79
Ritchie, William 112
Ross School (*see* Old Schoolhouse)
Roubilliac sculpture 227
Royal Edinburgh Hospital 97, 226,
    255, 256
Royal Hospital for Sick Children 196,
    197, 198

St Bennet's 21, 37
St Cuthbert's Coop Store 112
St Matthew's Iron Church 53
St Matthew's Parish Church 258
St Peter's Roman Catholic Church 145-149
St Roque's Chapel 119, 120
Scott, Sir Walter 9, 22, 25, 47, 48, 105, 106
Scott Monument 104, 106, 107, 108
South Morningside School 66, 69, 70, 178,
    179
Springvalley Farm 78
Springvalley House 74
Steel, Dr Thomas 6, 94
Steell, Gourlay 125
Stevenson, Robert Louis 4, 66, 192, 239
Streatham House (The Priory) 113,
    252, 253

Street sellers 223, 224
Syme, Professor James 120-123

Tanfield Hall 14, 16
Taylor, Wilfred 98, 111, 152
Telephone exchange, original 168
Tipperlinn Village 97, 154, 155
Torrance's tea rooms 177, 178
Trotter, Miss Menie 162
The 'Clan Chattan' 112
'The Last Emperor' 229
The Open Door 258, 259
The Plague 119
The Priory 113, 252, 253
'Villadom' 239, 240, 241
Volunteers Rest 91-94

Walls, George, architect 11
Westgate 11
Whitehouse 45
Wilson, Daniel 32, 33
Wilson, Professor George 32, 33
Wilson, James 128, 129, 131
Woodburn House 117, 118
Woodcroft 28, 29, 30
Woodville 128, 129, 131, 232, 233
Wright, Dick, blacksmith 75